A ZEAL FOR CHRISTIAN EDUCATION
The Memoirs of B.J. Haan

A ZEAL FOR CHRISTIAN EDUCATION

The Memoirs of B.J. Haan

by

B.J. Haan

The cover was designed by Jake Van Wyk.

Copyright 1992 by
Dordt College Press

ISBN: 0-932-914-24-1

Printed in the United States of America

Contents

	Page
Dedication	7
Acknowledgements	9
Preface	11
Chapter One
An Iowan By Birth and By Choice	13
Chapter Two
Rekindling the Flame of Christian Education	32
Chapter Three
The Story Behind Life's Story	48
Chapter Four
They'll Never Stop It	65
Chapter Five
The Sapling Takes Root	84
Chapter Six
The Politics of Growth	108
Chapter Seven
Gaining Accreditation and Credibility	123
Chapter Eight
Expanding Facilities	138
Chapter Nine
The Gathering Storm	153
Chapter Ten
The Storm Erupts and Subsides	168
Chapter Eleven
Beyond Liberal Arts or Vocational	192
Chapter Twelve
Observations	204
Educational Task of Dordt College	218

It is with loving heart and sincere appreciation that I dedicate these memoirs to my wife, Deborah, with whom I have spent fifty years in blessed holy wedlock and without whose many gifts and helpful partnership the accomplishment of anything of value in my labors would have been virtually impossible.

Acknowledgements

I am grateful to the Dordt College Board of Trustees for the encouragement they gave me to write my memoirs. I also appreciate the support and cooperation of both the college administration and the Dordt Press in getting these memoirs published. I wish also to express special thanks to J. Van Wyk, professor of art, for the attractive and meaningful cover. However, I owe a particular debt of gratitude to Mrs. Calvin Jongsma (Sally) for her journalistic and editorial expertise. Her readiness to spend numerous hours offering suggestions and working over the manuscript were of inestimable value to me.

It is my prayer that this publication may be used for the promotion of God's kingdom and bring glory to the name of our faithful covenant Lord.

B.J. Haan

Preface

One day while walking with a visitor over a flourishing and expanding Dordt College campus, I was asked if I ever felt like Nebuchadnezzar looking over the great Babylon he had built. My immediate and emphatic reply was "No, never." It is true that we all like credit, we all seek praise and honor, and there is sin in all that we do. However, when it comes to the establishment and development of Dordt College, I know better than anyone how little man did and how much the Lord did.

It often happens that one or two persons receive credit for something many made possible. I am extremely grateful to the Lord for men and women of dedication, wisdom, talent, and willingness with whom I worked shoulder to shoulder over the years. I am utterly amazed at how God in his providence so often had the right man or the right woman at the right time and place to make possible the successes that we together have experienced in our lifetime.

Obviously I can only write as I personally experienced things and saw them happening. In order to spark my memory and ensure the authenticity of my account, I have also researched various documentary sources. However, there are many significant and interesting details that minutes and other records do not reveal and that ought to be told. As I relate what I judge to be significant and interesting facts, the reader will have to trust my memory and my discernment.

Writing about one's self can easily create the wrong impression. I could appear boastful and proud. I could be accused of exaggerating or twisting the facts in such a way as to make myself look good. I suppose these are the risks of writing an autobiography. Yet God does use persons as instruments to accomplish his purposes. Not to tell what God has done would be an injustice both to history and to the God who makes history.

Let it be said at the outset that if there is anything in my life or accomplishments that has lasting worth and value, it is God alone who deserves the credit. I sincerely hope that what appears in these memoirs will clearly demonstrate this.

If the writing of these memoirs can help bring about a greater commitment to and labor for the coming of Christ's kingdom on the part of coming generations, it will have been worth the effort.

Chapter One
An Iowan By Birth and By Choice

I was born on April 24, 1917, in Sully, Iowa. They tell me it was a very stormy night. That I was born in Sully, Iowa, is significant for what transpired in my life. To demonstrate the importance of the spirits operative in my background, I want to trace briefly the history of my father.

Father was a son of the Rev. Enno R. Haan, a missionary from the church of the secession in The Netherlands. Grandfather was born in Delfzijl, Groningen. He served without furlough for ten years in the Dutch East Indies where my father was born. When he finally returned to the church in The Netherlands from which he was sent, he planned to return to the Indies after his furlough. However, he was a strong believer in the covenant and when he was told that his children could not go back with him, he decided to accept a charge in The Netherlands. This covenantal emphasis had a solid effect upon my father and upon our home.

Abraham Kuyper was in the heyday of his career during my grandfather's ministry. He became an ardent supporter and advocate of Kuyper's way of thinking and was influenced by Kuyper's program of Christian action. The name Kuyper had a definite ring and meaning in our family. Kuyper vigorously promoted establishing Christian schools. As a result a strong Christian education movement grew in The Netherlands. These efforts profoundly influenced my father's thinking on Christian education in the years ahead. When grandfather accepted a call to the United States in 1889, the Kuyperian influence came with him.

Ironically, due to a lack of good communication, grandfather was unaware of the differences between the Reformed Church of America and the Christian Reformed Church. He accepted a call to the Reformed church near Midland Park, New Jersey. However, he soon discovered that his views had greater acceptance in the Christian Reformed Church. Two of his sons were planning to study for the ministry, and he became convinced that they should affiliate with the Christian Reformed Church. The result was that grandfather left the Reformed Church of America and founded the Midland Park Christian Reformed Church. It is interesting to note that nearly seventy percent of the new members of this church came from the Reformed Church of America of which grandfather was minister for only one year. This tells something of my grandfather's concerns, convictions, and charisma, the strength of which I also felt in my training.

Some years later grandfather accepted a call to the Grandville Avenue Christian Reformed Church in Grand Rapids, Michigan. It was here that my father met his wife and my mother-to-be, Katie Deunhouwer, and it was here that father became actively involved in Christian education. As a young man he was chosen to be treasurer of the Christian school board. During his service as treasurer, he established a close friendship with Mr. Bernard John Bennink. Bennink, the principal of the Grandville Avenue Christian School, had an interesting connection with my own history that I shall relate at the proper time.

Mother also immigrated to the United States from The Netherlands. She was born in Puttershoek, a lovely village close to Dordtrecht. She first settled in Detroit, Michigan, and later moved to Grand Rapids, where her parents became members of the Grandville Avenue Church. After a happy courtship, father and mother were married. For the first ten years of married life, father operated a general store in Grand Rapids. Six of their fourteen children were born during this time. They then moved to Sully, Iowa, a small town a few miles from Pella. This move was supposedly for the benefit of mother whose physical welfare, my father thought, could be served by a change of environment. I am inclined to think that the move was more the result of an adventuresome spirit in my father.

Not long before I was born, Mr. Bernard John Bennink visited us in Sully. Knowing my father very well and with a twinkle in his eyes, he suggested that since he had no children of his own, if the child was a boy my father ought to consider giving him the name Bernard John. When I was born, my father and mother decided to honor Mr. Bennink by giving me his name. It is rather significant, I think, that both Bernard John Bennink and I were very much involved in Christian education.

Bernard Bennink later moved to Rock Valley, Iowa, and was for years the principal of the Christian school there. He was a staunch Calvinist, a follower of Kuyper, a highly respected leader in Christian education, and the author of a book on church history used in many of our Christian schools.

Two events that occurred while my parents lived in Sully had a major effect upon my thinking and the direction of my life. One was the arrival of the Rev. Henry Danhof, and the other was the establishment and protection of the Christian school in Sully. The Rev. Danhof came to Sully at the same time my parents did and was minister there for five years. The parsonage was directly across the street from our house and our two families quickly formed a lasting friendship. It was not so much the friendship as the tremendous influence of the Rev. Danhof's preaching and teaching upon my parents that is important for my history. So strong and lasting was this influence that even though I was born in Sully five years after Danhof had left for another charge, the effects of his ministry on my parents and their later affiliation with him helped shape my own development.

Through the Rev. Danhof different strands in our Reformed tradition came to expression. Danhof, together with the Rev. Herman Hoeksema, was put out of the Christian Reformed Church in 1924 and formed the Protestant Reformed Church. The issue in dispute was common grace. Danhof and Hoeksema opposed common grace as proposed by Abraham Kuyper and as generally upheld by the Christian Reformed Church. Hoeksema and Danhof insisted that there is only one kind of grace, namely, God's special redeeming grace in Christ. They were convinced that to teach another grace for the unregenerate opened the door to an unbiblical alliance between the redeemed and the unredeemed. Once that happened, they feared, worldliness would dominate God's people. Kuyper held firmly to the view that we can be saved only by God's special grace, but he believed the Bible also taught another kind of grace which was the result of the general operation of the Holy Spirit upon the unregenerate. Without regenerating the heart (saving grace), such grace laid the groundwork for the unregenerate to engage in so-called good works in such areas as civic and moral activity. This work of the Holy Spirit Kuyper called common grace—an undeserved gift of God.

Because of God's common grace, believers and unbelievers could work together in some areas. However, Kuyper insisted that such activity had to be consistent with God's Word. Whenever working together was in conflict with Scripture, it had to be opposed. It could never lead to an unbiblical fellowship that would wipe out the antithesis between the two. In that sense common grace was not a bridge for God's people to cross over into the world of the unregenerate. The lines of demarcation had to remain strong.

Although Hoeksema and Danhof opposed Kuyper to a large extent because they feared a danger in common grace, they did have a great deal of appreciation for much of what Kuyper wrote and espoused. It was this "No" and "Yes" to Kuyper's ideas that played a large role in the history of our churches and also in my own history.

When my parents arrived in Sully, Iowa, there was no Christian school. In Sully, a group of immigrants from The Netherlands who had obviously been influenced by Kuyper had carried to this country strong convictions about Christian education. The arrival of Danhof at approximately the same time my parents came to Sully strengthened the movement for the Christian school. Danhof was in solid agreement with Kuyper on the urgent need for Christian education even though he did not accept Kuyper's view of common grace.

A short time after Danhof and my parents came to Sully, a society for Christian education was formed and a school erected. The battles involved in establishing and maintaining the school placed an indelible stamp upon our family. During World War I, a strong anti-German, anti-Dutch feeling prevailed. Church services were allowed only in the American language, and the Christian school was threatened because it was a so-called "Dutch school." The supporters of the school were accused of being anti-American, unpatriotic, and even subversive.

One night the Christian school in Peoria, only a few miles from Sully, was destroyed by fire. For a long time after that incident, members of the school society, by turns, guarded the Sully Christian School each night with guns. One night the guards decided to go home early. The enemies of the school, who were constantly waiting for the right opportunity, quickly moved in and set the building on fire. Fortunately, the minister, the Rev. J. Haverman, had arisen early to study for a funeral sermon since it was difficult for him to preach in English. He could see the school from his study. Looking out, he saw the fire in the basement of the school. At once he and his wife aroused my parents. Together, with the help of my oldest brother, Enno, they formed a relay team, pumping water and passing the buckets along. The school was saved.

The determination and deep commitment of these advocates of Christian education affected me greatly, even though I was born a few years after the Christian school was opened. Hearing my father and others relate the struggles and exciting experiences involved in funding and protecting the Christian school in its early history not only fired my imagination but also served to instill in me an unshakeable belief in the significance of Christian education. This background led me, early in my life, to search for a deeper basis for Christian education.

I wanted to be able to defend and promote this most worthy cause with the best arguments. I soon found that not all proponents of the cause argued from the same standpoint and not all had the same perspective. I came to realize that my own thinking was somewhat influenced by these opposing and contradictory viewpoints.

Our family lived in Sully, Iowa, for eleven years. These were beautiful years. My parents and older brothers and sisters spoke with the fondest memories of their experiences in this small farming community. But father, thinking it best for the family, purchased a general store in Orange City, a Dutch community in Northwest Iowa, two hundred and fifty miles from Sully. I was three years old when we moved to this town.

We lived in Orange City only three years, but they were very happy years in my life. Normally impressions formed from ages three to seven are not as strong and lasting as those formed later. At least memories about events and experiences that transpired are usually not too clear. Strangely, that was not the case with me. I recall that when we returned to Orange City several years later, my memory of the city was sharper than that of my older brother and sister. I only call attention to this fact because it had a great deal to do with my coming to Northwest Iowa as a minister, with the role I was given in promoting Christian education in Northwest Iowa, and with my work in establishing Dordt College. When I look back, I can clearly see the leading of the Lord already early in my life. There is indeed a direct link between the aspirations implanted, stimulated, and cultivated in my early years and that which transpired later in my lifetime.

The Lord built up in me a strong and fond attachment to Orange City and Northwest Iowa during those early years. It is difficult for me to explain this. I recall looking out of my classroom window in Grand Rapids, Michigan, and thinking rather longingly of Iowa even though I was happy where I was. My wife was surprised and really could not understand when I said to her early in my ministry that I would like to get a call from Northwest Iowa. Opportunities to serve churches elsewhere seemed quite promising and forthcoming, but Iowa was the place that drew my attention. When that opportunity was given by the Lord, there was no doubt about my decision to accept.

It was also in Orange City that I developed a rather early interest in and attachment to the church. My uncle, Dr. Ralph L. Haan, was the minister at that time in the First Christian Reformed Church of Orange City where we were members. As a little boy I was so fascinated by the church and the preaching of my uncle that I wanted to become a minister. That desire never left me. I was convinced already then that my calling in life was to be a minister of the gospel. They tell me I loved to play church. I was always the preacher. What I said in my "sermons" I don't really know. I do remember, however, that my family was quite amused by it all. One time we had a visit from my uncle John Hekman, a wealthy baker from Grand Rapids, Michigan. He was an elder delegate to the Christian Reformed Synod in 1922, which dealt with the highly controversial Jansen case. While he was at our home he wanted to watch us play church. So we arranged a service. I was the preacher and my brother, Chris, was the deacon. When the offering was taken, I was very interested in it because my brother and I were to share it. As the collection plate was passed around, it came in front of my uncle John. I looked with big eyes at that plate to see what was going to be placed in there by my wealthy uncle. He didn't disappoint us.

The manner in which I related Bible stories when we played church amused my family. My talents reached the ear of the principal of the Christian school, Mr. Chris Aue. One day, when I was in the first grade at the Orange City Christian School, he called me out of the room, brought me upstairs and set me on the desk in front of his seventh and eighth grade pupils to tell his class a Bible story. I don't know what the story was about nor what the class's response was. I do have the impression, however, that it must have been rather humorous.

We moved back to Grand Rapids, Michigan, in 1922, and I was enrolled in the Grandville Avenue Christian School. I attended that school for the next eight years, graduating from the ninth grade in 1932, the year that Franklin D. Roosevelt became the president of the United States.

These were by no means dull, peaceful years. In the Christian Reformed Church the Hoeksema-Danhof controversy over common grace was reaching the boiling point. Living on the southwest end of town, we again joined the Grandville Avenue Christian Reformed Church. The minister at that time was Dr. Y.P. De Jong, father of Dr. P.Y. De Jong. We belonged to that church for only about a year, but it was an eventful year. I shall never forget the first Sunday School Christmas program. I had to give the welcome speech. Several people spoke to me about that little speech and encouraged me to become a preacher. These incidents stuck in my mind and heart and were an incentive to me. Later as a boy I remember sitting in church and becoming very nervous about the fact that maybe someday I would have to stand up in front and preach. As I got older I still battled stage fright in my speech classes. Nevertheless, it did not deter me in my desire to be a minister, and gradually this fear was overcome.

In the controversy over common grace, my parents soon felt that the church was not dealing justly with Danhof and Hoeksema. I well remember the arguments over common grace that took place between my father and our minister, Dr. De Jong. Eventually my parents decided to transfer their membership from the Grandville Avenue Church to the Eastern Avenue Christian Reformed Church, where the Rev. Herman Hoeksema was the minister. We lived on the other side of the city and had no automobile, so we attended the Grandville Avenue Christian Reformed Church in the morning and on Sunday evening drove to Hoeksema's church with a middle-aged couple who were also avid Hoeksema followers.

I remember vividly sitting on a chair next to my father directly below the pulpit. Father was hard of hearing and wanted to sit close to the front. The church was jammed to the rafters. I could observe very carefully every move of the preacher. What a powerful preacher he was. Of course, at that age I did not know what the sermons were all about, but I do remember how deeply committed I became to both Hoeksema and Danhof and their cause. The intense loyalty and firm conviction of my parents deeply influenced me.

The fierce battle over common grace resulted in the deposition of both Danhof and Hoeksema in 1924. Several other ministers and many of the laity joined these men in establishing what is known as the Protestant Reformed Church. We went along with Hoeksema and joined his large congregation, which met in the downtown St. Cecilia building in Grand Rapids while a new church was being built. We began meeting in the basement of that church as soon as it was ready. Unknown to me, in that assembly was a little two-year-old girl who would later become my wife, Deborah Cornelia Harkema. Deborah has had a most pronounced influence upon my life. She was baptized by the Rev. H. Hoeksema, was catechized by him, and made confession of faith in his church.

Because there were several families in the southwest part of Grand Rapids who were staunch followers of Hoeksema and Danhof, it was decided to set up another congregation of the Protestant Reformed Church in that part of the city. We called it the "slide-off," on Roosevelt Avenue. We were in this church only a short time before there was a sharp rift between Hoeksema and Danhof. They soon parted from each other. This, of course, was a sad experience and one wonders what would have happened if they had remained together, for many leading preachers and lay people were sitting on the fence and leaning in the direction of the Protestant Reformed Church. The break between these two men proved to be a serious blow to the cause and stifled, to a large extent, the growth of the Protestant Reformed Church.

When Hoeksema and Danhof parted company, my parents joined Danhof's congregation in Kalamazoo, Michigan. My parents were very close friends of Danhof and could not understand why Hoeksema was so stern, cold, and unrelenting in his attitude toward Danhof. To this day I really do not know what the issue was that caused the rift between these two men of God. It could be, knowing the character of these two men, that there was a struggle for power, for a position of strength within the movement.

For several months we traveled to Kalamazoo every Sunday. Often we had dinner at the Danhof parsonage. I recall, too, that for a short time Danhof came weekly to our home in Grand Rapids to teach us catechism. I can still picture the scene in our family playroom. We learned, among other songs, a couple of Dutch psalms. However, it was impossible to make the trips regularly to Kalamazoo. Our family eventually returned to the Christian Reformed Church. We then became members of the Bethel Christian Reformed Church, where father served as elder.

These experiences created in me a very strong desire to understand the issues. Sometimes my parents, and more often my brothers and sisters, chided me for being so inquisitive. In fact, they used to call me "big ears." My persistency in wanting to know the meaning of things at times exasperated them. I recall, early in my youth, discussing and debating the issue of common grace with anyone who was willing and interested enough to participate. What I cannot quite understand is that in my early opposition to common grace, I never developed antipathy toward Abraham Kuyper. Strangely, the battle, as my parents became involved in it, somehow cast no negative reflections upon Kuyper. In fact, my mother, who read a great deal, was extremely fond of Kuyper's meditations. Mother was an avid reader of both fictional and devotional material. She was a deeply spiritual person with rich spiritual insight and much sanctified common sense. Being steeped in Kuyper's meditations, she found ample occasion to relate much of Kuyper's ideas to me. When I was a senior in high school mother suggested that it would be good for me to read occasionally before bedtime a meditation from Kuyper's *To Be Near Unto God*. This I did and found it to be a source of great strength. All of this formed in me an early and deep attachment to Kuyper as a person. I looked upon him not only as a giant with immense capabilities and knowledge but also as a beautiful child of God. For that reason it was not difficult for me later to open up to more of Kuyper's works and thinking. This gradually led me away from the strong anti-common grace position that I persistently maintained practically all the way through college.

I recall in that connection some rather interesting experiences. Already in high school I encountered various students with whom I discussed the question of common grace. This led me to read further and study the issue. In college I was known by my fellow students as being against common grace. In fact, in either my junior or senior year, as a member of the pre-seminary club at Calvin College, I participated in a debate with Harold Dekker, who later became professor of missions at Calvin Seminary. He argued in favor of common grace, I in opposition to it. Looking back, I suppose it was a bit dangerous on my part, since I wanted to be a preacher in the Christian Reformed Church, to be so strongly opposed to common grace. I do not regret that I fought against common grace. It made me study and think, and it alerted me to the dangers of aspects of common grace that not only must be avoided but must be opposed.

I spent four and a half years at Calvin College, graduating in 1939. Since I had graduated from high school in February, I decided to enroll immediately at Calvin College. It was possible to finish college in three and a half years with heavy loads, but I decided against that. I was quite young and felt that four and a half years of college could well serve my purposes. It gave me an opportunity, because I took heavy loads, to broaden my thinking and my education. I was able to major in both philosophy and classical languages with strong minors in history and English. This proved to be very valuable when I became president of Dordt College.

Although I majored in philosophy, I was also interested in the course taught by the late Dr. H.H. Meeter on Calvinism. Meeter was perhaps the best authority on Calvinism in Christian Reformed circles at that time. I took the course during my third year at college. Sad to say, few students appreciated the course. The students of philosophy, in particular, spoke critically about it. Philosophy seemed to get at more of the real problems, and philosophy's rather speculative character had greater appeal to the novice in academic study. I happened to be different on that score. I appreciated very highly Dr. Meeter's courses. This must have gotten through to my philosophy teacher. I can still hear him chide me by saying "Haan, you always want to answer philosophical questions with a theological answer." That bothered me. Later I came to think that what I was really seeking was not a theological answer to a philosophical question but a scriptural answer or basis for a philosophical issue. This was considered by others as being too theological.

What impressed me most in the course on Calvinism was how Meeter presented Kuyper as developing solidly out of a Calvinistic mindset. Meeter made it very clear to me that Kuyper built upon Calvin. The manner in which Kuyper drew upon, further developed, and applied Calvin's thinking was to me, as a philosophy student, very fascinating and enriching. Those who claim that Kuyper had a viewpoint that differed basically from

Calvin are simply mistaken. Meeter's book, *The Basic Ideas of Calvinism*, actually equates Calvinism with Kuyper's concept of the sovereignty of the social spheres. It was in this course too that I was introduced to Abraham Kuyper's Famous "Stone Lectures," delivered in the United States at the Princeton Seminary in 1898.

Upon graduation from Calvin College I had an attractive opportunity to study philosophy further at the University of Indiana under the late Dr. Harry Jellema, but I felt deep down that this was not the direction in which I should go. Here again, I look back and sense the remarkable leading of the Lord. I was eager to get into the ministry. I wanted to complete my seminary training and preach. This decision turned out to be a very important one in my life.

After graduating from Calvin College, I enrolled in Calvin Seminary. My three years in the seminary were extremely valuable. I'll never forget the course I took the very first semester with Dr. Clarence Bouma. It was a course titled "Encyclopedia." I had, in my early years, developed a rather strong antipathy against Dr. Bouma because in my home he was looked upon as an ardent supporter of common grace and a central figure in the battle against Danhof and Hoeksema. The fact that my parents did not speak highly of Clarence Bouma had its negative effect upon me. However, already as a senior in high school I heard Dr. Bouma speak on the question of our Christian responsibility as a citizen. He was running for office in Grand Rapids, Michigan, at that time. I was deeply impressed by that lecture and could sense the beginning of a new attachment to Dr. Bouma, who was also an ardent disciple of Abraham Kuyper.

In his course in seminary, I was introduced for the first time to Kuyper's major scientific work, *The Encyclopedia of Sacred Theology*. I cannot think of any experience in my early history that had a more significant and lasting influence upon my thinking and my life activity. As a philosophy major at Calvin, I had come to accept an idealistic coherence theory of reality and knowledge that came close to a pantheistic system. Kuyper opened my eyes to the biblical view of reality and knowledge that God is the creator who, while being the one through and in whom we live and move and have our being, is separate from and above his creation. God and the cosmos are different. This is extremely important in understanding man's relationship to his creator.

Kuyper's view of the created order as an organic whole governed by laws that are interrelated and give meaning to that creation was an eye opener for me. Kuyper's view of societal spheres and the distinct laws under which they function, all under the Lordship of Jesus Christ, lays the foundation for a magnificent Reformed world and life view. Each sphere, while distinct and having its own task, is still interrelated with all the others. Man, created in God's image, is at home in the cosmos because the laws that govern all of God's created order, including the laws for societal spheres, correspond to the laws by which man functions in creation. He is equipped to know, to investigate, to interpret, and, in fellowship with God, to develop creation toward its high goal.

Kuyper gives a clear picture of man's call to be a partner with God to keep and unfold the garden, that is, His kingdom. Because of sin, that call is now to reform creation by obeying the will of Jesus Christ our king in every sphere and activity of our lives.

I spent hours trying to master the contents of Kuyper's work, to understand the implications of its ideas for all scientific endeavor. I was so impressed with Kuyper's thinking that after graduating from the seminary I took a graduate course with Dr. Bouma called "The Epistemological Implications of the Reformed Faith." This course included studies on Augustine, Aquinas, Calvin, Kuyper, and Barth. Once again I was busy with Kuyper's *Encyclopedia of Sacred Theology*. I can still see myself in the parsonage of the Ridott Christian Reformed Church in German Valley, Illinois, working on this course, striving to broaden and deepen my understanding of Kuyper's principles. I did not realize at the time that within a few years I would be involved in the establishment of Dordt College. Nor did I realize that I would be part of Dordt's education committee that would, among other things, be called upon to write an educational statement of purpose or philosophy for the college.

It was during my seminary years that I began to see the error in opposing common grace. This was primarily due to the influence of Dr. Bouma and Prof. Dietrich Kromminga, professor of history at Calvin Seminary. Gradually it dawned upon me that to deny common grace was basically unscriptural, and even though I avoided some of the extremes in the views of those who held to common grace, I nonetheless came to feel very much at home with the position of the Christian Reformed Church in its opposition to Danhof and Hoeksema.

I did sense, however, both in my college and seminary years that the Christian Reformed Church, by and large, had significantly departed from the teaching of Abraham Kuyper, particularly with respect to his idea of a world and life perspective and his view of the Christian's calling under the Lordship of Jesus Christ in all areas of life. I sensed this mostly in Calvin College. I was not unappreciative for what I had learned at the college and for the many fine dedicated men and women teachers, but at the same time I detected a different influence coming into the academic world of the Christian Reformed Church. This bothered me and others. It probably had something to do, maybe a great deal to do, with my attitude toward the establishment of a Christian college in the Midwest. I was convinced that to answer the problems that faced us in America and in the world around us, Kuyper's principles and world view were of utmost importance.

As I look back to those years, I realize that another experience also helped prepare me for the years ahead. While I was going through high school, college, and seminary, I worked in the market owned and operated by my older brothers. I spent most of the summer in those years and every Saturday from ninth grade on, working in my brothers' meat and grocery market. In those days the hours were long and the pay very small. For several summers I received only ten dollars a week. This job managed to get me through high school, college, and seminary financially. But in fact it did more than that. It kept me close to the business world, and it put me in close contact with the general public. I always loved that part of my work. I enjoyed nothing more than to visit with people, and the grocery-meat market was an ideal place to carry on a wide variety of conversations. Although I was thankful that I did not have to spend my life doing that kind of work, I consider it to have been an extremely valuable experience. It taught me how to work, it taught me how to be patient, and it also taught me how to deal with people.

I met my wife-to-be, Deborah Harkema, the summer before my last year in seminary. We met through my brother Arthur, who was the director of the Radio Choir of the Protestant Reformed church of which Deborah was a member. Arthur asked me to go along with him to listen to a practice session of the choir. Deborah sang a solo. I was impressed both with the voice and the girl. This led to a closer acquaintance, to courtship, and marriage. Deborah was entering her third year at Calvin College when we met. Her plan was to graduate from the college with a degree in education. She was a very good student with special talents in public speaking and music. However, since I was about to graduate from the seminary and to declare myself a candidate in the Christian Reformed Church, we faced a real problem. Should Deborah continue her education, complete her college training, and I go into a parsonage alone for a year? Or would it be better that we marry and that she, at least for the time being, forego the last year of college and join me in the ministry? We finally decided that it was better to marry and to go together into the parsonage wherever the Lord would call us.

It was truly amazing how much our thinking coincided. We were in basic agreement on practically every theological and philosophical question. We shared the same views of the purpose of God's people, the high importance of the church and Christian education, and the need for strong covenantal family life. We were truly united in our hearts and in a basic understanding of our calling before the Lord. Throughout the years this proved to be of inestimable value and significance. It is often said that behind every successful man is a good wife. I cannot possibly imagine how the things that were accomplished could have taken place without the assistance of, the backing of, and the insights of my wife.

We were married on July 21, 1942. I shall never forget the wedding and those early days and months of our married life. They laid the groundwork for a life of mutual interest and cooperation. We knew that we were partners in the work of the Lord. In a true sense, these memoirs are not mine alone but of Deborah and me together.

Our marriage was blessed with six children, three girls and three boys: Katie Lynn, Charles Elson, Mamie Lou, Deborah Bernice, Bernard John, Jr., and Enno Ryan. We were a close-knit family. Our vacations were always family affairs. We spent many weeks at a cottage in Northern Minnesota and on trips throughout the country. Four of our children graduated from Dordt College. The other two attended Dordt for three years. We gratefully acknowledge the Lord's faithfulness to His covenant promises in the life we shared with our children and grandchildren. Truly children are a joy in the Lord.

At the time of my graduation from seminary there were very few vacant churches. In those days a candidate seldom could expect to get a call to a reasonably large church. Most candidates were happy if they received a call from a church of around fifty families. The Lord had to teach Deborah and me a good lesson in humility and patience at that time. I suppose I was too confident that I would receive a call quickly. That did not happen. All of my classmates, eight of them, received calls and were being examined and ordained. Reading about these events in the church publication, *The Banner*, gave me a strange feeling. For the first and only time I wondered whether I had missed my calling. Deborah was a bulwark of strength during these trying days. But it was good for us to go through this. I took a job in a grocery store because I had to make a living for the two of us. Finally in the later part of October, I received not one but two calls: a call from Bemis, South Dakota, a church of some fifty families, and one from Ridott, Illinois, German Valley, a church of approximately sixty families. You can imagine how grateful we were when we received these calls. I had a rather difficult time making the decision. I traveled to Bemis, South Dakota, all alone, preached there and met with the consistory. I also went to German Valley and did the same there. It's very difficult for me to know why I decided to go to German Valley. Probably because it was closer to home and probably it had other advantages that appeared to me at that time to be more important. But there is no question about it that the Lord's hand was in this.

Ridott, Illinois, proved to be an ideal place to prepare me for the work that awaited me elsewhere. The congregation was comprised of nearly all German people. In fact they were Oostfriesians. While there were many points of similarity between my upbringing and what I experienced in Ridott, there were also significant differences. I was brought up in a rather conservative and somewhat traditional, pietistic context. When I came to German Valley, I faced a people who had a different tradition and different practices. My wife and I loved them dearly and the years we spent there were indeed delightful, enjoyable years. But I had to adjust to their ways, to their circumstances, and to their needs. I had to reappraise some of my own thinking, some of my attitudes toward tradition. I found this to be very valuable for me. I also was called upon to make very clear in my preaching precisely what I considered to be the biblical Reformed view of life.

For many years the church had been lax in the discipline of its membership. It surprised me how many members of the church would refrain from attending the services for various periods of time, who would neglect the Lord's Supper, without being visited by the consistory. I also inherited a weak, inadequate catechetical program. But the people were responsive to my desire to strengthen the church in these areas. I can recall the beautiful meetings we had with the consistory, the wonderful hours we spent family visiting and the marvelous cooperation we had in setting up a solid, strong catechism program. To this day the German Valley Christian Reformed Church emphasizes solid, Reformed preaching. Not that I was the only one to bring this attitude about. There were others prior to my coming there and subsequent to my being there who contributed toward these endeavors. However, as a young minister facing these problems, I approached them with the kind of zeal that tested my abilities. The experience led me to become cautious and yet persistent, to be loving and yet uncompromising, and to learn that the Lord blesses such labors. I also had an opportunity to engage a congregation in a sorely needed building program. It seemed almost impossible to them to accomplish it. But we did it with success and with blessed fruits.

I was ordained in Classis Oostfriesland, now called Classis Northcentral Iowa. It was at Classis Oostfriesland, which I attended eight times while minister in Ridott, that I first came to learn of Grundy College. Grundy College was a thriving institution. It had a large enrollment, outstanding professors, and was providing a great service to the churches of the Midwest. However, plans were being made to set up a seminary at Grundy. This caused a sharp conflict within the Christian Reformed Church, resulting in the church refusing to recognize credits of pre-seminary students from Grundy College. Consequently, many supporters of Grundy College throughout the Midwest withdrew their support, and the college had to close its doors. That was a sad experience and caused many hard feelings. I personally feel that the church made a very foolish decision on this matter. Grundy College could have served a stellar role in the building up of the church throughout the Midwest, especially among the Oostfriesians. It had everything going for it.

Being in this classis at the time they were liquidating properties, I learned much about the Grundy College situation. I could sense a heavy, sad spirit on the part of many of the people in the classis when they discussed the Grundy matter. Later, when I became involved in the establishment of Dordt College, I profited a great deal from what I had learned through the experience of Grundy Center. I was able to answer many arguments opposing the establishing of a junior college by pointing to the fact that Grundy College did not fail for lack of students or lack of support, and that given the right situation with the right demands and the right needs, a junior college would certainly be successful in this part of the country.

We established some beautiful relationships with many people in Ridott. Today, some forty-five years later, when we go back to our first charge, we still feel like it is a homecoming. It is truly a joy and most rewarding to go back and meet the dear people who are still living, as well as their children and grandchildren.

I vividly recall the first time I received payment for services as a minister. The salary was by no means excessive. In fact, it was quite the opposite. I was called at that time on the salary of $1340 per year. My earnings were $55 every two weeks; $110 a month. But when I received that first $55 check, you can't imagine how satisfying and gratifying it was. I had been brought up in a large family with thirteen children and had gone through the great depression years. We had very few conveniences. In fact, while we were in Grand Rapids, my parents never owned a car. We struggled along. There were times during the depression that several of my older brothers were without work. Only my father had a reasonably good job. We were satisfied with a little, and we did a great deal with a small income. So when I received that first paycheck, even though it was meager, to me it was a great step forward in my finances. We lived frugally, and the people were gracious to us, generously giving us all kinds of meat and other foods. The congregation sensed and met our financial needs. When we were there barely two years, they presented us with an automobile. We were delighted with the car and very thankful for it.

After only two years in Ridott, I had received three calls: one to a smaller church in rural Western Michigan, another call from Morrison, Illinois, which was only fifty miles from German Valley, and a call from Ackley, Iowa, which was a member of Classis Oostfriesland. I was not given the freedom to accept these calls. I kept thinking about Northwest Iowa.

In the spring of 1945, I was notified that I was on trio at the First Christian Reformed Church of Sioux Center. My interest was aroused immediately. However, I didn't get the call. But I watched *The Banner* and I noticed that three or four ministers, called after this first trio was made, declined. Then I was placed on trio again. I felt quite confident that I would get the call, and I had already determined in my mind that if I did get the call, I would accept. At about the same time, there were church leaders advising me to be a bit patient because other churches were interested in calling me. As a matter of fact, I was told that a church in Grand Rapids, Michigan, was considering putting me on a trio. But that didn't impress me. I eagerly awaited news from Sioux Center. I recall very well that the congregational meeting was held on a Monday night. I knew that the mail would come on Wednesday if I received the call. I can still see the automobile of the mailman driving up to our mailbox. I went out to the mailbox fully confident that the call letter would be in the box. I reached in, and sure enough, there it was, a call to First Sioux Center. It was the month of June, and my father and mother were visiting us. I quickly ran into the house holding up the call letter. I said "I'm going to accept this call." My wife Deborah began to cry because she really loved the place where we were and felt badly about leaving. But it was clear in my mind that Sioux Center was the place I had to go.

Although we loved the life in Ridott, Illinois, and truly loved the people, the congregation was rather small and there was no Christian school. Looking to the future, it did not seem to be the place where we could serve the Lord most effectively. When we received a call from Sioux Center, the people pleaded with us to stay, and even suggested that if we stayed, we would soon have a Christian school there. That made us feel very good; we were thankful for that commitment. It meant that all we had taught and all we had preached had been appreciatively and lovingly received.

Later I received a number of calls while in Sioux Center. But not once did I feel inclined or have the freedom to accept. I was in Sioux Center to stay. The Lord, in an unusual and unique way, tied and held my labors in His church and kingdom to Northwest Iowa.

When I got the call to Sioux Center, I was also informed that I would have to preach a sermon in the Dutch language once a month. Although I knew some Dutch, I had not joined the class in seminary for students who planned to preach the Dutch language. I really was not qualified to handle a Dutch service. Yet even this did not stand in the way of my desire to go to Sioux Center. I'll never forget either that when I did move to Sioux Center the very first sermon I had to preach was in Dutch. How I ever managed to get through the first year preaching those Dutch sermons I'll never know. But the people were kind to me, especially the older ones who wanted a Dutch service. I made a point that first year of faithfully visiting these sheep of the flock and a bond of mutual love and understanding was formed. I knew that they felt very sorry for me. In fact, when the consistory decided to discontinue the Dutch language entirely, there wasn't a single objection, not one complaint. That made me happy and served to cement an even stronger tie of spiritual friendship. Oh, what enjoyable, blessed years were experienced in our life with the congregation of First Sioux Center.

It was in Sioux Center that the more important events of my life took place. If it were not for these events, there would be little need or purpose for writing these memoirs. Although my early history was very important in preparing me for what was to come, it was what transpired while I was in Northwest Iowa that should be related and passed along to posterity.

A very humorous incident took place upon my arrival as a minister in Sioux Center. I was often playfully teased about this by members of my congregation in years to come. My father and mother and, of course, our two oldest children, Katie Lynn and Charles Elson were with us when we traveled from German Valley to Sioux Center. We had a good car, the automobile that had been given to us in Ridott. But being a product of the war years, there were certain defects. Just as we entered Sioux Center, full of excitement, for some reason or another the horn on the automobile began to blow. There was no way I could stop it. This embarrassed my parents and especially my wife. They chided me as though I was to blame. Of course, this was not true. I remember saying to them, "Well, I can't help it so what do I care. If it blows, it blows!" So we came into Sioux Center with great fanfare, the car horn blowing incessantly.

This incident was frequently referred to in later celebrations. It was said, humorously, that I came into Sioux Center blowing my horn and that I continued to blow it ever after. There may have been something to it, though, that was symbolic, even prophetic. If it is true that my horn was blowing ever since arriving in Northwest Iowa, I sincerely hope and pray that it was a trumpet call to arm for the battle and to carry on the work of the Lord in the coming of His kingdom.

Chapter Two
Rekindling the Flame of Christian Education

We came to Sioux Center thankful that there was a Christian school to support and promote. I was firmly convinced that no congregation could carry out its responsibilities effectively, in agreement with the demands of the biblical Reformed faith, without participating in and giving support to Christian education. If we truly believe that our children are the Lord's and are citizens of his kingdom who share the calling to live out their faith in all areas of life, they must be educated in schools that stress their high calling in God's kingdom, schools that articulate a Christian perspective in all fields of learning. The church order of the Christian Reformed denomination states clearly that consistories shall see to it that there are good Christian schools where children can be educated according to the demands of the covenant. I, therefore, maintained that it was the duty of the church, particularly the consistory, to promote Christian education. Not to do so would be contrary to the stand of the denomination.

I was hardly in Sioux Center for two weeks when I began to detect that support for the Christian school, even on the part of my own congregation, was not at all as anticipated. I sensed quickly within both the congregation and the community that there was a sharp difference of opinion about the need for Christian education. Several families in the congregation sent their children to rural public schools. Although this was understandable, it was not a healthy situation. However, what concerned me even more was that several families in town were sending their children to the public school.

I saw a division within my own church between those who sent their children to the Christian school and those who sent them to the public school. The situation was no better in the Second Christian Reformed Church, now known as Bethel Christian Reformed Church. While approximately sixty percent of the children of my congregation, the First Church, were enrolled in the Christian school, hardly forty percent of the children in the Second Christian Reformed Church attended the Christian school.

I made it known at the outset that I intended to promote Christian education and rally God's people behind it. Shortly after I began my ministry in Sioux Center I was confronted by some influential members of the church

Rekindling the Flame of Christian Education 33

who were strong advocates of the public school. They tried to persuade me to go cautiously and to support those behind the public school as much as those behind the Christian school.

I will never forget two instances of such attempts to restrain me on the issue of Christian education. A prominent community member, one who backed the public school and who had a measure of influence within my congregation, stopped me on Main Street. He told me how he felt about my actions and my position on the Christian school question, and let me know, in no uncertain terms, that if I continued to press the issue, I was heading for trouble. He pointed out that the former minister had treated both groups within the congregation equally and did not stir up the nest on the touchy issue of Christian education. He was not at all pleased when I informed him that as a minister in the Christian Reformed Church, I was wholly committed to Christian education and that it was my duty to stand behind that commitment. In response he took a paper match folder and said to me, "This is what you're going to do to this church." He slowly tore the match box in half. I responded by saying that if that was really true, then it better happen, and I challenged him: "Why can't we all rally together behind the Christian school and make it the kind of institution that will be a strong witness in our community and command respect?"

About the same time I visited one of the chief officers of the local bank. He was a member of my church and also an ardent supporter of the public school. He gave me a long lecture on how I should conduct my ministry in this community. He tried to impress upon me that Sioux Center was a unique community where everyone worked together. Being very involved in the Sunday school of my church, he urged me to put my full effort behind the Sunday school, making it a truly effective instrument rather than to belabor the issue of the Christian school.

My wife recalls vividly how I came home from one such encounter and said to her and to my parents who were still visiting with us, that if I did not know before why I had to come to Sioux Center, I now knew very well.

A bit later I found out through a member of the church who had been an advocate of the public school, but who had changed his mind as a result of my preaching, that an elder of my church had visited him following a Sunday afternoon service. He came to talk about the division that I, this young upstart minister, was creating within the church, and asked what to do about it. Evidently when he discovered no sympathy for his actions, he became more cautious and nothing threatening developed.

It was true that I was very young, only twenty-eight years old. However, despite my youth, I had done my homework carefully. Past thinking, the many discussions on the subject, and my family's history in Christian education equipped me to deal with the questions calmly, lovingly, and without anger. Fortunately, from the very first Sunday I stepped up to the pulpit, my preaching was very well received. Attendance at the services increased and one could feel a welcome stir within the congregation. The supporters of Christian education were obviously delighted by the sermons and looked for the dawn of a new day for Christian education in our community.

Before I go into further detail on the struggles in promoting Christian education, we should look at the historic background of the situation. That history is a story in itself and had a direct bearing on the conditions present in both the community and the churches when we arrived in Sioux Center.

Already early in Sioux Center's history, a rather significant number of families were strongly committed to Christian education. The result was that in 1905 a Christian school with four rooms was erected. Even though many members of the church sent their children to rural public schools, the church solidly supported the Christian school. One knew that if the day came when the rural country public schools would go out of existence, families with children in these schools would align themselves with the town Christian school and gradually with the proposed Christian high schools.

Until 1922 there was only one Christian Reformed Church in Sioux Center. It was a large congregation and a very influential one. This church had enjoyed the leadership of a few prominent ministers who did much to shape the lives of the members and deepen their convictions in the Reformed faith. Members were loyal to the church and to the principles upon which it was established.

However, certain events took place that threw serious roadblocks in the way of commitment to Christian education in the Sioux Center community. The predominant factor was the strife that developed within the Christian Reformed Church of Sioux Center. Seldom has there been a rift in a congregation accompanied with more misunderstanding, anger, hatred, and enmity. The struggle reached its peak during the ministry of the Reverend C. De Leeuw.

I was determined to find the real cause of the rift. It was a fruitless endeavor. No matter with whom I talked or what I read, I simply could not find the true cause of the division. There were so many different opinions about it. One reason that stands out as a prominent cause of the trouble was the argument over the use of the Dutch language. However, there must have been other related incidents and experiences that combined to create such a bitter spirit among the members of the church.

In 1922, therefore, the Second Christian Reformed Church was formed.

The Synod of the Christian Reformed Church, which ultimately had to address the issue, decided that the families of what was later the First Church were in the right and should remain in possession of the properties and the name, First Christian Reformed Church of Sioux Center. This group was also obligated to assume the indebtedness on the property, which was no small amount.

Approximately eighty families formed the Second Christian Reformed Church of Sioux Center, later named Bethel. They met for one year in temporary quarters, which, after that year, was converted into a roller skating rink. There apparently was more wealth in the Second Church than in the First Church. Consequently, although First Church had possession of the building, they were unable to meet the payments on the indebtedness. As a result, after one year, they were forced to evacuate the building and turn the building over to the Second Christian Reformed Church. The strange situation arose in which my congregation retained the name First Christian Reformed Church, but the Second Christian Reformed Church occupied the building that had on its cornerstone "First Christian Reformed Church."

The First Church met for approximately five years in the public school auditorium. In 1929 a new building was erected that the First Church congregation occupied for many years. It was in that building that I preached the gospel for eighteen years.

The rift in the Christian Reformed Church in Sioux Center had its adverse affects upon the development of the Christian school. Since a majority of students in the Christian school were from the First Christian Reformed Church, many in the Second Christian Reformed Church did not care to affiliate with or support the Christian school. It should be noted, however, that there were a few families in the Second Christian Reformed Church who remained wholly and completely dedicated to the cause of Christian education and throughout the years have given their full support to the local Christian school. But for some time the Second Christian Reformed Church refused to give financial support to the local Christian school. I was told on good authority that the minister, the Rev. L. Ypma, who was the first minister of the newly formed Second Christian Reformed Church, promoted Christian education in his way and the church did take offerings for Christian education. However, the minister saw to it that the money did not go to the local Christian school but was sent to the Christian school in Minnesota where his daughter was a teacher.

Obviously these circumstances made it very difficult to promote the local Christian school in Sioux Center. Many rural families who continued to send their children to the country public schools were not easily convinced of the need for Christian education. When these children graduated from the country schools, it was only natural that several of them would attend the local public high school. No one gave strong leadership urging them to attend the Christian high school. Furthermore, because of the struggle, several families left the Christian Reformed Church and affiliated with the Reformed Church of America. Generally these families also were lost to the Christian school. It happened frequently in those days that when a young man courted a girl from the RCA and married, their membership was transferred to the Reformed Church of America. In most of these instances, support for the Christian school ceased.

Another disconcerting fact was that the local community centered its social and community life around the public school and its activities. The local public school was an influential, popular institution. The Christian school was made to appear needless since teachers in the public school were Christians. For many it was the "in" thing to attend the public school and thus become an integral part of community life and action. The Christian school, on the other hand, was weak, unattractive, and had very little status in the community. It faced an uphill battle all the way. The result was that even in the First Christian Reformed Church people easily sent their children to the public school, both elementary and high school. Their status, both in the congregation and certainly in the community, was in no way hurt.

The Great Depression added to the woes of the Christian school. There was no money, times were hard, and even some of the supporters of Christian education felt relatively at ease sending their children, upon graduation from elementary school, to the local public high school. Such was the setting when we arrived in Sioux Center in 1945.

Although I learned within the first few weeks I was in Sioux Center that there was serious disagreement about Christian education, I did not become aware of the extent of the problem until the later part of August when I attended the society meeting of the Christian school. The meeting was held in the basement of the Protestant Reformed Church of Sioux Center. That church was one hundred percent behind the Christian school, but it was a very small congregation of about twenty-five families. The minister, with whom I worked closely and with great pleasure, was the Rev. James Van Weelden. He, later, was the first among the Protestant Reformed ministers to seek and receive entrance into the Christian Reformed Church. I went to the meeting full of enthusiasm and anticipation. I was not at all ready for what I met when I arrived outside the church. There were only about twenty people present at that meeting including the board members of the Christian school. I was stunned. Where were my people? Where were those who had their children in the Christian school? Even they seemed to have very little feeling for the school. Standing outside the building with these few people, I asked what was going on. I was told that this was nothing unusual; that interest in the cause of Christian education was very weak; and that very few appeared ready to tackle the problems and move forward in the cause.

I suggested that we begin the meeting and discuss the situation. Regular business was set aside. We just talked. I proposed that as early as possible the Christian school board invite the two consistories to a meeting to discuss the matter. Immediately the next morning, I visited with the minister of the Second Christian Reformed Church, and we agreed that such a meeting could be valuable. But then I had to face my own consistory. I knew that this would be a delicate situation because at least two members of the consistory had children attending the public school. That meeting also proved to be historic. When I brought up the subject, it became very tense and quiet in the room. I clearly articulated the stand of the church. I also stated my convictions as a minister of that church, that I was firm in my view, and that the consistory had to stand behind me in the promotion of Christian education. I said that I would find it very difficult to go family visiting and promote Christian education with a member of the consistory who presented an opposing view.

How it happened I will never know, but the consistory took a definite stand behind me. It was quite evident that the church, with the backing of the consistory, was committed to doing more to promote the cause of Christian education.

The meeting did not mean that we were free from further struggles within the congregation and in the community. Not at all. But the back of the opposition to Christian education was broken, at least in my congregation, by the decision of the consistory.

There was some uneasiness that we could lose families to the Reformed Church of America over the Christian education issue. Many of us were amazed to find that even though a couple of families left our church, the church as a whole stood solidly together. Even the majority of those who had their children in the public school were friendly and quite encouraging. For me this was a major breakthrough.

The meeting with the two consistories and the Christian school board was another vital step in the process. The minister of the Second Christian Reformed Church, the Rev. Oliver Breen, convinced his consistory to join with our consistory and the school board for this meeting. It was held in the basement of the Second Christian Reformed Church and was another meeting that I will never forget. The problems of the Christian school were candidly and openly stated and discussed. No one was left in the dark as to the true state of affairs. At this meeting I realized that even though there had been many past arguments and divisions, and even though there had been bitter feelings, the principles of the Reformed faith and Christian education, having been deeply instilled, were still alive. Beneath all of the recent events and all the history, there remained the conviction, deep down, that Christian education was of vital importance.

It was agreed at this meeting to call another Christian School Society meeting. The board decided to come with a mandate, an ultimatum, to the people. The question was, "Will we continue to have a Christian school in Sioux Center or not?" Even though we formulated the announcement that way, we did not seriously think the Christian school would be discontinued in Sioux Center. Our aim was simply to emphasize the seriousness of the situation.

Although there were only some twenty present at the earlier fall meeting of the school society, there were no less than 150 at this meeting. Even the mayor of Sioux Center, the late Maurice Te Paske, attended. Mr. Te Paske, though a strong supporter of public education, did not like to see the Christian school of Sioux Center closed. It was his conviction that the Christian school helped to keep the public school on its toes and helped to preserve good morals and high standards in the public school.

But in 1945 the Christian school was in a sad state of affairs. These years were not depression years. People were going ahead financially. In spite of this, the Christian school operational budget had run behind by nearly $6000. In those days, that was a lot of money. If you stop to consider that I was called that same year to Sioux Center on a salary of $2800 and that this salary was considered to be relatively high, then you can see what $6000 indebtedness in the operating expenses of the school implied. Furthermore, the physical facilities of the school were run down. There were only eighty-seven students, and it was almost impossible to find a principal for the school. Something radical had to take place. The people who attended the meeting were aroused and filled with eager anticipation. A meaningful buzz filled the room.

The speaker for the evening was Mr. Peter De Vries, an elder in the First Reformed Church and one of the few members of that church who was an enthusiastic backer of the school. He was also one of the county supervisors. He spoke on the *Song of Solomon*, chapter one, verse six, "They made me the keeper of the vineyards; but mine own vineyard have I not kept." One could hardly imagine a more appropriate text from which to speak nor a message that was more applicable to the situation in Sioux Center with regard to the Christian school. Needless to say, Mr. De Vries made a profound impression upon the audience.

After hearing all the facts about the financial plight of the school, a recommendation by the board to conduct a drive to liquidate the $6000 debt was unanimously adopted. That very night the mayor of Sioux Center gave a contribution of $100 to the cause. This action on his part made it very difficult for those who might be opposed within the community and within the church to speak with disfavor about what was decided.

Interestingly enough, it was decided that if funds beyond the $6000 were raised these should go toward the building of a new Christian school.

The drive was highly successful. We raised not only enough money to pay the debt but also an additional sum to be used toward the building of a new Christian school. A new spirit of hope and optimism filled Christian school supporters, but we were still a long way from being out of the woods as far as the successful operation of the school was concerned. To most people, even those within the Christian school, the thought of a new school building was an idle dream. We also knew that it would take a lot of work to convince those who were in the public school to join in the Christian school movement. But it was a new beginning. From there all it took was wise planning and loving but persistent prodding.

Women played a major role in the activity of the school and in its promotion in those early years. When we came, a Women's Christian School Society met regularly. This was a very dedicated group of women, who came forward and pledged to donate money toward a new Christian school building. However, because Dutch was the only language spoken at their meetings, it was a very small group of women. I saw great possibilities for this society and knew that it would be tremendously important to get all of the younger mothers into that society. But to do that they had to do something about the language problem. I suggested that my wife, who knew no Dutch at all, join the group. One other young mother attended the meeting who also knew no Dutch. My wife was somewhat reluctant to go to the meeting but upon further thought decided to attend. It was our hope that if the minister's wife, who knew no Dutch, would come to the society, it would not be long before they would switch from the Dutch language to the English language. When that happened we would encourage a host of young mothers to join the society. That is exactly what happened. Shortly after my wife became a member, the women decided that they should have the after-recess program in English and not long thereafter, it was decided to conduct meetings entirely in the English language.

In no time a large number of women joined the society, and it became a flourishing group. I seriously doubt whether the new Christian school building would have been built if it had not been for the energetic activity of this group of women. Even to this day, the Christian School Guild, for that is its name, renders wonderful service to the school. The amount of money that they raise through soup suppers and other projects is simply amazing.

There was some genuine humor associated with my wife's joining this Dutch school society. The name of the society was Dragt Elkander's Lasten which means "share one another's burdens." Now that was a very appropriate name. However, my wife, not knowing the Dutch language at all, came home from the society one evening and said to me, "What does that name mean anyway?" When I explained to her what it meant, she said, "Oh. It sounded to me like 'Drag it to the laundry.'" This little story rapidly made the rounds in our circles and received a good deal of hearty laughter. The people appreciated my wife, Deborah, and found nothing at all of ill will or negative criticism in her comment.

Something else happened at this time that was exceptional, if not radical in character. In 1947, after the Rev. Breen left, the Rev. and Mrs. John Brueker from Muskegon, Michigan, took a call to the Second Christian Reformed Church. Not long after they were in Sioux Center they began to press for allowing women to attend the Christian School Society meetings with the right to vote. I was pleased with their desire. The matter was presented to the board and somewhat to our surprise a proposal was adopted by the board and recommended to the society. It carried by a substantial majority. This decision later proved to be a key factor in the vote on whether or not to proceed with the building of a new Christian school.

I recall the mild criticism we ministers received from a few men not in favor of pressing for a new building. They claimed that we played politics by getting the women to vote and thereby win the vote on the issue of a new building. To this criticism we made it very clear that we were not at all sorry or apologetic and if confronted again with a similar situation we would do the same.

A severe test of my role in Christian education and the kind of leadership I would be able to give came in the spring of 1946, only seven or eight months after I arrived in Sioux Center. This was an extremely delicate but crucial matter. Each year the graduating class of the public high school selected a preacher for the baccalaureate service held on the Sunday prior to graduation. Being young and having gained favor with young people of my church and the churches around Sioux Center, I was selected to be the speaker. But it was up to the local Ministers' Association to approve the class decision. When I was asked, or rather, when I was assigned the task of speaking, I promptly refused. My refusal was received with consternation. Other Christian Reformed ministers before me had been willing to speak at these baccalaureate services, why not me, they asked? But I stood my ground. I made it known that given the present attitude of some members of the Christian Reformed Church toward Christian education, it was my duty to build a stronger commitment to it. I was in no position to advance or confirm public education by preaching at the baccalaureate service.

When I asked one of the ministers of the Reformed Church if he would be willing to speak at the graduation of the Christian school, he replied that he could never do that. His people would not understand, and, after all, the public school was here first. My response to this comment was that neither could I speak for the baccalaureate of the public school since many of my people would not understand and my role in promoting Christian education would be seriously weakened.

Many people and even leaders in the Christian Reformed Church were outraged by my refusal to preach at the baccalaureate service. Several members of the graduating class belonged to my church and other families had their children in the public high school. I went through a period of soul-searching, consulted several of my trusted friends and continued to hold to the position that, for me, at that time in history, to preach the baccalaureate sermon would jeopardize Christian education.

Although there was displeasure and tension within my congregation over the matter, I did not feel anger or disrespect. The people already knew how much I appreciated them. They knew, too, how convinced I was that the goals and purposes I was pursuing were in the long run in the best interest of the church.

Despite my stand I did understand why some were displeased with my decision. The class valedictorian was a member of my church. She was extremely disappointed with my refusal to speak. She came to me after a catechism class, and, with tears in her eyes, wanted to know why I could not preach the baccalaureate sermon. I said to her, "Come over to my house and let's talk." We had a beautiful meeting. She told me that her father, who was fairly strong in his commitment to the public school, suggested that she ask me why I had made that decision. To my surprise she said that her father told her that Rev. Haan usually did not take a stand without good reason. That was an opening for me, so I asked her, "What kind of a minister do you want me to be? Must I be a minister who bows to the wishes of the people and the community, or may I have some convictions of my own? If I am convinced that Christian education should be promoted for the welfare of the church, and if I am convinced also that to participate at this time in the baccalaureate service would jeopardize my goals and purposes in the church, why should I bow to the wishes of the people?" The young lady accepted my convictions very graciously and apparently was satisfied with my explanation. We remained good friends thereafter.

Another incident also illustrates how, although outwardly there was dissatisfaction, deep down there was a growing respect for my stand. I went to visit a good family of the church, who also had a son graduating from the public high school. They, too, wondered why I could not preach this sermon, but appeared content with my reply, for they were also strong advocates of the Christian grade school. But they mentioned that it was difficult to make their son understand. Our discussion seemed to have had a significant effect. Later, this son was uptown with a group of his classmates and other friends from the community, and I was viciously maligned for my actions by one of the young men. They tell me he pressed the young man up against a building and said to him, "You take that back right now." When I heard this, I was floored, but grateful for his support.

Upon graduation this young man attended Calvin College, was married, and had a family. Hearing that I was in Grand Rapids attending a session of the Synod of the Christian Reformed Church, he invited me to have lunch

Rekindling the Flame of Christian Education   43

with him. He wanted to talk about the past. About that incident he said, "We opposed you on the surface, but we applauded you in our hearts." He told me that he was active in the church and Christian education in Grand Rapids. I thanked God.

Another unusual thing also took place. Each year, a Sunday or two after baccalaureate Sunday, the American Legion held a big Memorial Day service in the First Reformed Church. This was a truly big affair. The officers of the American Legion had to select the minister for that service. They met in the telephone building where two young women from my church worked as telephone operators. They told me of the following incidents.

The members of the Legion discussed who should speak, and someone brought up my name. These men had been displeased with my decision not to deliver the baccalaureate sermon. Confident that I would turn it down, they thought it would be interesting to see once if I would deliver the Memorial Day sermon. When I received the call, I asked a few questions about who was to supervise the service. I saw no reason to reject it. In fact, when I accepted at once during the telephone conversation, they were utterly amazed. So I was told by the two young women, who were amused by the reaction of these men especially when they said, "He accepted without even asking his consistory." My congregation was obviously delighted that I was going to be the preacher at the big Memorial Day service.

At certain times in life you know that the significance of that moment or event is crucial, and you lean particularly heavily upon the Lord. The Memorial Day service fit into that category. I was nervous, and I prepared diligently for the service. I chose to preach on Hezekiah, pleading for more time to live in order to carry on the program of the Lord. When I came into the building I was shocked by the huge audience. Many people wanted to hear what this young preacher would say, what kind of sermon he would deliver. The Lord was truly good to me that night. I was surprisingly calm and evidently the sermon was well delivered and received. I was greeted with an overwhelming response of appreciation on the part of many in the audience, several of whom were members of the Reformed Church.

The following week on the street people said to me, "Now you delivered that sermon for the Memorial Day service, why couldn't you have given a sermon like that for the baccalaureate service?" I do not know exactly what I replied. I do recall, however, one main theme in my reply. I let it be known that I had no axe to grind with the people of Sioux Center. To show that I thought very highly of many of them, I said, too, that I hoped I could stay long enough in Sioux Center to demonstrate to all that I intended good rather than evil for the community. After that I received the distinct impression that even though there had been an uneasy feeling toward me in the community, I had gained their respect. This incident had a positive effect on my own congregation.

One good side effect of these actions in Sioux Center was the sparking of a new interest in Christian education in several neighboring communities. I was asked to speak at several Christian school society meetings. I was also chosen to be the graduation speaker for Western Christian High School, which I accepted. This created no small stir. Many eyes were on Sioux Center to watch the developments there.

But the struggles in the local Christian school were by no means resolved. We had our work cut out for us as we faced problems of poor facilities, small enrollment, and financial difficulties. The coming of the Rev. John Breuker, whom I mentioned earlier, played an important role in this struggle. He was an older man, experienced, a good preacher, and wholly committed to Christian education. We owe this man of God a great debt of gratitude for the courageous service he rendered in promoting Christian education. Breuker turned things around in the Second Christian Reformed Church of Sioux Center on the issue of Christian education. It was a joy and a blessing to work together with him.

I had been an advisor to the Christian school board for two or three years, from 1945 through 1948. This was unusual. Prior to this, while ministers may have helped to support the school, they stayed as far removed from the operation of the school as possible. That was not my view of the relationship of the minister of the church to the Christian school. I was fully convinced that the relationship between the minister and the principal and the board of the Christian school should be close and supportive. This relationship turned out to be a real boost to the Christian school. When the Rev. Brueker came, I thought it best that he become the next advisor to the board. Steps toward building a new Christian school had already been taken, and we were fairly well along the way. But the going was a bit rough. Rev. Breuker helped to turn the tide.

A number of people believed that it would be impossible to raise the funds needed for a new school. Others disagreed on the kind of school to be built. Some wanted to build a more economical wooden structure, some were determined that the new school should be brick. However, considering the past grim experiences of the school, several strong supporters of Christian education retained a certain amount of hesitancy and uncertainty. It was difficult to come to the point where all were convinced that it was possible to gain a large enough group of supporters to maintain a new Christian school building.

Rekindling the Flame of Christian Education

But support was steadily growing among the people. There was an increasing awareness of the urgent need to go forward, to take some calculated risks for the sake of the cause.

After the decision was made to build a new Christian school, there were issues to confront. How were we to raise the money? How much money would we need? How costly a school should we build? But the momentum was growing and one could sense that these obstacles would be overcome. The people would not rest until that happened. A special spark to ignite the flame and create a spirit of aggressive optimism among the people was needed.

Two such sparks stand out in my memory. After the board decided to build a new school, we had to make plans. An architect from Sioux City was hired and asked to draw a plan for a four-room brick school. When the plans were ready, three of us, two members of the building committee, Mr. John Broek, Sr. and Mr. Albert Kraayenbrink, and I traveled to Sioux City to look at plans and discuss them with the architect. We were very impressed with what we saw. After looking over the plans, the all important question had to be answered: how much would this cost? You must remember that for our people, money was no simple matter. The original school had cost approximately $5000 in 1905. Things had changed considerably but even at that time $1000 was a lot of money. Our hope was to avoid a wooden structure by getting a brick school for approximately $30-35,000. When the architect gave an estimate of $45-50,000, my heart sank. There was a moment of silence. As we left that office and went down the elevator, neither one of the gentlemen said a word. We came out of the building and, standing on one of the main streets of Sioux City, Mr. John Broek, Sr. said, "Now when we show these plans to the society, we must not tell them immediately what the cost of the building is." After that statement, and Mr. Kraayenbrink's nod of agreement, I knew that they were in favor of the proposal even if it cost that much. They were already planning how best to convince the people. To me, we were well on the road to having a new Christian school building.

But we had to raise money. Somewhere there had to be a group of people ready to set an example and give the fundraising campaign a vigorous boost. My wife and I were fully aware of the need for this and discussed the matter carefully and prayerfully. I was still advisor to the board and pressing on all fronts for a new school building. We decided that even if we had to borrow it from the bank we would go to the board and offer a gift of $200 toward the new school. In those days that was no small sum. Since

I had been called to the church of Sioux Center a year or two before on a $2800 salary, you can well imagine how much this meant.

At the board meeting we discussed the campaign. At a proper moment I presented them with the $200 gift. There was silence in the room for a

Sioux Center Christian School

few minutes and then one of the members said, "Well, if Rev. Haan gives $200 then I have to give $500." About a dozen men were present at this meeting. One of the most significant things that happened, which really made it possible to have a successful drive, was that from these men that night we raised $7-8000. We set the goal for the initial drive at $20-25,000.

I should relate a rather humorous exchange between myself and one of the board members about the drive for funds. He was not too optimistic about the outcome so I challenged him. In a playful spirit I said to him, "If we fail to reach the goal, I'm obligated to give you a box of cigars, but if we make the goal then you owe me a box of cigars." We had a good laugh about this and awaited the result of the campaign.

The Rev. John Brueker, the Rev. James Van Weelden, and I worked like beavers to rally people behind the campaign. We were well-organized and carried out the drive in a very systematic way. When the results were finally

Rekindling the Flame of Christian Education 47

in there was great rejoicing. We had reached our goal. A few days later, the board member with whom I made the wager came to the parsonage and handed me, with great joy and delight, a box of Dutch Masters cigars. No matter how much I protested and insisted that it was just a playful wager, it was to no avail. I had to keep the box of cigars.

At this time there were also other communities where Christian school supporters were facing serious problems. Their schools were so dilapidated and out of date that action was required. I am sure that what happened in Sioux Center was a strong motivation to them. Our prediction that other communities would follow suit if we built a brick structure certainly proved to be true.

Near the end of the building project, representatives of two communities came to Sioux Center to look at our project. Five men from Sheldon came to the parsonage to discuss their needs and what they were planning to do to achieve their objectives. I do not recall the advice given them. What I remember is that they wanted a brick school and that each of the five men were going to contribute $5000. I was very pleased. Today Sheldon continues to have a thriving Christian school. The excellent brick structure, later enlarged, is a tribute to the cause. Likewise, the Christian school society of Leota, Minnesota, shortly after our school in Sioux Center was constructed, built an exact duplicate of our school. De Stigter Brothers Construction was the contractor for both schools. Today Northwest Iowa is blessed with beautiful schools in Orange City, Rock Valley, Hull, Hospers, Ireton, Sanborn, Inwood, and Doon. And there are six Christian high schools in our Tri-State area, not to mention several other fine elementary schools in Minnesota, Iowa, and South Dakota.

Chapter Three
The Story Behind Life's Story

The battle over whether to have a theater in Sioux Center was a struggle that caused no small stir in the community. Sioux Center was in the spotlight of the nation. *Time, Life, The Des Moines Register, The Sioux Falls Argus Leader,* and others came to Sioux Center for a short time to cover the story. Little did we realize when we began our fight against the theater that it would have such wide repercussions.

I am still puzzled by it all. Why and how it happened remains a mystery to me. Local and national news reporters suddenly arrived. It was a strange situation. People have often asked me how I responded to that publicity, and I have never been able to put into words precisely how I felt. On the one hand I was not ashamed of the wide attention we received, but neither did I delight in it. For several weeks after things quieted down I tried to assess the pros and cons of what had taken place. I sincerely believed then, and still believe today, that the Lord had a definite purpose in it all. This conviction not only comforted me and encouraged me but also served to keep me humble. When the Lord leads you through such an extraordinary experience, you come to know your own insignificance and His greatness.

Before recounting the story of the controversy, I should make a comment about the people involved. I certainly do not want to convey the idea that those who were opposed to the theater were the good people and those who were in favor of it were the bad people. In the heat of the conflict actions were taken and things were said that cannot be condoned. Nevertheless, it is important to tell the story exactly as we experienced it, without respect of persons.

People often support causes for different reasons. To me the struggle over the theater involved basically the same issues as those we confronted in the struggle for Christian education. I say this even though many public school supporters stood shoulder to shoulder with us in opposing the theater. The fundamental question was this: who would determine the policies and set the direction for the citizens of our community? Were policies to be formed by community leaders reflecting a kind of civil religion, or were we to honor the Lordship of Jesus Christ and follow His will as expressed in His Word?

The Story Behind Life's Story

Sioux Center was too much under the dominance of a kind of civil religion. To be a good citizen was to cooperate with and bow to the will of the community. We were determined to break through that barrier and give the Christian school and the principles it advocated a place of influence and respect in the community. I believe that in the theater controversy the Lord provided us with a fitting opportunity to achieve our purpose.

In the aftermath of the battle over opening a theater, the lines became more sharply drawn, but there also emerged a more respectful attitude toward Christian education in the community. This spirit proved important in the establishing of Dordt College years later. The same community that had engaged in such an intense struggle, later became known as a place where cooperation between various groups of the citizenry was exemplary. Today there is an underlying sense of fair play and an admirable spirit among the people of Sioux Center.

Looking back I find it amazing that some of those against whom I fought at that time later became good friends. One of my closest friends and golfing partners was a man who stood on the opposite side of the fence on the theater issue. I had the highest respect for him as a dedicated Christian and was deeply gratified when I was asked to speak at his funeral. The same can be said about my relationship to the churches in town. They became increasingly cordial. Without compromising my principles, I gladly accepted several invitations to preach in both of the Reformed Churches of America in Sioux Center. I was very grateful that I was warmly received on the pulpits of these churches.

But to return to the story, most people have the wrong idea of what actually happened in this conflict. I suppose misperceptions are understandable when you take into account the report of the battle by *Life, Time,* and various leading newspapers. Although we were opposed to the theater and theater attendance, the opening of a theater in Sioux Center by itself was not the real issue. The issue was whether the American Legion, which included many members from our church, should own and operate a theater. If some individual had decided to invest in a theater, we would not have objected. I would have preached against attending such a theater, but we would not have opposed its coming into Sioux Center. I know several people who would have opposed a theater even if it was owned and operated by an individual, but that was not my position.

Nor was opening a theater the problem my consistory addressed. If the American Legion owned the theater, then members of our church would be the actual owners of the theater. Our denomination had taken a strong stand against the theater and theater attendance. Furthermore, our denomination also maintained the principle of corporate responsibility. Corporate responsibility means that if you are a part of an organization whose practices are contrary to the principles upon which your church stands, then you are co-responsible for the condemned practice.

To get the full picture of the theater conflict, we must go further back. During the war years, the local minister's association sponsored community prayer services. At these prayer services we prayed for our servicemen and our nation. Since most of the men were still in the service and in the process of returning home when I came to Sioux Center in 1945, these services continued for approximately another year. I recall addressing two of these well-attended services, meetings that were enjoyable, profitable, and meaningful.

An offering was always taken to raise money to express our gratitude to the fighting men when they returned home. Funds were quite naturally placed in the hands of the American Legion. Shortly after the men returned home from duty, the American Legion announced that they wanted to use the money to benefit the whole community. The majority of the Legion's members agreed that sponsoring a theater would be an appropriate way to serve the entire community. Naturally the funds that had been raised at the prayer services would be used for this purpose.

For some time certain members of the community, along with a few older, influential leaders of the American Legion, had been eager to have a theater in town. However, since there was some opposition to having a theater in town, no individual stood ready to provide the necessary capital. The supporters of the idea figured that having the American Legion open the theater was a good way to overcome the opposition. People would hardly dare object to having the young men who fought against our enemies own and operate the movie house, they reasoned. Who would have the audacity to speak out against what these young men desired?

The city council had already leased the Town Hall to the American Legion for the theater when the news of the decision was released. You can well imagine the storm of protest that came from several members of the community. Many were incensed at the thought that money contributed at prayer services for the welfare of returning servicemen would be used instead to establish a theater.

As was to be expected, the churches quickly and vigorously voiced their disapproval of the plans. Without exception, the ministers of the local ministers' association were against the proposed theater and immediately took steps to prevent its coming under the Legion's ownership. A committee composed of all Sioux Center ministers and a lay representative from

The Story Behind Life's Story 51

each church was organized to supervise the opposition to the theater. The fight was on.

Due to changes in the personnel of the minister's association, I was chosen to be the chairman of the group. For that reason, at the age of thirty-one, I became a central figure in the ensuing struggle. I was strengthened by the backing of the churches of the community, and especially by the support of my own consistory. This was very important to me. It was my policy never to engage in any activity without the knowledge and support of my consistory.

The ministers put a great deal of pressure on the city council. This pressure put the council in a difficult spot since they had already leased the Town Hall to the American Legion until April 1, 1948. For their part, the Legionaires had been so confident their plans would be realized that they had invested $10,000 in equipment.

Although the committee made their major appeal to the city council members, there was also a heated encounter between the leaders of the Legion and the ministers. After a good deal of argument and debate, the city council finally decided to settle the issue the American way by calling a referendum vote on the matter.

January 6, 1948, was the date chosen for the voting to take place. For at least two weeks prior to the vote, there was a flurry of activity from both sides. The *Sioux Center News* was full of advertisements and special articles with urgent appeals from both the Legion and the ministers.

On January 1, those opposed to the theater held a special mass meeting in the Second Christian Reformed Church (now Bethel). The church was packed. The Rev. H. Colenbrander, minister of the First Reformed Church of Orange City, Iowa, and speaker for the meeting, spoke strongly and effectively against the theater. The Sunday before the election, I, and perhaps other ministers, preached a sermon dealing with the issue. Even the mayor was in attendance in my church to hear the sermon.

Somewhat to our surprise, those resisting the Legion received solid support from a large number of local farmers. These farmers, of course, were not given the privilege of participating in the referendum. As a result they prepared a petition signed by 450 farmers pleading for opposition to the theater on the part of the voters. They placed a prominent ad in the *Sioux Center News* the week prior to the election.

The Legion also had its propaganda machine. In the January 1, 1948, issue of the *Sioux Center News*, the following advertisement appeared:

> But now some folks want to take away our license to operate. They have asked for a vote. The date is January 6th. We wish they had been

here all their lives like we have instead of just a little while. We wish they had been with us when we went to war. They would understand us better. They would know that we love our community and have only its good at heart. We know that some spiritual leaders here who oppose us are lenient and liberal as to their own habits. But some of our boys and girls are too young to take up smoking and drinking just yet. God give us strength to offset the example they are setting for the youngsters of this community. We are asking the people of this town to support us with our project of nice pictures for nice people.

Some leaders of the Legion resorted to slanderous attacks on my person in the struggle that followed. Certain leaders of the community and many of the citizenry were strongly opposed to smoking and drinking. The large majority of the members of the Christian Reformed Churches in Sioux Center and the Protestant Reformed Churches were, at that time, not opposed to moderate smoking nor to moderate drinking. We continued to have wine in our communion services. The Legion leaders focused on this issue. Many young people from the public high school also got involved in the campaign. Often in the morning I would come outdoors and see my lawn littered with empty beer bottles. A rumor spread that I had no milk in my refrigerator for my children, only beer. Another rumor claimed that I frequented the only cafe where beer was sold, Doc's Cafe.

One day a community leader called me into her office and asked me how I, a minister, felt about drinking. She wondered if I was setting a good example for the young people by patronizing Doc's Cafe. I replied, "I never go to Doc's Cafe. The only time I ever entered Doc's Cafe was my first week in Sioux Center. My mother and I were walking down the street when we saw a sign for 'Ice Cream' at Doc's Cafe. Without thinking or even knowing the situation, I went into Doc's to buy some ice cream."

She answered, "Well then we must stop this awful rumor." In response to that comment, I made it very clear that I was not about to run down rumors. There were so many false stories afloat that I could spend all of my time just tracking down negative rumors. In the long run false rumors do little harm, especially when you are in the heat of a battle for principles based upon the Word of God.

Despite some slanderous attacks on my person, I refused to react in kind. For example, I urged people to trade with local businesses. I always advocated doing business in our own community, so that we could build a thriving community, promote a good spirit, and make a good living. Even during this conflict, I did most of my business with the local merchants.

One of the leaders of the Legion even remarked that more people from Haan's church traded with him than from his own church.

After one heated argument between Legion leaders and the ministers, the president of the Legion approached me somewhat nervously, asking me what I intended to do. I asked what he meant by that. "Well," he said, "I'm a young, new veterinarian in this community and I have several good clients from your church. You can make it rough for me."

I promptly replied, "Well, Doc, don't worry. If you think that's the way we carry on a fight, you're badly mistaken. I have no intention of trying to get my people to cut you off. To boycott someone in that manner is totally unChristian." He was obviously relieved. Later, I heard that in a meeting of the Legion, when some uncomplimentary remarks were made about me, this doctor stood up in my defense.

A similar incident occurred later. One morning I visited an elderly couple in my church. Their physician was a prominent doctor in the community and highly appreciated by several of my church members. He was an ardent and influential backer of the Legion and argued passionately for the theater. He, very unprofessionally I thought, talked loudly about all the young people who were going to other communities and practicing questionable morals. He thought that a theater in our town would keep these young people home. When I called on the elderly couple they informed me that their doctor had just been there and spoke quite negatively about me, their pastor. He must have been shaken when this couple told him that Rev. Haan always spoke highly of him as a doctor and assured them that they could place full confidence in him as their physician.

One incident that took place just prior to the election finally opened the eyes of several members of my church who were public school supporters. The public school firmly supported the American Legion and the theater. In fact, they staged a parade in which many of the students participated, carrying banners calling for the people to vote "Yes" in the election. Among those marching were young members of my church who attended the public school. The experience proved to be very embarrassing for several of the parents.

As was to be expected, there was a heavy turnout for the vote on January 6th. To the dismay of the members of the Legion and their followers, they lost by a vote of 488 to 427. However, our assumption that the vote settled the matter was by no means verified. We knew that the struggle was not over when we read the following statement in the January 8 issue of the *Sioux Center News*:

The proposition was admitted by both sides to be a directive to the city council and not an official mandate. Apparently both sides meant to carry their case beyond the election in the event of defeat. That just simply was not true. We did not believe that the fight would continue after the election, and we certainly assumed that this was an official mandate, not simply a directive.

In the same article of the January 8 issue of the *Sioux Center News*, we read,

> Legion officials said after the election that their future course would depend on decisions by the local Legion Post.

They pointed out that their present license ran until April 1 and that they had already invested $10,000 in equipment, which they felt obligated to protect. The vote confirmed for them that if 427 voters favored a theater, their rights to see pictures should not be ignored.

An article in the *News* prior to the voting stated that the election had attracted attention from outside the community. I quote from the article printed the morning before the election:

> George Mills, ace reporter for the *Des Moines Register*, accompanied by a photographer, flew to Sioux Center by plane to get a complete story on the theater fight. He interviewed city officials, legionnaires, and several of the pastors. Stories were carried in daily newspapers and on radio stations in the middle west. The novelty to outsiders is that a town of this size doesn't have a theater, and the intensity of the battle in the articles and advertisements in the last issue of the *News* was exciting. The public loves a tough fight, but whether this fight is a credit to Sioux Center is highly doubtful.

Anyone can see how biased these comments were and what side the *News* was on.

A new phase of the battle began about two months later when the city council had to decide whether or not to renew the license of the American Legion to operate a theater in the Town Hall. Since new council members had been elected in March, the majority of the members were in favor of granting the license to the American Legion. In spite of efforts by the Rev. John Breuker, the Rev. James Van Weelden, and myself to convince the city fathers to abide by the advisory vote of January 6th, they decided to grant the license for another seven months. The following reasons were given:

1. Authority for licensing is vested solely in the council under Section 368.8 of the Code of Iowa, 1948.

2. Town Hall facilities had been granted twenty-five years ago to Veterans of World War I.

3. For many years the Town Hall had been leased for commercial purposes, during which period the community used the Legion Hall.

4. The American Legion's request for the use of the Hall was originally made and granted over a year before equipment was purchased and operation commenced.

5. The original request was made shortly after the termination of hostilities of World War II, and the council then in office granted the request of the American Legion.

6. The majority of the council agrees with those who conscientiously feel that there is less danger to the morals of our young people by permitting the local showing of a safer and higher type of picture than they would see in other communities in this area. Carried by a vote of 4 to 1.

This decision of the council was not only unprincipled and contrary to the democratic process, it also proved to be quite foolish. Although many members of the Reformed Church of America in Sioux Center were displeased and disappointed with the council's action, the leadership in the RCA was ready to acquiesce in the matter. Now it was only the Rev. Van Weelden, the Rev. Breuker, and myself who continued to oppose the Legion.

One of the leading ministers of the RCA met me at this time in the post office. He did not feel we should continue the fight over the issue and felt that it probably wouldn't be all that bad to have a theater in Sioux Center after all. But the two Christian Reformed Churches of Sioux Center felt differently. They published a joint statement that membership in the American Legion under the present circumstances and membership in the Christian Reformed Church were incompatible. This meant we were asking our boys to discontinue their membership. Although forty Christian Reformed young men pulled out of the American Legion, others were unhappy with the decision of the church. But something happened that quickly led them to change their minds. The same RCA minister who had spoken to me earlier about going along with the council's decision spoke to a couple of the young men in my church who were not too happy with the decision. He suggested they come to his church where they would not be bothered. The young men were angered and soon decided to quit the American Legion. Despite these actions, the American Legion moved ahead with its plans, and the theater came to Sioux Center.

The conflict surrounding the city council's decision brought a wave of reporters to our city. *Time* and *Life* were soon on the scene, sensing the possibility of dramatic news. We were fairly pleased with the articles in the *Des Moines Register*, written by George Mills, and with the *Time* articles on the subject. But we were very displeased with the way *Life* treated us and presented the case.

Being young and naive about news reporting, we were caught off guard by *Life* magazine. The two reporters from *Life* who came with their cameras ready to shoot claimed that they were interested in the strength of religion and churches in our rural communities. The struggle over the theater, according to them, confirmed this fact. Now it is true that at that time, and even today, church attendance was very high. Most townspeople were members of one of the Sioux Center churches and faithful participants in the life of their church. The city was governed by high moral standards. The late mayor, Mr. Maurice Te Paske, often took pride in the fact that at that time there was only one divorce in Sioux Center. So it was not dif-

The Story Behind Life's Story

ficult for us to fall for the trap. We cooperated fully with the *Life* reporters. In fact, the Sunday they were in Sioux Center, we invited them to our house for dinner and had what I thought was a very friendly and meaningful conversation. They even attended my church on that Sunday afternoon. They took pictures of several of our churches and the crowds attending them. They also asked to take pictures of me, to which I foolishly consented. In fact, we were fairly well convinced that these two reporters intended to give an honest report of the event in Sioux Center. We heard shortly after these men left town, however, that just prior to their leaving, one of the leading citizens of Sioux Center, the publisher of the *Sioux Center News* cornered them and gave them an entirely different picture of the event, which, evidently, these reporters accepted.

When *Life* magazine appeared on the streets, we were stunned, almost shocked. We had expected something better. They treated the whole issue as a rural, small town fight between religious conservatives and progressives. To our surprise, though, we soon discovered that thousands of people from all over the country were pleased with the stand that we had taken. It is a pity I did not save all the letters I received from various parts of the world. The vast majority of them were complimentary. Some objected to the fact that I was not opposed to moderate drinking or moderate smoking. I was even invited to speak at a large gathering of Christians in California who were battling the moral issues of the day. But by this time I had had my fill of publicity and notoriety. I wanted to get back to the normal life of a minister. Evidently, the other members of the special committee set up to supervise our actions felt the same way. We could have brought *Life* to court for false representation, but we decided against that. Perhaps the unexpectedly favorable response of so many throughout the world prompted us to leave the issue well enough alone.

But the *Life* article also brought a good deal of ridicule from outsiders. Those who supported the theater in Sioux Center were very much ashamed of what had taken place and were angry with me for a time. I was presented as a saint from afar who came to Sioux Center only to bring trouble and to break up the unity of the community. Some even told people in my congregation that they would be stuck with me for the rest of my life because no one else would want me. However, I continued to enjoy the good will and respect of people in my congregation and in surrounding communities.

Nevertheless, I was grateful when, shortly after all of those events had taken place in Sioux Center, I received two calls to other churches. One of these calls was from a local church—Leota, Minnesota—and the other was from Munster, Indiana. The members of my church, almost without exception, urged me not to leave. This was a mystery to many of the people of the community. They were completely dismayed and confused.

In those days of trial, stress, and strain, the Lord was very good to me. During the next few years, which were crucial for the cause of Christian education in Sioux Center and the coming of Dordt College, the Lord literally flooded me with calls. The records will bear out that I received approximately fifty calls, several of them from large and influential churches. At times I wondered what the Lord expected of me. Did he want me to leave Sioux Center or were these calls just an encouragement to me in my work? I have no doubt that those calls strengthened me in whatever role of leadership I was called to exercise.

Some in the community were eager to see me leave. I remember after receiving several calls that one leading woman in Sioux Center said to a member of my church, "How loudly and how long must the Lord shout in that young man's ears?" The implication that I paid no attention to the will and the calling of the Lord troubled me somewhat. When I next visited Grand Rapids I called upon the late Henry J. Kuiper, editor of *The Banner*. After discussing my situation he assured me that often ministers who were the most effective in the life of the denomination remained in one church for a lengthy period of time. He assured me that if I did not feel called to leave there was no reason to be disturbed about declining these calls.

The Lord had his own way of keeping me in Sioux Center. Although I did not want to leave Sioux Center and felt obliged to stay because of the work that I was involved in, several personal experiences made it impossible for me to accept a call elsewhere even if I had wanted to. In the end, it was not so much I as the Lord who kept me in Sioux Center.

Today, looking back on those events it is interesting to note that from the day the theater opened in Sioux Center, it was a losing proposition. Attendance was poor. Even those who fought to get the theater hardly dared attend it because of the attitude of many citizens of Sioux Center. Some business people didn't dare to attend the local theater for fear of the effect it might have on their business. They would go out of town instead where they wouldn't be seen. With the advent of television in the home, the doom of the theater was sealed.

As a result of the theater controversy, the American Legion lost much of their influence in the community. The men who left the American Legion began a new organization called "The Veterans of Foreign Wars." With a competing organization in town, the American Legion never regained its former influence.

Only two members of my church asked to have their membership transferred to another church because of our stand on the movie question. The spirit in First Church during these times could hardly have been better. Various factions within the church pulled together with a new goal and a new purpose. Those were truly exciting days. Plans for the new Christian school were presented to the people, a campaign for funds was under way, and hope for the future was bright. Not only that, the battle over the theater question caused several of the members of my church whose children attended the public school to take a new look at Christian education. By the time the new school building was ready for occupancy, several of these families took their children out of the public school and enrolled them in the Christian school. The increase in enrollment was most gratifying, and we praised the Lord.

Something else began to happen at this time. Earlier, if a young man from our church married a girl from the Reformed Church of America, he would usually join the RCA rather than remain with the CRC. Now the tables began to turn. In several instances a young man from the community who had gone through the public school system married a girl from my church and became a member of my church. Some of these new members became ardent Christian school supporters. In fact, one of these young men who joined our church later became president of the board of the Christian school.

You can hardly imagine how many marriage ceremonies I conducted during those first few years after World War II. One week I had no less than four weddings. With so many young married couples, I considered it important to bring them together around God's Word to discuss the issues we were confronting. The Gleaner's Forum was one of the first societies of married couples to be organized in the churches of our area. It served a vital role in the promotion of Christian education. It was a healthy society, a place for couples to let their hair down and speak out forthrightly on all matters of principle. We had such wonderful times together and the result of the activities of this group cannot be over-emphasized. This was a group alive with kingdom vision.

In the fall of 1948, the Christian school received a real boost with the coming of Mr. A.J. Boersma as principal. He occupied that position for twenty-three years. He not only did a superb job as the administrator of the school, having a profound influence upon the spiritual direction of many of the pupils, but he also brought something unique to Sioux Center. He had a love for flowers, trees, and birds. He soon planted and maintained a lovely display of flowers on the grounds of the Christian school. It wasn't long before Sioux Center became noted for its flowers. The city of Sioux Center, particularly under the influence of Mayor Maurice Te Paske, soon engaged Boersma to take charge of the planting on Main Street and in the city parks. When Dordt College started, the college hired Mr. Boersma to plant beds of flowers on campus. To this day Dordt College is known for its flowers and attracts visitors from miles around to see its beauty.

The struggles over the theater and Christian education drew the attention of many other communities. Prior to this time Sioux Center was hardly known throughout the Christian Reformed denomination. Now there were very few who did not know about Sioux Center. Sioux Center began to take a leadership role in Christian education and other related matters. This eventually proved to be a vital factor in the establishing of Dordt College and the choosing of Sioux Center for its location. It is doubtful whether the momentum needed to establish Dordt College would have been there if Sioux Center had not gone through the struggle over the theater and had not championed the cause of Christian education.

Furthermore, the fact that advocates of the Sioux Center Christian School gave such vigorous support to Christian secondary education in Hull, Iowa, showed that Sioux Center was not selfish in its pursuit of Christian education but was ready to cooperate with others for this worthy cause. During these early years I was laboring just as diligently and hard for Western Christian High School as for our local Christian school. Each one of my six children graduated from Western Christian High School. Over the years people from Sioux Center have been strong supporters of Western Christian High in Hull and later of Unity Christian High in Orange City.

My church was also strongly behind Calvin College in those days. One year there were thirteen students from my church attending Calvin College, confirming a solid interest in Christian higher education.

In spite of the battle that raged, a basic unity, though somewhat broken for a spell, was soon restored in Sioux Center. I am convinced that the friendship that developed between Mayor Maurice Te Paske and myself during these troublesome days helped restore peace. We came to respect each other, and our ties were cemented by the fact that both of us wanted what was best for the community. He understood what we were after as promoters of Christian education. Our position on such questions as the ownership and control of the theater by the American Legion could be appreciated by him. He was indeed gracious and charitable. It was therefore relatively easy, once the dust settled, for the members of the community to come together in a new relationship and work for the best interest of the town of Sioux Center.

Gradually the tension between Christian and public school supporters lessened. We cooperated with the citizens of Sioux Center where we could.

The Story Behind Life's Story

When they proposed a new gymnasium-auditorium, we threw our support behind it. It was because we were willing to do this that the bond for the school project was approved. Mayor Te Paske was so pleased with the outcome of the vote that he contacted me immediately to thank me for our cooperation. I was out of town but he located me and called me out of a meeting to let me know his appreciation.

Two special experiences that my wife Deborah and I enjoyed indicated how good the feeling was between us and the community in Sioux Center. I commemorated twenty-five years in the ministry in 1967. We had been in Sioux Center for twenty-two years. Dordt College was already in operation and flourishing. My church had celebrated this event but the city council, under the guidance of Mayor Te Paske, also decided to do something special for Deborah and me on this occasion. At a dinner sponsored by the city council, we received a special plaque that contained a citation for distinguished citizenship. The plaque read as follows:

CITATION FOR DISTINGUISHED CITIZENSHIP

For the twenty-three years Rev. B. J. Haan has been an esteemed citizen of the City of Sioux Center, Iowa;

For the many ways in which he has been a positive influence for community development and service through Church, Education and Government;

For the twenty-five years of dedicated service in the Christian Ministry through which he has made a valuable and permanent contribution to the spiritual and material strength of our Community;

For the significant role which Mrs. Haan has taken throughout this distinguished career in affording her gracious cooperation in these mutual endeavors;

The Council of the City on this 24th day of November, 1967, with thanks to Divine Providence which has directed these steps and actions in our midst, proudly and gratefully cites for

DISTINGUISHED CITIZENSHIP
Rev. and Mrs. B. J. Haan

In response to this gracious act of the city council, I wrote the following letter:

Esteemed Brethren:

Mrs. Haan and I were overwhelmed by the honor which you, the city fathers, conferred upon us at the commemoration of our twenty-five years of service in the ministry of our Lord. During our twenty-two years in Sioux Center we found it a real joy to be part of community progress. This is the place which we love, the place where our children were reared in an atmosphere of the highest friendliness; this is the place where we have many dear friends and a host of cherished memories. We labored with delight together with many others who gave so much to improve the quality of our fair city.

No wonder then that we were pleasantly surprised to be so generously remembered for our work which we performed without any thought of merit or deserving special recognition. Just to enjoy together the fruits of the efforts of many zealous civic-minded citizens is reward enough. Obviously, however, we are very grateful that you have judged our labors worthy of this tribute. This humbles us before the Lord who has been so good to us and our community and to whom we give all the praise.

Permit us to extend a special word of thanks to our dedicated and gifted Mayor Te Paske. His message of congratulations in the name of the City Council touched us deeply and warmed our hearts. The beautiful flowers grace our living room and inspire us to work even more vigorously with you in making Sioux Center an even better place in which to live.

Cordially,
B. J. Haan

The second incident concerns a gracious offer of Mayor Te Paske to me and my wife. He told me one day that he and his wife Vera wanted to do something special for us. He mentioned the fact that we had both worked together in the promotion of Sioux Center in various projects. He also let me know that, being the attorney who handled my income tax, he knew that my income was rather meager compared to his. He said, "We want to take you and your wife on a trip with us to Cairo, Egypt, and to the Holy Land." So it came about that, all expenses paid, we traveled with the Mayor, his wife, and one of his children to Egypt and the Holy Land. Mr. A. J. Boersma, who as a bachelor lived with us for many years and who worked very closely with the mayor and myself, also accompanied us on this trip. It was one of the most delightful trips we have ever made. I write these things only to demonstrate that whenever one endeavors to live his convictions and his principles, he will not suffer shame. Often the rewards will follow.

I would do an injustice to my own congregation if I did not record the many times that they demonstrated their appreciation for the work that my wife and I were doing among them and in the community. We were in Sioux Center only a year when the young people presented us with a beautiful brand new piano. And in subsequent years, four times, the congregation supplied the money necessary for us to trade in our car for a new one. Whatever we had to pay in addition to the money allowed for our old car, the congregation provided. And at the time of our twenty-fifth anniversary, we were the recipients of an attractive stereo-radio-phonograph console. We were truly blessed with several tokens of appreciation during our eighteen-year ministry in First Christian Reformed Church of Sioux Center.

Pat Haveman, who grew up in First church, wrote this poem about one of her memories of those early years.

Christmas in the '50s
I remember in the '50s
    when the children's program took place on Christmas Eve
    not on a Sunday or two before,
    when it was traditional to go home after the program and open presents.

Ah, those programs!
    girls in dainty dresses, boys in ties,
    adorable speeches, cherished carols.

But the highlight, yes, the highlight of the evening
    was Rev. B.J. Haan
    At the end of the program he'd walk proudly to the front of the church.
    He'd turn his head from side to side, beaming at everybody.
    He'd rub his hands together and say, "My, my, my. That was the best
        program we ever had!
    Then he'd go on to ask,
        "How many kids are going home to open presents?"
    After a nearly 100 percent show of hands, he'd ask,
        "Did you all buy a present for your parents?"
    Another good show of hands, and then came his favorite question,
        "How many of you bought your dad a tie?"
    Some hands would go up hesitantly, afraid to reveal a secret.
    One year the inevitable happened.
    A little Douma girl, on seeing her sister's hand raised,
        spoke up—hurt and angry—
        "BETH-Y!! You TOLD!!"

While she choked back the tears, the audience stifled chuckles.
Rev. Haan rushed into his closing prayer.

And it was over.
The elders and deacons handed out candy
while Mrs. Gerritsma played the recessional.

I loved Christmas in the '50s.
I loved the sparkle and exhuberance Rev. Haan displayed.
I wonder where he'll be this Christmas Eve.
I wonder if he'll get a tie.

The first three years of my ministry in Sioux Center seemed to be packed with significant events. One would almost think this would be enough for a life time. However, it was only the beginning, like the bud of the flower. The most significant was yet to come. I will now tell the story of events leading up to the establishment of Dordt College and of the twenty-five years that I served as its president.

Chapter Four
They'll Never Stop It

Dordt College began in 1955 with five professors, thirty-five students, and facilities costing approximately $100,000. The campus, consisting of one building, was located on a small plot of ground seven acres in size. Today, some thirty-five years later, it is a thriving institution with eighty professors, nearly 1100 students, and a campus consisting of more than two dozen buildings. It covers forty-four acres and is valued at nearly $15,000,000. In addition it owns and operates the Agriculture Stewardship Center.

My purpose in the following chapters is to present a personal history of the college in its formative years. Other publications, particularly *A History of Dordt College: The B.J. Haan Years*, by Dr. Mike Vanden Bosch, professor of English at the college, take a broader institutional perspective. I will instead share how I saw the institution, under the amazing blessing of God, wrestle its way into existence, continue to maintain itself in the face of threatening obstacles, and enjoy surprising successes. My account will not be that of a reporter's, but the account of one who had a vital part in the rise and growth of the college.

By the year 1935, four years after the demise of Grundy College, Calvin College appeared to be firmly fixed as the only Christian Reformed college owned and operated by the denomination. The failure of Grundy College was looked upon as proof that it would be impossible for a junior college to exist apart from Calvin College. The attempt to prevent the coming of another college by pointing to the failure of Grundy College did not prove to be very effective, however. No doubt to the surprise of many, it was Classis Ostfriesland Iowa, the home of Grundy College, that began the move to establish a junior college in the Midwest. This noble and unselfish act demonstrated clearly that there was no bitterness from the Grundy experience and that there continued to be among the people of this classis a strong vision for the expansion of Christian higher education. As a result, classis appointed a committee with representatives from five Midwest classes to discuss the possibility of a junior college in the Midwest. The committee came back to these classes recommending that they establish such a junior college. It is interesting to note the grounds given for this action:
    a. It can help to provide Christian education for many of our young people who now are seeking higher education in other institutions.

b. It can serve as a feeder school for Calvin College.
c. The unity of our system of Christian education calls for it. A junior college will help our Christian grammar and high schools as well as the reverse.
d. It will be a powerful instrument for helping our people maintain their distinctively Reformed position.

The Calvin board appointed a committee to meet with the committee from the Midwest classes to discuss the matter. The committees discussed establishing a branch of Calvin in the Midwest. In fact, on July 10, 1940, the Calvin committee was ready to recommend establishing some kind of higher educational institution in the Midwest.

Two persons who played vital roles in fostering a Midwest junior college were the Rev. Dick Plesscher from Kanawha, Iowa, representing Classis Ostfriesland, and my uncle, Dr. R.L. Haan, minister at Hull, Iowa, representing Classis Sioux Center. Plesscher continued until his dying day to be a firm and ardent supporter of a junior college in the Midwest. In fact, after his death his widow remained a solid supporter of Dordt College and made several significant financial contributions.

Dr. R.L. Haan was also committed to the expansion and spread of Christian higher education in Reformed circles. He gave leadership not only to the junior college movement but also to the revival of Western Christian High School. Western Christian High, formerly Western Academy, had gone bankrupt during the Great Depression. But Haan had a lively spirit and predicted that a wave of enthusiasm would sweep over our Reformed people and Christian junior colleges would be established in various parts of the Christian Reformed denomination. He based that observation on the historical development of the junior college movement.

When I became actively involved in the junior college cause in the early 1950s, my father, a brother of R.L. Haan, was a bit uneasy about my actions. He wondered whether I was wise to go against the powers that be in the Christian Reformed Church. Only after I revealed all that his brother had done toward establishing a junior college, did my father change his mind. He stood behind me in the battle for a junior college until his death. I was grateful for my father's support since I always had the highest respect for his judgment.

The declaration of war against Japan brought an abrupt end to further negotiations with the Calvin College board of trustees. With the coming of war, enrollments in colleges, including Calvin, dropped rapidly. It is hard to imagine what would have developed between 1940 and 1945 if war had not interrupted the work. But by the time World War II had ceased, so had the labors of one of the leading spirits in the junior college movement. Dr. R.L. Haan died in 1943, after having given much time and study to this project.

Significantly, after the war it was not the Midwest classes that introduced the matter again. The Alliance of Christian Schools of Northwest Iowa, Minnesota, and South Dakota, formed its own junior college committee to study the matter and come with a recommendation. At the same time Classis California overtured the Christian Reformed Synod of 1946 to establish junior colleges in areas of the denomination needing such institutions. Upon the recommendation of a study committee, the Synod of 1948 declared that there was a definite need for junior colleges and appointed another committee to further study the issue. The report of this second committee at the Synod of 1950 caused a great disturbance, leading ultimately to serious action on the part of the Alliance of Christian Schools in Northwest Iowa. The committee recommended that synod continue to maintain Calvin College and Seminary and do all in its power to strengthen and expand these institutions. It also recommended that no further educational programs be supported that would necessitate the curtailment, retrenchment, and stunting of Calvin College and Seminary programs. For political reasons, however, the committee proposed a screening committee to handle all requests that might come from areas seeking to establish other higher educational institutions.

The people of the Midwest realized that this screening committee was only an attempt to placate those busily engaged in setting up a junior college in the Midwest. But instead of curtailing plans for a junior college in the Midwest, synod's action did the opposite. It stimulated, all the more, the desire for a junior college.

At this point I became directly involved in advancing the junior college cause. Not long after synod's 1950 decision on the junior college, I appeared at an Alliance of Christian Schools meeting. During the business session of that meeting, the committee on junior colleges, which had been inactive while awaiting synod's decision on the matter, arose to give a report. The committee reported that nothing much had been done, and it was not prepared to come with any recommendations at this time. At that point I asked for the floor and talked for perhaps ten minutes during which I called the body to action. I do not recall the content of what I said. But I do know that it ignited a spark and engendered intense excitement. The atmosphere was charged, and people were determined to go forward. As a result of this dynamic spirit, the committee for a junior college was enlarged and given the mandate to take concrete steps toward the establishment of a junior college. Shortly thereafter, I was appointed a member of the committee.

The committee, called the Alliance Committee on the Junior College, met once a month in the Rock Rapids Christian Reformed Church consistory room. I will never forget the first meeting. I was concerned about what might happen. I knew that not everyone on the committee was enthusiastic about the junior college. Although I had a wedding in my church and could not be present at the first half of the meeting, I asked my wife to take my place as the Master of Ceremonies at the reception so that I could attend part of the meeting. When I arrived, I sensed a spirit of dejection among the committee. Fortunately, in the month preceding the meeting, I had given a great deal of thought to setting up guidelines for our work. I presented an outline that detailed an overall program complete with necessary committees and a timetable for our work. With a positive program of action on the table, spirits revived.

Each of the men on the committee was a leader in his own way. One member possessed exceptional qualities, with a great deal of vision and wisdom plus the remarkable ability to use the right words at the right time. Although a quiet man, Mr. Egbert Meyer from Volga, South Dakota, possessed unusual powers of persuasion. He stands out in my memory as a giant, one of the most influential persons in the early history of Dordt College.

During the first few months of work, some members continued to seriously doubt whether a junior college could be established. One member, Mr. James Geels, voiced this reservation to me one night on the way to Rock Rapids. He asked me if I didn't think that we were really on a wild goose chase. We traveled to Rock Rapids every month. Committees were working diligently and with a lot of determination. But was it really worthwhile? Would anything really come of it? He asked the question very seriously.

Strangely enough, I never had any such doubts. I don't mean to say that I never wondered at times when it seemed everything was against us, but something in the movement itself convinced me that we would ride out the storms, overcome the obstacles, and in due time give birth to a college.

Five or six months later, the chairman of the committee, Mr. Arnold Christians, and the Rev. S. Kramer revived the questions. They had talked as they drove to the meeting and expressed serious doubts that we would ever accomplish the goal. It was a memorable night. Mr. Egbert Meyer, in a very quiet manner, gave a most stirring defense of the work of the committee. That little speech carried enormous weight. Never again did anyone within the committee raise questions about the validity of the work we were doing.

It is easy to understand why some members felt uncertain about the endeavor. One of the original members of the committee, Mr. John Vander Ark, strongly opposed the movement. He was a member of the board of Calvin College and made it clear that he saw no need for a junior college nor any real hope of achieving it. John Vander Ark and his wife, Julia, were our friends. When we came to Sioux Center, John was principal of Western Christian High School. I worked closely with him to promote Western and its expansion program. Because it was difficult to raise funds for Western, John was pessimistic about starting a college in our area. His negative influence lingered among some members of the committee. I felt it was fortunate that soon after the committee was organized, he received an appointment to a position outside of our area and accepted it. Later as director of Christian Schools International, John was very supportive of the college. Despite Vander Ark's opposition most of the leading educators in the area were strong supporters of the junior college movement. The majority of ministers, however, were either outspokenly against it or refused to speak in favor of it. Strong opposition also came from Grand Rapids, Michigan.

But there were encouraging sides to the situation. Several leading ministers in our area accepted calls to other churches at this time. If these men had continued to remain in our area, their influence, which was predominantly anti-junior college, pro-Calvin College, likely would have made it difficult, if not impossible, to launch an effective movement for the college.

One example of this was in the leaving of Dr. Herman Kuiper, a member of the synodical committee on junior colleges that came with a "thumbs down" recommendation in 1950. Dr. Kuiper accepted a call to Redlands, California, in 1952. Deborah and I invited Herman and his wife, Josie, to a farewell steak dinner at our home. When they were about to leave, as we were standing at the door wrapping up our conversation, Dr. Kuiper said words to the affect: "Bernie, you'll soon be leaving this area, too, with all the attractive calls you're getting. After all, Northwest Iowa isn't exactly the most exciting and influential place in the church. I know you are interested in the junior college but you and I will both be long dead and buried before anything comes of it." These comments only made me smile and did not dampen my spirits one bit. But I knew that Kuiper was not the only reputable minister who felt that way.

It is only fair that I mention Kuiper's later radical change of attitude. While a professor at Calvin Seminary in the mid 50s, he looked to our area for a revival of the Reformed faith, which he saw losing ground elsewhere. In fact, Dr. and Mrs. Herman Kuiper later generously supported Dordt College.

Because so many ministers left the area, the few remaining preachers were called to be counselors to more than one church at a time. I served as counselor to at least three churches. Taking advantage of the situation, I worked diligently to unite the leading laity of the area into a solid group of supporters for the junior college. I often said to the lay people that we should form such a mighty army of supporters among the people that no coalition of ministers could stop the movement. The support we received convinced me that nothing would be able to stop the coming of the junior college.

This grass roots support was important for another reason. I was convinced that no kingdom venture, no Christian educational institution, could truly be an instrument in the hands of the Lord for the effective promotion of the kingdom if it was not sustained by the people. I am glad to say that, even to this day, Dordt College is known as a college of the people of God. That is its chief strength.

If I did emerge as a leader of the college movement, it was only because of these close ties and intimate relationships with the leading laity of the area. So strong was the backing of many of the leading members of the churches that new ministers who moved into the area were reluctant to say anything against the junior college movement. In fact, even if they didn't support it, they did not openly oppose it.

I do not mean to leave the impression, however, that there were no ministers who supported the college movement. Several young ministers in Classis Sioux Center were a great help. The Rev. Henry Van Deelen was particularly active in promoting the college. As the minister of the large Hull, Iowa, Christian Reformed Church for several years, his support was of inestimable value at that particular time in the history of the college. The majority of the members of Classis Sioux Center also backed the college. This proved to be a great benefit.

Classis Orange City was at the time composed of several strong-minded ministers who posed a real threat to the coming of the junior college. However, the influence of these ministers was offset by the presence of just enough ministers who, together with a solid force of laity, remained firm in their backing of the proposed college.

As I said earlier, during the early 50s the Lord gave me numerous calls to other churches in the denomination. Some of them were large and prestigious congregations. The fact that I received these calls solidified my position among the people. When I continued to decline these calls, people felt assured that I was not intending to leave them in the lurch, and my position among them was strengthened.

I also gained more stature and respectability in the Christian Reformed denomination during these years. I was elected a delegate to the Synod of the Christian Reformed Church three times within five years, serving as reporter on advisory committes dealing with important problems in the denomination. A strong bond of mutual love, trust, and respect developed between leading Midwest churchmen and myself. No doubt my previous labors on behalf of Christian education and the controversy with the American Legion over the theater issue contributed to forming this bond.

Perhaps the most significant stimulus for the junior college movement was the Christian school movement itself. After the war, the number of Christian grade schools grew dramatically. Several Christian high schools were also established in the Midwest. But as the number of Christian schools grew, we were confronted with a serious shortage of teachers. To deal with this critical problem the National Union of Christian Schools (now Christian Schools International) made some decisions that helped the junior college movement. Because of the teacher shortage crisis and the general interest in the college issue, the National Union of Christian Schools invited me to debate Dr. Cornelius Jaarsma, professor of education at Calvin College, at the annual convention in Chicago. Many delegates attended even though it was held near the end of the convention after many delegates normally left.

It would be presumptuous to claim victory in the debate. Dr. Jaarsma was knowledgeable in education. He was a qualified speaker, and no doubt presented his side of the question very effectively. However, I do recall that through this debate the junior college movement gained respect and support from many teachers, principals, and board members of our Christian schools.

At this time the Iowa Education Board began to raise its requirements for teacher certification. For years the state had allowed teachers to receive a temporary teaching certificate with a high school diploma and six weeks of summer college work. Now they were demanding a minimun of two years of college to obtain a teaching certificate. Even though it took time for the state to enforce this requirement in its own public schools, we knew that we would not be exempt and that shortly we would be caught in a serious bind. Something had to be done quickly. Since Calvin College was not prepared to provide enough qualified teachers to meet the new demands, the door was open for the start of a junior college.

One concern still plagued us. Western Academy, after several successful years, was forced into bankruptcy during the Great Depression. Several people, out of love for Christian education, had invested a great deal of money in the school and lost it. Resentment and bad feelings divided the supporters of Christian secondary education. Even though the institution had reopened under the name of Western Christian High School and was growing, it was not easy to raise the funds needed to keep the institution going, and it was even more difficult to gain support for a needed addition to the school.

Confronted with growing enrollments, the board of Western had to do something. It was impossible to operate under the present crowded conditions. A remodeling and expansion plan was proposed, and a drive was held to raise the funds. I recall vividly the difficulty we had getting that money. Many felt we should raise money to pay off those who had lost their money before we should talk about expanding the building. In spite of this noble sentiment, few were ready to donate funds for a project that aimed to pay back those who had previously lost money.

It is not difficult to see what this might mean for the junior college movement. If people were not prepared to give money for the Christian high school, some said, how could we possibly raise the funds to begin a college in the area? However, many of us knew there was sufficient material prosperity among our people to support both Christian higher education and Christian secondary education. We believed that building a junior college would spark a new interest in Christian education, substantially increasing the amount of funds contributed to Christian education generally. History proved us right.

I would like to say at this point that in all of our publicity, there was never any trace of bitterness against Calvin College or criticism of its program or teaching. The junior college was not born in reaction to what was going on in Grand Rapids. We did not intend to set up an alternative to Calvin College. Rather the movement grew out of our obvious need for Christian teachers.

That does not mean to say that all of us were fully satisfied with the philosophy of education that prevailed at Calvin College. Not at all. In our discussions about the coming junior college, some of us spent a good deal of time talking about the emphasis at this new institution. We were determined to have a college that operated on the principle of the lordship of Jesus Christ as expressed in a covenantal-kingdom perspective. We were eager to promote the best in the Reformed tradition as it came to us by way of such men as Groen Van Prinsterer, Abraham Kuyper, Herman Bavinck, and Herman Dooyeweerd. In other words, since we were starting a new Calvinistic college, we aimed to do so in the finest sense of the term.

I am quite sure that Dr. William Spoelhof, the very capable president of Calvin College at the time, sensed what some of us were eager to promote. I was in Grand Rapids once and stopped to pay a visit to Dr. Spoelhof. In the conversation, he said to me, "Bernie, what do you intend to do? Set up a college that is more 'Calvinistic' than Calvin College?" He, of course, knew that we were not happy with the philosophical direction in which some at Calvin College were heading.

I responded to Spoelhof's question by raising my eyebrows in a look of surprise as though this thought had not occurred to me and said, "That might not be a bad idea."

The Alliance Committee on the Junior College, meanwhile, spent many hours preparing a provisional constitution that gave direction to the society and suggested the organizational structure under which it was to operate. After a year's work, we were ready to call together the people to form a society under the provisional constitution. The date of the meeting was set for January 31, 1953, and it was to be held in the Rock Valley Christian Reformed Church. It was the heart of winter, and we knew a bad storm could prevent many people from coming to such a meeting. With some anxiety we awaited the meeting, wondering how many people would attend and whether or not we should have coffee and donuts after the meeting. Looking back, it is amusing to recall the discussion we had. Some suggested that we have 100 donuts; they didn't think we would have more than 100 people at the meeting. I suggested that we be more optimistic and order at least 250 donuts, arguing that we could always get rid of the excess. With a little laughter we decided to buy 250 donuts.

January 31, 1953 turned out to be an extraordinarily beautiful spring-like day. I arrived at the meeting a bit late. As we approached the church, I asked those with me if there was another meeting going on in the church because there were so many cars. There was even a bus there. Due to my shameful lack of faith, I didn't think all these people could possibly be at the meeting for the junior college society. But to my amazement and joy, the building was packed with nearly 600 men. And we had only 250 donuts! Mr. Arnold Christians, chairman of our committee, and Mr. Leonard Haan, the secretary, appeared on the platform. It was suggested that I sit in the audience toward the rear of the building and be prepared to answer questions should that be necessary. You should have heard those men sing at the opening of the meeting. It was not only thrilling; it indicated the spirit with which they had come to the meeting.

A provisional constitution was read and time was given for questions and comments. Sitting across the aisle from me, was a leading minister, the

Rev. D.D. Bonnema from Hospers, who was not in favor of the junior college movement. Bonnema, who had just moved into the area, could speak with great force and conviction. He stood up and called out in a very loud, ringing voice, "Mr. Chairman, I've got a lot of questions." He proceeded to ask one question, implying that more would follow. The audience immediately became very quiet. They sensed that the stage was set for a real battle. Evidently, the chairman of the meeting was not prepared to enter into the foray. He looked over the audience as though trying to locate someone, and said, "I see Rev. Haan sitting there in the audience. Perhaps he would be ready to reply to the question of the brother."

I was ready and eager to answer Bonnema's question. In fact, I knew from other sources what questions were on his mind. When he asked his first question, I was prepared not only to answer it but also to deal with all of the questions that were in his mind so that he would not have an opportunity to present those questions later.

I don't recall how long I spoke. All I know is that as I was speaking, the minister who raised the question, showed signs of becoming increasingly uncomfortable. To the amazement of the audience, Bonnema never stood up to ask any more questions during that meeting. When the time came to vote on the provisional constitution, all 600 men were ready to let their feelings be heard and to let them be heard distinctly. You should have heard the vote of those 600 men. It rang through the church like the roar of a cannon.

That was truly a momentous, historical moment in the life of the junior college movement in the Midwest. I came out of that meeting fully confident that regardless of what obstacles still stood in the way, nothing would be able to stop the movement from realizing its goal. That did not mean that there would be no further problems to overcome. In fact there were many. However, the momentum and strength of the movement was such that it could rise above these obstacles and overcome them on the road to success.

Between the time that the society was organized in January, 1953, and the day the college opened, several events of note took place. First, as required by the constitution, a board was elected with representation from five districts. The first meeting of the board was held in the Bethel Christian Reformed Church in Edgerton, Minnesota. At this meeting Arnold Christians was elected chairman, and I was named vice chairman. Many committees were appointed, including a place committee and a promotion committee.

As expected, the location of the junior college was a chief concern to the newly established board. The board had appointed a subcommittee composed of men from several places to avoid the criticism of playing politics in the matter of selection. The committee established some basic guidelines for determining the location. First, wherever the college was to be located, there had to be a strong representation of Christian Reformed churches and schools, both in the immediate community and in a larger surrounding area. It had to be in a community willing to support the new college and in a place that was convenient for a large part of the constituency. After much study, the choices were narrowed to four towns: Pipestone, Minnesota; Rock Valley, Iowa; Sheldon, Iowa; and Sioux Center, Iowa. Rock Valley expressed considerable interest and was ready to offer the college a piece of ground somewhere along Highway 18. After a full investigation, the committee concluded that Rock Valley would not be the most suitable of the four places. The Sheldon church showed very little interest and was unwilling to give any assurance that it would support the new college financially. I remember that the minister at that time in Sheldon was not at all interested in the junior college movement and so put a damper on any initiative that might have been present in his church. Interestingly, the community of Sheldon showed more interest than the church. The city of Sheldon was ready to offer the college a piece of ground.

Pipestone was another story. A large Indian reservation in that city was ready to be auctioned off to the highest bidder. The reservation included several buildings and for a short time the committee seriously considered this option. I recall being asked to go along with the group to look over the facilities. But after all was said and done, the cost was prohibitive. The upkeep and financing that would have been required to convert the buildings into useful facilities for the college were too staggering. Furthermore, the place was too far removed from a strong nucleus of Christian Reformed churches.

In the end the decision to locate in Sioux Center was made not because other places were unsuitable, but because Sioux Center offered more advantages for a college. I was happy that I was not on the search committee, because when I knew that Sioux Center was high on the list of possibilities, I went to work to get our people to demonstrate their readiness to give solid financial and moral support to the college. I called together approximately twenty men of my church and presented them with a challenge. By the time the slip was passed around, these men had promised approximately $20,000. I then went to the consistory with this pledge. The consistory called a special congregational meeting to challenge the congregation to add another $10,000 to the $20,000 already committed. After a lengthy discussion, the proposal passed by an overwhelming majority. However, there was a condition. Other churches in the area would also have to raise a considerable amount of money before the $30,000 from First Church would be given.

Second Christian Reformed Church of Sioux Center, now known as Bethel, was ready to add $10,000 to the $30,000 from First. By 1954 the two churches in Sioux Center were ready to give $40,000 to establish a junior college.

The site committee was finally ready to come to the society to recommend Sioux Center as the location for the college. The meeting, held in the Hull Christian Reformed Church, was well-attended and this time included many women. Although the meeting was charged with excitement, there was also a certain amount of tension. Some people were not eager to see the college built in Sioux Center. One individual from Sheldon stood up during the meeting and said that he had received a vision. In that vision he had been told that the college should be in Sheldon. Now, what do you do in a moment like that?

Here again Mr. Egbert Meyer provided wise leadership. He stood up and in a very kind and quiet but forceful manner addressed the audience. In response to the gentleman from Sheldon, he said, "We sought the guidance of the spirit of God. We opened all our meetings with prayer seeking divine guidance, and we felt all along the way that we were being directed by the Lord. We didn't have a vision, but we are confident that what we are recommending is the result of prayerful reflection and consideration and evaluation of all the particulars in the case." Meyer's statement evidently satisfied the overwhelming majority of the people present because the vote was strongly in favor of building the college in Sioux Center.

The board favored building a new structure rather than purchasing an older facility such as a large home in Sioux Center. An architect was hired, plans for the building were prepared and approved, and the goal to raise $150,000 was set. We pulled out all the stops to publicize the decision and encourage support. Materials were sent out, meetings were held, speeches were given.

Finally it was time for the drive. The results were very disappointing. Although the two churches in Sioux Center had been willing to offer $40,000, the total income from the rest of the 25-30 surrounding churches amounted to only $35,000. We only had $75,000—half of our goal. That created a real crisis because my church had said that it would only give its $30,000 if all of the outlying churches together raised the remaining $110,000. Now that these churches had given only $35,000, would my church still want to release the $30,000 for the junior college building?

We held a meeting, and it was a stormy one. But we pleaded, saying that this would be the crucial point in the junior college movement. Everything depended on getting the building started. Otherwise, the whole movement could quickly collapse. After much debate and strong argumentation, which was done, nevertheless, in a good spirit—the vote was finally taken. By a large majority our church was willing to give its $30,000. Bethel had no strings tied to their contribution, so we could figure on the $10,000 from them. But the question now to be answered was, what kind of a building could we put up for $75,000?

Something very interesting happened at that time. The De Stigter brothers, who built the first unit of the Dordt College campus and later on built several other units, were all members of my church. I went to them and said, "You've got to come up with a plan that will cost us $75,000 and still give us a building that is decent, respectable, and serviceable. It should be a building that has at least four classrooms, an office, and toilet facilities. But we want it to be a good looking building." The De Stigter brothers said to me, "It's impossible to do that. We don't know how it can be done." But I didn't give up. I even went to some of their wives. I pleaded with them, saying, "We've got to get the boys to do this."

The upshot of the matter was that finally they came up with a plan for the first unit of the college campus. But for that price it would be a bare concrete and brick building with as little of the trimmings as possible—no terrazzo floors or lockers in the halls, no tile floors in the classrooms.

I was very happy, however, when this plan came to the board. Even though they were pleased that De Stigter Brothers was ready to put up a building for $75,000, they saw that it was not really adequate. The college owes a great deal of gratitude to Mr. John Bonnema from Prinsburg, Minnesota, who was on the executive board at the time. He stood up and said, "We've got to be ready to put another $10,000 with this. We need to have tile on the floor. We have a Christian high school in Prinsburg that is a better building than what we're proposing here. How would it look to have a college that was inferior to one of our Christian high schools?" Although the board had previously decided not to go into debt for building facilities, after a bit of discussion, the board decided to add another $10,000 so that the building would have an atmosphere suitable for a college building. When the general board met, they adopted this plan and the building process was initiated. The new junior college in the Midwest was born by that action.

Another significant event was the appointment of the Rev. Cornelius Van

Schouwen to be the first employee of the college. He was appointed a public relations representative the year before the college actually opened. The assumption was that he likely would continue on as one of the teachers. We were happy when he accepted this appointment because having a full-time employee gave a certain amount of stability to the movement and demonstrated that we meant business and intended to move ahead. Van Schouwen did a great service for the college that year and in the following years. He organized the drive, wrote public relations materials, and did a variety of other services for the college.

The first publication sent out to inform and raise support was called the "Monthly Newsletter of the Midwest Christian Junior College." I forget how many issues were sent—I'm sure at least five or six. But we soon began to feel that it was inadequate for our purposes. The promotion committee was asked to give recommendations on how to improve our contact with the public. I will never forget one meeting held in our parsonage. The committee was made up of five men, one of whom was the Rev. Bonnema who raised his voice at the organizational meeting in Rock Valley. I proposed to this committee that we begin a regular publication called the *"Voice,"* which would be printed quarterly. I also suggested that we make Reformation Day a special event for the promotion of Christian higher education, particularly for our junior college.

Bonnema objected to all that was proposed. He argued that the Reformation belonged to the church rather than an educational institution. I was both disgusted and amused by his arguments. I knew that the other men on the committee were also frustrated with the spirit of his remarks. Finally I said to him, "Well I have presented several proposals, all of which you find unacceptable. So you tell us what to do and we'll do it." To my surprise this turned the brother completely around. He went along with the *Voice* and the Reformation rallies.

A struggle developed over the organizational structure the new college was to have. Should it be church owned and controlled as Calvin College, or should it be a society owned and operated institution like Christian elementary and high schools? Our first proposal combined both approaches, making the institution society-controlled but with representation from six area classes. We brought our proposal to the classes for adoption. Although a few voices were raised in opposition, the plan was adopted by an overwhelming majority in the Sioux Center classis.

It was a different story in Classis Orange City where a group of ministers opposed the building of a junior college. They used whatever means they could to discredit the college and hinder its growth and development. It

They'll Never Stop It

seemed as though they chose to use the issue of organizational structure to create a disturbing influence.

I was appointed to go to this classis and present the board's plan. It was a strategic meeting. The chairman of that classis was none other than the Rev. D.D. Bonnema, who had attempted to throw roadblocks in the path of the junior college ever since the society had been organized. I knew that I was going to be in trouble. I could feel it from the moment I stepped into that meeting. But I argued fiercely, pulling out all the stops. It was indeed a heated debate. What amazed me was that those arguing against the proposal insisted that the college had to be strictly a society owned and controlled institution. Several ministers stated frankly that establishing Calvin College as a church-controlled college was a mistake we should not repeat with a junior college. Even though I knew that I was not going to win on that point, I argued as cogently as I could, hoping that when the proposal was rejected, as it was, classis would at least recommend the junior college for financial and moral support. I felt then, and still believe today, that it would have been difficult to obtain moral and financial support if that had been our only request. However, since our proposal on ownership and control was rejected so strongly, it was a relatively simple matter to get the classis to recommend the college for financial and moral support.

Shortly after this, the Rev. Bonnema suffered a serious heart attack, was hospitalized, and died. I was asked by his widow, at his request, to take part in the funeral service. I did so with deep gratitude to the Lord, because it helped me see the true childlike, humble, and gracious attitude of my colleague. The event taught me a good lesson. At the funeral, his oldest brother, one of several in our immediate area, thanked me for being present and offering prayer at the funeral. He told me that he and his brothers deeply respected their departed brother. But he said to me, "Rev. Haan, we let our brother know how much we trusted and stood behind him, but we also told him that on the junior college issue we differed with him. We stand behind you." This affected me profoundly; I was encouraged and yet humbled.

Despite Classis Orange City's rejection of the proposed organizational structure, we were not too disturbed. In fact, we were ready to come to the society with a revised plan, a strictly society operated school. This meant, of course, that we would have to struggle to get any kind of official financial support from the churches, especially by way of denominational quotas. I will write about that struggle later in these memoirs.

The February 18, 1954 issue of the "Midwest Junior College Newsletter" says that the education committee was given permission to begin interviewing prospective teachers. This statement deserves comment. Many people in Grand Rapids and many educators throughout the country were convinced that we would never be able to get qualified teachers. So when the request for applicants for teaching positions was published in *The Banner* of the Christian Reformed Church, we awaited the outcome with some apprehension. The education committee was surprised, relieved, and encouaged to receive forty-two inquiries! This removed our doubt about procuring an adequate faculty.

I recall being in Grand Rapids during this time. The late Prof. Henry Schultze, professor of New Testament at Calvin Seminary and a former president of Calvin College, asked me what kind of response we received from *The Banner* ad requesting applications. When I told him the result of these ads, he was simply floored. I do not say this to imply that he had opposed the junior college movement. Based on his experience teaching at Grundy College he knew the injustice that had been done by the church to the Grundy institution. He seemed to have an understanding sympathy and appreciation for the work that we were doing.

Although we had received forty-two responses to our *Banner* ad, we could only appoint four or five to the faculty. We decided that our first priority was in the field of education. We needed someone qualified to teach courses that would meet the state requirements for certification of teachers. We also looked for persons in the areas of history, Bible, English, classical and foreign languages, biology, and mathematics. From the applications, we soon discovered that it would not be too difficult to hire faculty members in these fields who had at least earned their master's degree. We received a big surprise with our applications for education. Mr. Douglas C. Ribbens from Sheboygan, Wisconsin, had exactly the qualifications we needed. We called him in for an interview. I remember his visit with me in my home. We had a good discussion about the philosophical and theological direction of the college. His acceptance of the appointment proved to be an enormous benefit to us. As is well known, Dr. Ribbens remained at Dordt College and served not only as professor of education but also as academic dean. Ribbens was a person with unusual abilities and talents, a man who could give needed direction to the proper  development of the educational program of the college. He also gave leadership in our effort to achieve state approval and North Central accreditation. The college owes Dr. Ribbens a great debt of gratitude.

The other four men appointed were: Mr. Leonard Haan to teach English; Rev. Van Schouwen to teach Bible, doctrine, and educational psychology; Dr. Peter Van Beek to teach German, Latin, and Greek: and Mr. Nick Van Til to teach history and philosophy.

An interesting difference of opinion developed in the board during the interview of Mr. Nick Van Til. One of the ministers on the board, the Rev. Peter Van Tuinen, a philosophy major during college, was an ardent follower of Dr. Harry Jellema. This gentleman was not pleased with Van Til because he was a dedicated disciple of his uncle, Cornelius Van Til, a well-known apologete in Reformed circles. The minister pointed out that the first philosophy teacher at the college would have a profound influence on its future direction. The "Van Tilian" emphasis was not the kind that he would support over against the thinking of someone like Dr. Harry Jellema. Most of the rest of us had the highest respect for Cornelius Van Til, and it soon became evident that the board was not ready to accept the advice of this fellow minister. Van Til was appointed to the position. He, too, remained with the college until the day of his retirement. The college owes a great debt of gratitude to him for his unstinting labors on its behalf. He taught a variety of courses, was very cooperative, and brought a scholarly influence to the faculty and the students that was invaluable to the college.

The college movement also owes a special tribute to the late Tim Fikse of Hills, Minnesota. A successful businessman, Mr. Fikse was appointed to the board of the college in 1953 and contributed a good measure of experience, wisdom, and insight to the movement. He was of great help to me personally. I can recall going with him and our wives into the Dakotas to promote the college. His confident spirit affected us all. Sad to say, he was suddenly taken home by a heart attack. I was asked to preach at the funeral held in Steen, Minnesota. It is one of those moments in the history of the college that was truly painful. I was deeply grieved and stunned. However, his passing opened the way for another member of the Fikse family

It has been a great joy to me and to others to have had his son, Everett Fikse, take his place. Everett served on the college board for several terms, and I cannot say enough good about his contributions to the development and growth of Dordt College.

I should mention, too, that in the fall of 1954 the Rev. J.B. Hulst, now

Dr. Hulst, president of Dordt College, accepted a call to Ireton, Iowa. A young minister with many gifts and talents, he was soon seen as a rising leader in the Christian Reformed Church. He immediately took an interest in the college. The strong support of this gifted young man had a significant effect on many others. Popular in his congregation, he was soon known as an outstanding preacher. He was destined to have a great deal of influence in the church and in the field of education. He was for me, in a very real sense, a God-send. We had many meaningful conversations together. We shared vacations as families and enjoyed many other social activities. Dr. J.B. Hulst later served as chairman of the board, became the dean of students and Bible teacher, and eventually succeeded me as president of Dordt College.

When I look back over these first four years of the college movement and my participation in it, the amount of work done seems almost incredible. But the Lord was good to me, providing health and strength and allowing me to share and enjoy the many blessings showered upon the college. I especially enjoyed working with all the people, to feel their support, and to know that we were engaged in something of genuine meaning for the coming of God's kingdom. However, if I thought at the time that my work for the college was completed, I was certainly mistaken. Although those were difficult, trying, but very profitable years, the years to follow were as much so or more. In the following chapters I will sketch the story and what was behind the story of Dordt College from opening day in the fall of 1955 to the time of my retirement in 1982.

During the early years of Dordt's history, when the movement needed to build momentum and enthusiasm, I was often called upon to speak on behalf of the college. I used to tell a story that is not my own but that served the purpose very well. It went like this: years ago when the first train came into the west, the children and the grandchildren of a certain elderly man thought it would be nice to bring him down to the station to see that mass of iron. When he saw the big machine standing on the tracks, he stroked his beard and shook his head saying "They'll never start it. They'll never start it." Then the engineer threw some coal on the fire, built up the flame and the steam, and pretty soon he pulled the throttle. The mass of iron began to move. The wheels began to turn. When old grandpa saw this he said, "They'll never stop it. They'll never stop it."

The point is clear. People had said the junior college movement would never get started. But once it was beginning to roll, people began saying, "They'll never stop it."

Chapter Five
The Sapling Takes Root

Ground breaking for the new college occurred in the spring of 1955. We proudly watched each step of the building progress. Needless to say, the spring and summer of 1955 were busy times. Many men and women came to clean up the new property. They washed windows and helped get the building ready for the arrival of the students that fall. The cornerstone was laid in September in a ceremony held just before classes began.

The first class of thirty-five students, though small in number, gave encouraging promise that the student body would represent a wide area of the Christian Reformed denomination. Already in that first class, there were two students from California, one from the Chicago area, and two from Wisconsin. The attendance of these students proved to us that people outside of our immediate area also felt the need for a college like Dordt.

We wanted the opening exercises of the college to receive due attention so we asked Dr. William Spoelhof, then president of Calvin College, to be the speaker. Considering his attitude toward the junior college movement, I thought it would be a rather difficult assignment for him. He graciously accepted the invitation and delivered an outstanding address, which was printed in one of the first editions of the *Voice*.

I'll never forget that meeting, which was held in the new Sioux Center public auditorium. The place was packed. I recall vividly sitting in the back of the auditorium. Dr. John Masselink, who had strongly opposed the coming of the junior college, spotted me sitting on the bleachers and said to me, "You shouldn't be sitting here; you should be up there at the front." Coming from him, the remark surprised me, but I smiled and said "No, I feel more comfortable sitting back here." I always felt that I could accomplish more by working behind the scenes than by occupying center stage. Not that I was without ambition or didn't take pride in being recognized. We are all human. But I sincerely believed that it was better for the movement that I stay in the background at these strategic public meetings.

You can hardly imagine what a stir the opening of the college created. We had gone through a long struggle to get the college movement to the point where we could actually erect a new building. Now college doors were about to open. We had our teachers, our board, our students, and the enthusiastic support of a large constituency. We were very excited and abundantly grateful to the Lord.

An important financial breakthrough came during the summer of 1955. The synod of the Christian Reformed Church decided to recommend that all churches of the denomination take one or more offerings per year for the Midwest Junior College. This was a major achievement since it kept the name of the college before the churches and paved the way for people from all parts of the country to make financial contributions.

* * * * *

To understand the significance of this decision we need to backtrack a bit. Obtaining denominational support for the college was not easily accomplished. We went through a lengthy battle before it came about.

The struggle began in 1953 when we sent an overture to synod requesting that, when the college opened, those areas supporting the college be allowed to hold back twenty percent of their Calvin College and Seminary quota. The reaction to this overture showed that synod was very cautious in reaching its decision. The advisory committee of synod in 1953 proposed that they reject the overture. Two grounds were given. First, synod said that as long as the denomination owned and operated Calvin College every church in the denomination was obligated to pay equal support to that college. Secondly, synod decided that allowing some to reduce their quota by twenty percent would be unfair because other churches would have to make up the difference.

It was at this Synod of 1953 that I gave one of the more significant speeches of my career. I was a delegate to that synod and will never forget the number of people who asked me when the junior college issue was going to reach the floor. Many were following the issue closely. When it did reach the floor, a large number of visitors were present. The discussion sparked intense debate. Many opposed the request of Classis Sioux Center, but a surprising number of highly respected persons supported the proposal. One such person was Gerrit Heyns, a recognized leader of education in the Christian Reformed community. He had served as the principal of Western Academy, now Western Christian High School, in Hull, Iowa, and later as superintendent of Holland Christian High School in Holland, Michigan.

In the course of the debate Heyns rose to make a plea for the junior college movement in the Midwest. That appeal carried considerable weight. Later, I was granted the floor and spoke fervently on behalf of the college, defending the request for the twenty percent rebate. I can say without boasting that this speech was highly effective. It so convinced the majority of the members of synod that the advisory committee's recommendation not to grant Sioux Center's request was tabled and referred to the board of trustees of Calvin College and Seminary for special study. Some who supported the recommendation to have the Calvin board study the quota issue did so because they knew that I, as a new member of the Calvin board, would be there to represent the thinking and the wishes of the junior college people.

I was somewhat surprised to be elected to the board of trustees of Calvin College and Seminary at this time. But the time spent turned out to be interesting, and I learned a great deal about college administration. At first those who stood strongly behind Calvin College were worried that I, a proponent of the junior college movement, would prove to be a thorn in the flesh. I tried my best to be objective at board meetings and not show favoritism to the junior college. I was grateful that when I retired from the board six years later Dr. Spoelhof expressed appreciation for the manner in which I had carried out my responsibilities. He felt that as part of the junior college movement I was able to give helpful advice on crucial matters before the board. I worked as hard as possible to promote whatever was good for Calvin College.

Because of initial opposition to Classis Sioux Center's request, I was afraid the board would make a strong effort to squelch it and reject it. The matter was placed in the hands of a committee composed of a group of members

The Sapling Takes Root

from the Chicago area. The chairman of that committee was also the chairman of the board of trustees, the late Rev. Gerrit Hoeksema. Rev. Hoeksema was an unusually gifted man, an outstanding leader, and had been chairman of the board of Calvin College and Seminary for many years. He was often referred to as the "lawyer preacher" in the Christian Reformed Church. Many hoped that with Hoeksema as chairman the committee would snuff out for good any requests for quota relief for the junior college movement.

I vividly recall the committee's first meeting. Hoeksema asked me if I would attend and present my side of the story. We met in the old faculty room of the Franklin Street campus of Calvin College. There they sat, six men of considerable reputation in the church, one of whom was a banker in Chicago, a man who did enormous service for his local Christian Reformed Church and for the denomination. I knew that I had to make a good case for our request or it would likely be the end of any hope for financial support. Hoeksema said to me, "Now, Rev. Haan, let's hear the story." Though I was a bit nervous, my mind was clear and my voice steady. I described the urgent need of the junior college and the justice and equity of receiving quota relief. To my amazement, the committee quickly concluded that synod ought to grant the request of Classis Sioux Center. I was delighted by their response.

However, the board of trustees was not ready to accept this recommendation. After the committee reported to the board, it became evident that there would be no quick and satisfactory solution. A more geographically representative committee was appointed to continue studying the matter and to report to the board as soon as possible. This second committee stated: "We trust that both synod and Classis Sioux Center realize that although much work has been done already, the board must have more time to do satisfactory work." They recommended that synod continue its study of the Sioux Center junior college matter and report to the Synod of 1955. The Synod of 1954 accepted that recommendation.

I clearly remember the strong debate that took place when the issue finally came on the floor of synod in 1955. I had sent a special communication requesting that the matter be thoroughly studied by a synodically appointed study committee rather than a Calvin board committee. My proposal was adopted. It is not necessary to go into all the details of the report of the special committee, but it is important to note that the committee came to the Synod of 1956 with a minority and majority report. The majority report favored a twenty percent reduction in quotas, but the minority report, consisting of one member, Julius Mellema, a banker from Detroit, opposed it. Synod accepted his recommendation, including the suggestion that Dordt

College receive support through one or more offerings each year. Interestingly, when the matter of quota support was addressed again by a later synod, Julius Mellema was on the committee that recommended the present quota relief program.

By 1956, the denomination also had to address the problem of overcrowding at Calvin's Franklin Street campus. The coinciding problems of whether to purchase the Knollcrest estate for the Calvin College campus and whether to support the junior college movement pushed synod to undertake a special in-depth study of the church's role in higher education. A one-year study committee was appointed to look at the question of church ownership. Should the college remain under the control of the church or not? Then, too, what about the support of junior colleges, what about quota relief, and, furthermore, what about the needs of Canada?

The members of this study committee were carefully appointed. Each had a record of leadership in the denomination in the United States and Canada. Because of my association with the junior college, I was named to the committee. The committee came to the Synod of 1957 with a majority and minority report. I was the reporter for the majority committee, Rev. George Stob was the reporter for the minority committee.

Serving on this committee was one of the most stimulating, informative, and enjoyable experiences of my life. We soon split into two groups over the knotty question of church control versus society control. I remained with the group that favored maintaining Calvin College as a church controlled institution, even though, in principle I believed it better to be a society controlled college. I was convinced that to cut it free from the church at that time would be disastrous. Nor did I think this was necessary. Although some argued that because Dordt was not a church owned college it should not be allowed to have church quotas, I felt we could find a way to solve the problem of church support for higher education that would be equitable for both institutions. The majority committee proposed that Calvin remain church controlled and that quota relief be allowed. I wrote the majority report and defended it before synod.

Synod, to my amazement, adopted all of the recommendations of the report except the one granting a twenty percent rebate for the junior college movement. I was thoroughly frustrated and exasperated. But, thankfully, I kept my composure.

Synod did not completely shut the door, however, to granting quota relief. The problem was referred to the advisory budget committee of the Synod of 1958. Again the budget committee of synod recommended approval of a quota relief of twenty percent, and once again it was defeated by synod.

The Sapling Takes Root

You can imagine the anger and frustration of junior college supporters when again and again synod refused to grant their request even though, in principle, nothing was said against that request. It had simply become a political issue. I recall attending synods and facing those defeats but saying, "Fine, you have the votes. It's not a matter of principle any more, it's a matter of expediency. Some day we will have the votes as well as the principle."

The breakthrough finally came in 1960. Through Classis Orange City we presented an overture from the executive board of Dordt College requesting a special study of the quota system once again. Supported by Classes Minnesota South and Sioux Center, this report finally seemed to have an impact. Once again synod appointed a committee. Once again the committee was composed of strong, capable leaders. In addition, both Spoelhof, as president of Calvin, and I, as president of Dordt, were appointed to the committee. The recommendation of this committee finally resolved the problem. In fact, the system synod adopted that year is still in operation today. The decision was a great victory for the junior college movement and an enormous victory for Dordt College. It clearly indicated that support for the college was growing stronger among people in the denomination.

* * * * *

Two incidents that occurred during these years are worth recording. The first concerns a somewhat humorous but telling experience I had at one meeting of synod. As I came to the building where synod met, I approached a group of men talking together. One was a professor in the seminary, Dr. Henry Stob. Another was the Rev. Peter Eldersveld, the radio minister of The Back To God Hour and strong supporter of the junior college. Other friends and colleagues were also there. As I came towards them, Stob, in his sharp clear tenor voice, said, "Hello, Bernie. How's your little college coming along out there?" I was angry, though I tried not to show it. How I came up so quickly with a rejoinder, I'll never know. But I said, "Well, fellas, when you plant a little tree and every wind blows on it and every dog in the neighborhood takes a turn at it and the tree still grows, that is going to be a good tree." The looks on their faces were priceless. Some laughed, but they knew very well what I meant. I was so thankful that Dordt College was indeed a strong tree, right from the beginning.

Another incident involved the Rev. Gerrit Hoeksema. As I mentioned earlier, Hoeksema was chairman of the one-year study committee that dealt with denominational ownership of Calvin College and of the junior college quota relief. It was Hoeksema's custom, as chairman of a committee, to meet with the reporter before the entire committee met. Since I was the reporter, we agreed to meet in a hotel in Minneapolis, Minnesota. He came by train from Chicago; I by train from Sheldon, Iowa. We enjoyed two delightful days in Minneapolis, but of special importance was an hour we spent together after supper on the second day. He was being pressured on all sides to take a stand for Calvin and against the junior college movement. Even though he had heard my story before and showed support, he wanted to get things straight for himself. He said to me, "Now, tonight after supper, we are going to spend an hour together, and I'm going to look into your soul on this junior college business." So we sat together, he smoking his pipe, and I talking. I must have talked for half an hour. When I was through, all he said was "Let's get to work." His reaction was most gratifying to me because it meant that he was satisfied.

Even though I appreciated this kind of encouragement, I was not discouraged or sorely in need of outside support. I felt a good deal of support from people locally and across the denomination. In fact, as I mentioned earlier, I often used to say to people that I felt like the mouse that went over the bridge with the elephant. The mouse said, "Didn't we make the bridge tremble?" Throughout the history of Dordt College one factor that stands out most significantly is the way God's people stood behind the college. Their support was a great source of comfort, encouragement, and satisfaction.

* * * * *

Dordt College has always tried to stay close to God's people, believing that no kingdom venture can have the blessing of the Lord unless it represents and serves the people of God. One way in which we held local supporters close together was through an annual Reformation Rally. These were highly successful events in the early years of the college, drawing enormous crowds. The first was held in October of 1954 with Rev. John Piersma as speaker. In following years we had as our speaker such people as Dr. Dick Wolters, then president of Reformed Bible College; the Rev. R.B. Kuiper, then president of Calvin Seminary; Dr. William Masselink, a popular Grand Rapids minister; and more than once, speaking to packed houses, Dr. Peter Eldersveld. These meetings rallied the people around the principles for which the college stood and encouraged college personnel to be faithful to those principles.

I am reminded of another conversation I had in Grand Rapids around this time. In talking with a leader in higher education, I said that Dordt

College would depend primarily upon the support of God's people. In discussing whether Calvin College should continue to be church controlled rather than under a society, this man said, "If we had to depend upon individuals apart from church quota support for financial aid to the college, I would despair of any hope for a healthy college." To this I replied that I was confident people would give adequate support if the institution remained close to them and was willing to divulge all that was happening at the institution. I argued that college personnel should live close to the people. Faculty members, I said, as well as anyone else should be willing to visit with people and even, if necessary, to stand beside the manure pile with the farmer as they conversed. He was taken aback by that statement. In fact, he felt that to live that closely to the people would make it very difficult for a college to fulfill its obligation and responsibility. I thoroughly disagreed with that sentiment. History has proved that living close to God's people pays off handsomely in many ways.

* * * * *

During the thirty-five year history of Dordt College, the institution has gone through two major crises that threatened its very existence. Signs of the first crisis began to surface already in the spring of 1956 and continued to smolder during that summer. It broke into the open during the fall and reached its peak at the opening of the 1956-7 academic year. In writing about the fierce battle that raged for several months and caused many hard feelings a number of things should be remembered.

All of the men involved in the struggle were men of integrity, sincere faith, commitment, and loyalty to Dordt College. Each was convinced that his position was the right one. However, due to the sharp differences among the men involved and the intense feelings that they aroused, the conduct displayed and the procedures followed were not always exemplary. Things were said, accusations were made, and policies were adopted that cut deeply and led to hurts and grievances that were not easily resolved. Seldom does anyone who has been thrown into the midst of such a fierce struggle come out feeling clean. I find no joy in writing about these conflicts, and I sincerely hope that, as I relate what took place, it will not detract from those men who found themselves on the losing side. We owe a great deal to these men, and they should have a place of honor in our memories.

Bearing this in mind, it is nevertheless important to retell the story because of its impact on the history of Dordt College. Others involved in the conflict might present it differently, but I can only tell it as I experienced it.

The late president Harry Truman once said that a schoolboy's hindsight is better than the greatest statesman's foresight. Looking back we can see that the original organizational structure of the faculty was unworkable. It is obvious now that the operational structure for handling problems was inadequate. But that was not clear in the beginning.

The first faculty was too idealistic. They wanted a structure in which no one person would be given special power or authority to exercise leadership over another. There was to be no permanent president. Administrative duties were the responsibility of the entire faculty. Although there was a chairman of the faculty, he had no power and was responsible to the entire faculty on all matters. Finally, in order to give the faculty a strong hand in the direction and management of the college, the entire faculty met as advisors to the executive board.

The plan sounded good at first. However, anyone who has any knowledge of how educational institutions operate could have predicted that such a weak organizational structure was headed for trouble.

Within the faculty, people were sharply divided on how to run a college. Professors Leonard Haan, Van Beek, and Van Schouwen shared one point of view; Van Til and Ribbens favored another approach.

Because the chairman was responsible to the entire faculty for all decisions and actions, meetings often became a source of contention. The faculty held lengthy meetings every Friday afternoon, often about trivial matters that were not worth everyone's time. It didn't take long for the faculty to decide that not everyone should deal with routine details of administration. In January of 1956 the faculty chairman, Leonard Haan, was appointed dean of the college and made responsible for office supervision, keeping records, recruitment, general counseling, testing programs, and registration. He was also appointed registrar and librarian. Although there was still no plan to appoint a president, leadership of the college was shifting to one person.

But a more basic difference developed between the two groups in the faculty. Haan, Van Beek, and Van Schouwen wanted the institution to be strictly a teacher college. They argued that every professor should be certified for teacher education. Ribbens and Van Til felt that we should be a liberal arts college; the junior college would provide the first two years of a liberal arts program, and we should be ready to broaden our curriculum beyond teacher training. This difference of opinion polarized the group. Whenever they voted on an issue the vote was always three to two, the same three against the same two. The following year, George Pals, who had been a teacher for a number of years at Western Christian High School, joined the faculty. He was a close friend of the

The Sapling Takes Root 93

three who favored a teacher education college. The vote became four against two.

As dean, Leonard Haan's ideas about the direction of the college became more significant since he was backed by the majority of the faculty. A sharp breach grew between the faculty.

I will never forget a meeting I, as chairman of the education committee, had with Van Til and Ribbens. They told me that if the college continued to go in the present direction, they would not seek reappointment when their initial two-year term was completed. I was greatly concerned. I strongly believed that these two men were the kind of people the college needed. Although the board was not dissatisfied with the others, we preferred the direction of these two men and felt something should be done to support them. The matter eventually had to be resolved by the education committee.

In the summer of 1956 we began to discuss who we should add to the faculty. I found it disconcerting that the candidates several of us favored were not supported by the majority of the faculty. By that fall the board could no longer ignore the rift within the faculty. I was in the middle of the struggle since questions of direction of the college were addressed in the education committee. Feelings ran high and debates were sometimes heated at our meetings. We soon realized that, if we were going to avoid a serious break within the college, the board would have to take command, set specific administrative policies, and make faculty appointments. We spent much time that fall and early winter discussing the issues dividing the faculty.

The board, after listening to all sides, became more and more convinced that the organizational structure of the college had to be changed. The first thing they decided to do was to appoint a college president.

In all of these discussions I was impressed that a board composed of sixteen men came to practically unanimous decisions on each issue. These were men with a great deal of experience, wisdom, and leadership ability. I was always amazed at the talent represented on that board.

To understand the significance of these events, we have to consider the extent of the crisis the board was facing. The real question was, could the college survive a battle at this time in its history? The board felt that an upheaval within the faculty could threaten our existence. However, after looking realistically at the problem, all of the men on the board had the courage to stand by their convictions and move in the direction that seemed best. In my mind this was a heroic act.

Although the decision was made to have a college president, it was not deemed wise to appoint someone permanently. After all, this was a radical change of direction for the college. Furthermore, the board was uncertain who should be president. In the end, they decided that I should serve as "acting" president for two years. Such an arrangement would give the board time to consider various options and see what would develop during those two years.

Needless to say, this decision caused a stir among the majority of the faculty. We soon knew we were in for a titanic struggle. What added fuel to the fire was the February 1957 board decision on faculty reappointments. In taking responsibility for faculty and administrative appointments, the board dropped the position of dean. The board also decided to appoint Mr. Peter DeBoer to teach English and speech and to direct the choir. De Boer's appointment was strongly opposed by the majority of the faculty. It was difficult for the board to understand this opposition because DeBoer was a highly successful teacher at Western Christian High, showing great promise as both a teacher and a scholar. Ribbens, in addition to teaching education courses, was asked to teach psychology. Leonard Haan was appointed librarian.

As might be expected, these changes aroused the anger of the four faculty members, and they determined to do everything in their power to prevent the decisions from being carried out. Secret meetings were held between them and a few members of the central board. Without board approval these faculty members appealed to the people by way of a public letter. This action obviously caused a great disturbance among the constituents. The conflict was now out in the open and arguments for both sides were debated. Feelings ran high.

Since I was appointed acting president, I soon became the center of the controversy and came under severe attack. I was accused of being underhanded and of wanting to be the "Big Man," the one who held all the power. One man, a close friend of Leonard Haan but also a friend of mine and someone I respected, was so angry about the situation that he said I should be placed under censure. When I heard this, I went immediately to his home and made clear what he did not know, that these recommendations were supported by the unanimous vote of a board of sixteen highly responsible and qualified men. This satisfied him and our friendship was preserved. I suppose there was plenty of evidence for those who felt I was trying to get power into my hands. I had been appointed to several committees. I was serving on the denominational committee regarding divorce and remarriage. I was on the one-year special education committee appointed by the synod. I was on the board of trustees of Calvin College and Seminary. And within the college, I held the position of vice-president of the board and chairman of both the education committee and the promotional committee.

The Sapling Takes Root

At this time an anonymous article was published in the *Sioux Center News* in which one of those strongly opposed to my being the acting president listed all of my functions. The implication was that all I wanted was power. To be sure, all of us like recognition and perhaps don't mind being in a position of influence. However, I can truthfully say that not one of these appointments was something I sought or tried to attain by political maneuvers. The question remains, did my appointment to these committees indicate that I had the qualities necessary to give direction and leadership to the college or not? I leave that entirely to the judgment of others. In any case, the board at that time, knowing my activities, was ready to give me the position of acting president.

The consistory of my church stood firmly behind me during this period. Their support was a comfort and strength to me. But these were stormy days, and I was not happy about the stories being circulated or about the attacks on my person and character. It required a large measure of grace to stand up under the pressures and still provide the leadership expected of me.

Preaching was not easy during these months. Two of the opposition members of the faculty were members of my church, causing a spirit of unrest within the congregation and leaving me with a feeling of anxiousness. The majority of the congregation, however, were considerate of my situation and very supportive.

Before I could accept the position of acting president I had to get the permission of my consistory, since I would remain full-time pastor of First Christian Reformed Church of Sioux Center. Any feeling of dissatisfaction with my work would have become evident at that time. However, when the committee of the board visited with my consistory, the plan received the unanimous support of the consistory. I could feel, too, that the congregation stood behind the consistory's decision and appeared to be honored by the appointment.

However, I still had to decide whether to accept the appointment. The decision proved to be extremely difficult. Those opposed to me did everything in their power to prevent me from accepting the position. The four faculty members asked to appear before the board to present their point of view on the decisions that had been made—particularly the decision to appoint me as president. This was granted by the board.

Another issue added to the tension. The college was hoping to be approved by the state committee on secondary and higher education. Approval would mean that the credits of our students could be transferred to other colleges and universities. The faculty members opposed to my appointment publicly declared that if I became president it would be virtually impossible to receive state approval. They claimed that the board was taking a country preacher off the streets and making him a college president, a man without competence in academic affairs and who knew practically nothing about educational matters. Since state approval was such an important issue, the board decided to investigate this charge.

Shortly before the meeting between the board and the four protesting professors, the Rev. Paul Holtrop, then minister in Kanawha, Iowa; Arnold Christians, chairman of the board; and I traveled to Cedar Falls to meet with Dr. M. Beard, the chairman of the state committee on secondary and higher education. After presenting the case to him we asked him point blank whether my appointment would jeopardize our receiving state approval. Dr. Beard made it clear that, although institutions often found it difficult to survive when problems such as we were facing developed early in their history, the proposed changes would not affect the state's decision. Their judgment would be based on the quality of education, the competence of the faculty, and the adequacy of the curriculum and the facilities. With this information we were ready to face the opposition. I knew it would be a rough experience, but I was convinced that whatever happened, the college would be ready to move forward.

My confidence was inspired partly by the growth in enrollment in our second year of operation. The thirty-five students grew to seventy-two, and it looked as though we would have another sizable increase the third year. Our facilities were rapidly becoming inadequate. I had studied the problem and developed an expansion plan. The promotion committee decided to present this proposal to the board at the meeting in which the four faculty members would argue against my appointment.

The first half of the long-awaited meeting was given to the four faculty members. Although they addressed all of the changes the board was recommending regarding administrative personnel and faculty loads, they concentrated on the board's decision to appoint me as acting president.

Needless to say, there was an air of tension in the room. No one knew precisely what would come of this report of the faculty. The accusations and criticism brought against me were quite severe. I felt as though all the dirty linen in my life was suddenly hung out on the line for the members of the board to see. Although some of the accusations were a bit exaggerated, it struck me that much of what they said had a painful element of truth in it. In fact, I had the feeling that I stood condemned before the board. I was not prepared to counter with a defense. As the accusations continued to mount, I did not panic nor become angry. I simply accepted the fact that

The Sapling Takes Root

I would have to face them. Upon hearing these charges, I became more and more convinced that the board would find it difficult, if not impossible, to uphold their decision to have me become acting president of the college.

When the four members of the faculty finished their report, which lasted nearly an hour, I was given the opportunity to respond. My initial comment was that I really had nothing to say. I was not about to encourage anyone to bring out any more dirty laundry. I asked only who was responsible for the article that appeared in the *Sioux Center News* giving the impression that I had a lust for power. I was surprised to hear that one of the wives of the four members of the faculty had written the article and submitted it to the *News*.

The main argument against me was that I was not an educator but a country preacher who, if appointed, would seriously jeopardize the possibility of getting state approval. The four members of the faculty were obviously taken aback when they heard the report of our visit with Dr. Beard. However, it did not change the fact that, at this moment, I did not have a very lofty opinion of myself. I didn't think the board did either.

The four faculty members were dismissed with due respect. After they left the room, I told the board that, having heard these things against me, I felt there was sufficient truth in what had been said to make it unable for me to accept the appointment as acting president. At that point I experienced one of the biggest surprises of my life. To a man, each board member was still convinced that I should accept the appointment. They felt strongly that in battles like these none of us comes out clean; we all have our faults, we all make our mistakes, and sin attends all of our actions. Even though I had not been prepared to speak in my own defense, the board had done so in my stead. That was indeed a tremendous source of relief, comfort, and strength.

After the board recessed for lunch, I presented the plan for the expansion of the college. It was, I felt, necessary to inject a positive note into the meeting. The danger always exists in these crises that a negative spirit takes over. I did not want that to happen. As the board reviewed the plan and considered how to raise funds to carry it out, spirits revived. In the heat of the storm the board was determined to move forward. The expansion plan was recommended to the central board for adoption, together with all other administrative and faculty proposals.

When we adjourned, Albert Cooper, who had recently been elected to the executive board from Classis Northcentral Iowa, came to me and enthusiastically expressed appreciation for my readiness to move ahead in light of what had just taken place. He felt that this action was strategically a wise and laudable one. I was greatly encouraged by Cooper's comment. The Lord knows how much I needed it.

But the battle was not over. We still had to bring our proposals to the central board. The central board elected members to the executive board and voted on all crucial matters that the executive board proposed. A few of the central board members were upset with the decisions of the executive board. We knew they planned to bring a protest to the meeting. A certain element of the constituency was also upset over the issue. Once again I became the center of criticisms and objections.

In the days before the central board meeting, I did a great deal of soul searching. It was still not clear to me whether I should accept the appointment as acting president even if the central board would approve. I wondered if so much damage had been done to my reputation that I would be unable to give effective leadership. I knew that I had the board and my consistory behind me, but I was not sure how some of the lay leaders among the constituents felt. I also weighed my qualifications. Was it true that I was totally lacking in educational and academic expertise? I began to wonder, too, whether I would ever want to leave the pulpit for the presidency of the college. All of these matters stirred within me, making those weeks very difficult.

But I had to make up my mind and be at peace with myself after making the decision. Finally, after praying about this matter daily, it became clear to me that I should consult with someone who was responsible and highly respected among the people, one who could give me sound counsel. The man that came to mind was Mr. John Ten Harmsel from Hull, Iowa. Ten Harmsel was an extraordinary leader. He was highly respected; he had served as elder for many years; he was for years the treasurer of Classis Sioux Center; he had been on the board of Western Christian High School several times; and he was a member of the Hull city council. I loved him and held him in highest esteem. He was a wise man. And because he was a close friend of Leonard Haan, I knew he would be fair to both of us. I decided that whatever he recommended would be the Lord's answer to me. I'll never forget that Saturday morning. Before I could even tell him why I had come, he told me that he knew. Leonard Haan and his wife, Grace, had just left, he said, and they were not happy with what he had said. He had told them that I should be president of the college. I knew that Ten Harmsel was aware of the rumors and accusations that were flying around and yet he was convinced that I should accept the board appointment. What a relief that was to me! I knew then that my decision was

The Sapling Takes Root

made. I was going to accept the appointment to be acting president of Dordt College.

The central board was composed of several members from each of six districts. They represented areas of the college's constituency in Iowa, South Dakota, and Minnesota. I was extremely happy to learn that most of the opposition to my appointment had dissipated by the time the board met. I was astounded by the positive spirit that characterized this meeting. Only one man spoke strongly against the board's decision. It was clear that they, too, were ready to move ahead. The recommendations passed with only one dissenting vote. In the process of approving the plan for expanding our facilities, the dissenter stood up and said, "We won't need an addition to the building. With the decisions just made, we won't have enough students to justify what we are doing." The central board, with an air of determination and confidence, was undaunted by this comment.

Two of the faculty members opposed to the board's decision, Van Schouwen and Van Beek, decided to stay with the college. Leonard Haan accepted an appointment as principal of Central Christian High School at Prinsburg, Minnesota, and George Pals returned to teach at Western Christian High School. It was a sad experience, but we were happy these men found new positions and were honored among God's people in spite of the fact that their vision for the college was not fulfilled.

By this time it was April. The board immediately got to work on the proposed addition to the building. We had to move swiftly to finance the project and get it built by the time school opened in September.

We already had some debt from the purchase of a large home on Main Street used to house women students. Now we planned to add to that debt with the addition. How I watched enrollment prospects! We were eager to have an enrollment that would justify the addition. You can well imagine how delighted we were and what a tremendous morale boost it was when the fall enrollment was one hundred and seven students. We grew by thirty-five students, a fifty percent increase over the previous semester. I breathed a sigh of relief and thanked God for His goodness.

But with the departure of George Pals, we had no one to teach in the crucial areas of science and mathematics. I searched all over for a possible replacement. By some strange circumstance I learned of Mr. Ted Sjoerdsma, who was well qualified in this field. Sjoerdsma and his wife were on their way home from serving in Guam, but they had decided to travel around the world before they came back to the States. I tried all summer to locate him through his parents. Finally we contacted him. After a bit of persuasion he agreed to accept the position. Sjoerdsma was an excellent teacher. We were very thankful and grateful to the Lord for his arrival.

Other events occurred at that time that bolstered the growth of the college. First, we received notice from the state education committee that the college had been approved. Then in 1957, we appointed Dr. John Zinkand, a graduate of Westminster Seminary, John Hopkins University, Dropsie College, and Brandeis University. What a blessing that we could add to our staff, in those crucial days, a young man who had just earned his doctorate in modern and classical languages. Spirits were high when our doors opened in the fall of 1957. That fall I officially began my duties as acting president of the college.

* * * * *

As a side light, I should say something about my salary during those years. Some people thought that since I was both minister of the First Christian Reformed Church of Sioux Center and acting president of the college, I was probably receiving an enormous salary. That was not the case. My church was always very good to me. When I became acting president in 1957, I was receiving five thousand dollars annually from the church. Five thousand dollars, at that time, was an adequate salary. But the church believed that I should receive an increase. However, because I was acting president, I declined a salary increase from the church. The college, being somewhat limited in financial resources, was unable to pay me very much. During the first two years I received one thousand dollars. When I was reappointed acting president for a second two year term, the college increased my salary to two thousand dollars per year. I again turned down an increase from the church. Compared to most salaries at that time, seven thousand dollars was not excessive.

Looking back today, I still do not understand how it was possible for me to carry such a heavy load. I preached twice every Sunday, met with the consistory regularly, called on the sick, taught at least two catechism classes, led two societies, went family visiting, and did all the work that is involved with the church, such as attending classis meetings. In addition I was deeply involved in a college that was in its early stages. I had faculty meetings, board meetings, committee meetings, and I was expected to give leadership in recruitment and public relations. I often traveled around the area promoting the college. It was an enormous task. But I have strayed from my story.

* * * * *

Finding the appropriate organizational structure for the college was a trial and error effort. The unwieldy faculty structure was not the only unwise decision we made. We appointed a finance committee composed of men not on the executive board. They were responsible for raising funds for the school, handling unpaid pledges, appointing a collector for the college, and promoting denominational offerings and society donations. We soon discovered that it was difficult for an outside committee to understand the operational problems facing the college and make the right decisions about financing. Yet, once appointed, this committee seemed to feel it should be given control over the finances. It really became a board along side the board. That never works.

Although most of the men on the finance committee were close friends of mine, I knew that we should not have a committee operating separately from the board. The executive board agreed with me, and after a couple of years the board decided to discontinue the finance committee. This decision led to some hard feelings. In fact, later when we appointed one of these men to the executive board, he would not accept the position until he visited with me. He had a bone to pick, and it related to the original finance committee. After a forthright discussion, the air was cleared. We shook hands, he accepted the appointment to the board, and proved to be an outstanding board member.

It always impressed me how the Lord brought the right people at the right time to meet the needs of the college. One example of this was the coming of Miss Henrietta Miedema as secretary. She was a member of my church, and I knew she was an extremely competent young lady. A bright student, she was an excellent typist and knew bookkeeping. She held a good position in the office of the local creamery. I asked her once if she would be willing to consider serving the college as secretary. She appeared interested and received the appointment. To our surprise she declined it. We were disappointed. Sometime later I came to their home for family visitation, and I asked her, "You didn't feel free to accept the appointment?" She blushed a bit and said, "You know Rev. Haan, ever since I declined I haven't felt happy about it." I said, "What do you mean? Are you ready to accept the position if you get it?" She said, "Yes, I think I would."

I went back to the board with this information. They immediately gave her another appointment, which she accepted. Miss Miedema was my secretary for several years. She later became the secretary to the academic dean, Dr. Douglas Ribbens. She has served as registrar of the college even though she never held the title. Many have said that Henrietta has been worth her weight in gold to the college. For over thirty years she has been esteemed by college administrators and faculty and loved by the students. What a blessing she has been for Dordt College. Later in 1989, after the death of Ruth Ribbens, Miss Miedema became the wife of Dr. Ribbens. I found it a distinct honor to officiate at that marriage.

* * * * *

Something unfortunate happened while we were seeking accreditation from the state. To be approved, our institution needed the endorsement of three colleges accredited by the North Central Association. After discussing the matter, we decided it might be wise, courteous, and proper to ask Calvin College, our sister and denominational college, to be one of the three to recommend us. Such a recommendation meant that the institution would be willing to accept the credits of Dordt students. Two accredited area colleges willingly gave us a recommendation, but to our amazement, we received a letter from the academic dean of Calvin College informing us that Calvin would be unable to do so. They felt that they might jeopardize their own accreditation by giving us such a recommendation. As a result we went to another area college, which gladly endorsed us.

Calvin College could easily have helped us without damaging their own image. I inferred that they had an exaggerated idea of the accreditation process. People at Calvin may have a different version of this incident, but I felt that they looked upon Dordt College as being far below accreditation standards and feared that recommending Dordt would indicate a lack of standards on their part. This reaction was a keen disappointment and difficult for me to understand.

Despite this disappointment, we were encouraged to learn that one of the higher ranking members of the state committee, Dr. Al Gowan, registrar and faculty dean of Sioux Falls College, thought Dordt College should seriously consider developing a four-year program. We had discussed the idea, but, because of strong feelings for and against, we had not moved ahead. Now, however, we were quick to make use of his suggestion. Many of us wanted a liberal arts college. We had already decided that Midwest Junior College would not simply be a teacher training school but a liberal arts institution with a strong teacher education program. That seemed to be the time to move ahead.

The decision also affected our name. We wanted to leave open the possibility of moving to a four year college by ridding ourselves of the word 'junior'. Besides, the name Midwest Christian Junior College was colorless and had little meaning. After searching for a name that would describe our educational principles and purposes, we settled on the name "Dordt," after the great synod of Dordrecht, where the confessions of the Reformed

Calvinistic churches were adopted. The recommendation to the executive and the central boards caused some controversy. Some did not like the name. Others thought it was ideal, giving us a chance to explain what we were to people who asked what the name "Dordt" meant. We also disagreed about how the name should be spelled. Some wanted D-O-R-D-T and some D-O-R-T. I favored Dordt. I had recently purchased the newly published book, *Barth of Dordt*. When I saw this spelling I was very happy. Eventually we came to agreement on the issue, and the institution's name was changed to "Dordt College."

Since that time, there have been some who considered the name to be a hindrance to the college. Several years ago a few people on campus suggested changing the name. I was, of course, pleased to hear that not only a majority of the students but also alumni were opposed to changing the name. The name "Dordt" had, as a rule, brought back happy memories for them. That response seemed to put an end to thoughts of changing the name of the college. Names are either liked or disliked depending upon the experiences that people have had with the names. People respond negatively to the name of a person they don't like. So it is with Dordt College. The name "Dordt College" is known and highly appreciated by many, and, I'm convinced, will stand as long as the institution exists.

* * * * *

In those first two years of the college, we kept busy trying to raise funds. At one point I came to the finance committee and suggested establishing the Special Subscriber Organization to bring in additional revenue. Although the committee liked the idea of raising more money, they didn't like the name "special" because they didn't want some givers to stand out over others. After considerable debate they finally decided on two names. "Patron" members would pay ten dollars annually above their regular contributions and "special" subscribers would be asked to pay fifty dollars annually above regular contributions. But some still were unhappy with the name special subscribers. They preferred the term "honorary subscribers" over "special subscribers."

The name notwithstanding, it was not easy to get the organization set up the way we wanted it. Finally, after a great deal of discussion the board approved the organization that still exists today. It was called the Special Subscriber Organization, and members were asked to pay a minimum of twenty-five dollars a year above their regular contributions. I mention this because the contributions from this organization have proved to be significant, giving the college a great deal of financial stability. It also gave the college a broad base of financial support from people around the country, and it provided the morale and clout necessary to get funds for facilities and new programs. The organization has grown to over a thousand members, so that today there is an endowment fund of nearly one million dollars. Today this group is known as the "Friends of Dordt."

We were fortunate to obtain the services of Mr. Marvin De Young to teach in our science department at this time. De Young joined the staff in 1958 and taught biology, chemistry, and physics. During his years at Dordt College he worked steadily toward a doctor's degree. We were grateful to have another faculty member wholly dedicated to the stated purposes of the college. The last years of his service were as manager of the Dordt College Bookstore. In this area De Young rendered particularly valuable service to the college until the time of his retirement.

Music has always been important at Dordt College. From the beginning Dordt was known for its excellent choirs and music program. One reason Dordt College gained a reputation for its choirs and music program was because of the director, Mr. Dale Grotenhuis. Prior to coming to Dordt, Grotenhuis had gained a reputation for his work at Lynden Christian High. He and his wife stopped in Sioux Center during the summer of 1956 on their way from Washington to Michigan. I will never forget their visit because I happened to be on the campus at the time. I had heard about the marvelous high school choir that Grotenhuis directed and that had toured around the country. I warmly greeted them and told them a few things about the college. In the back of my mind I thought, "Wouldn't it be something if we would get this person to teach at Dordt College and be the director of the choir?"

I should say that we already had a good choir. Peter DeBoer had done a wonderful job with the choir. However, music was not DeBoer's area of expertise; he had no advanced training to qualify him to teach music courses.

So in 1958 we began to look for someone who could not only direct the choir but also head a music program at the college. We placed an ad in the Christian Reformed Church magazine, *The Banner*, asking for applicants who could teach music and speech. Because of our size we needed teachers who could teach in more than one area. After the ad appeared, I came to my office one morning and saw a letter on my desk with the name of Dale Grotenhuis in the corner. I opened it hurriedly and read it. Grotenhuis was then at Unity Christian High in Hudsonville, Michigan, and simply wanted to inquire about the position. He was not eager to teach speech, but was at least interested in what we had to offer.

The Sapling Takes Root

An amusing story can be told about that event. Two days after mailing the letter, Grotenhuis and his wife Eleanor were sitting at their table in Hudsonville, talking about my reaction to the letter. They knew me somewhat because my brother Art was a good friend of the family. "Well the letter should be there by now and, if we know Rev. Haan, we should be getting a telephone call shortly," they reportedly said. They had no more than said this when the phone rang. I was on the phone, determined not to let him get away if at all possible. He objected, quite persistently, to having to teach speech, but I pleaded with him not to make so much of it and come out to visit. We would pay the expenses. He had nothing to lose and everything to gain, I told him. He accepted the invitation.

What an interesting visit we had! The choir was giving a concert at that time, and he was impressed with their quality. But teaching speech remained an obstacle. We all prevailed upon him. We probably owe thanks to Mr. and Mrs. DeBoer for their efforts to convince the Grotenhuises to come to Dordt College. He accepted, and we were overjoyed. The entire music program at the college blossomed. It also proved to be a tremendous public relations arm. I cannot say enough good about what the choir did for the college in those early years.

Grotenhuis accepted a two year appointment in 1959—even though he had to teach speech—and is still serving as professor of music at the college, over thirty years later. When he came, we were told that we could expect him to stay no more than four years at the most. The fact that Grotenhuis continued to teach at the college all these years says a good deal about the quality of the college, the excitement of being on the staff, and the importance of the principles for which the college stands. He has, in his own way, done much to promote the college. Our music department, particularly the choir, gave the college a good image among the supporters.

A primary concern of mine as acting president was to write a statement of purpose that was rooted in the best principles of our Reformed tradition. We were determined to be truly Kuyperian in our outlook and perspective, and we wanted to make sure that the faculty knew clearly where we stood and what we hoped to accomplish.

In preparation for writing a statement of purpose, I provided the education committee with material for study. My source was primarily Abraham Kuyper's *Encyclopedia of Sacred Theology*, a scientific work with which I was very familiar. The volume had formed much of my thinking and helped me arrive at a basic educational philosophy. I would formulate several propositions that would then be discussed and refined. Gradually a body of propositions was adopted.

As valuable as the final document was, the discussions held by the faculty and board on these propositions were even more important. They gave us an opportunity to reflect upon the basic principles of a philosophy of education. We spent several years on this first statement of purpose and grew significantly in our understanding of how these principles applied to campus life. The final document was adopted by the board and the faculty in 1961. Even though it later became necessary for Dordt College to have an expanded statement of purpose for accreditation purposes, the principles advanced in that first document are basic to the present statement of purpose. They continue to be reflected in all academic and non-academic activity on the campus.

* * * * *

By 1959, we again needed to expand our facilities. Although the board had originally decided that no buildings were to be erected until the funds were raised, they soon began to take a different approach. We decided that the operational expenses of the college should always be met, but we agreed that a reasonable amount of debt for capital expenditures would not be out of order. So the board decided to build an addition to the original building and dormitories. Ads went out explaining our need and the interest that would be paid on the bonds and notes. To our amazement we received more than we needed to complete our building program. In addition to the home on main street used as a women's dormitory, we purchased two other buildings in town on borrowed funds. We were always careful, however, to repay our debts on schedule. To do this we began a debt reduction program. Each March we conducted the Spring Debt Reduction Drive to pay off indebtedness on capital expenditures. We were determined to avoid what had happened to Western Academy. But times were also different. Money was much more available than during the Great Depression, and the enthusiasm of our supporters convinced us that we would be able to meet our obligations. God's people would not fail us!

The second major fund raising program was the Fall Foundation Day Drive. It raised money to offset operational expenses. I remember when we first set up the Fall Foundation Day Drive we decided to send out self-addressed return envelopes to a large number of people. I don't recall exactly how many went out, but it must have been close to five thousand. We eagerly waited the result. People were asked to give a donation and place it in the self-addressed, stamped envelope. I wanted to have volunteers go to the homes and pick up the envelopes, convinced that we would have a much larger response if someone would contact the people. The board was opposed to that method, feeling that it did not fit a college image. I could not understand this thinking. The result was that, while we were happy with the returns, they were not nearly as large as they could have been. We raised seven to eight thousand dollars a year through the Fall Foundation Day drives. After a couple of years, however, the board went ahead and set up a program with organized volunteers to contact people and pick up their envelopes. The next year contributions increased by approximately $10,000 over the year before. The Fall Foundation Day campaign has become one of the major sources of support for the operational expenses of the college.

Chapter Six
The Politics of Growth

Already in 1957 the board had appointed a committee to spell out the duties of the college president and the qualifications necessary for such a position. A nominating committee was appointed to find candidates, but because the committee was not yet ready with a group of suitable candidates, in 1958 I was reappointed acting president for another one-year term.

Finally the executive board, through the guidance of the presidential search committee, nominated Dr. Klaas Kramer and me. Dr. Kramer was principal of the Christian school in Pella. A well-known educator, he later became a professor of education at Colorado State University in Boulder, Colorado. Kramer came with high credentials and certainly was a good candidate for the position. We both had to appear before the central board and the faculty.

Klaas Kramer came to the campus to be interviewed by the board. He was shown around and given an opportunity to ask questions. He and I had a very cordial meeting, talking openly and frankly. When Kramer appeared before the board, he said he believed that my knowledge of the situation and my experience would result in good leadership. He was most sincere and gracious in his appraisal of me, pointing out that I had the confidence of the people and that having lived so close to the movement I would be the best prepared to handle the job.

But others were not quite ready to agree with Dr. Kramer.

During the nomination process Nick Van Til, professor of history and philosophy, confronted me on my candidacy for president. He was not too enthusiastic about some of the names being bandied about as nominees, nor was he exactly enthusiastic about me becoming full-time president. When he met me one day on the street, he suggested that he might throw his name into the ring as a candidate. In the course of the conversation he said to me, "I don't think you have the demeanor of a college president." I frankly agreed with him. And I told him so. I said, "I know that Nick. And I want to assure you that if I become the president of Dordt College, I'm not intending to change one bit." When the faculty finally took its vote, the vote was 14 to 1. Even Van Til voted in my favor. That vote was an encouraging sign for me and had an influence on the board.

The Politics of Growth

Some board members, though, did not favor my candidacy. They wanted a president with an advanced academic degree. I was strongly involved with the promotion and development of Christian schools and Christian education, but I only had an A.B. and a Th.B. During my interview I was asked if I would be willing to further my education. I said that I would be happy to do so if it became necessary. This never proved to be necessary, and I never did go on for further study.

The final board vote, 32-12, seemed to indicate that some still wondered about my qualifications. But the results also showed that a substantial majority-approved of my appointment.

I recall a conversation held after the board had chosen me to be the full-time president. Neal Boersma, who later become the college business manager and served the college with exceptional ability, came to me and said, "Are you sure you really want to be the president of the college? You have a family and you don't know what the future of this college will be. Aren't you taking a big risk?" His comment surprised me. Here was a man on the central board, just appointed to the budget and finance committee and getting ready to become the business manager of the college, still expressing doubts about the future of the college. I was not the least bit shaken by Boersma's fears. I was not at all worried about the future of the college, but neither was I convinced I should accept the full-time appointment to the presidency.

The main reason for hesitance was that by becoming full-time president, eventually my ministerial status would be questioned. I was adamant about retaining my status as an ordained minister of the Christian Reformed Church. In fact I felt and still feel so strongly about this, that if I had not been allowed to maintain my ministerial status, I would not have accepted the position.

To keep my ministerial status I had to go first to my consistory, then to classis, and finally to synod. I knew I could gain the approval of my consistory and of Classis Sioux Center, but I was not sure how synod would respond. Even though I had been officially chosen to that office, I decided that I would not accept the full-time presidency until synod made its decision. I continued as acting president of the college while appealing the matter to synod. I also continued to be minister of the First Christian Reformed Church of Sioux Center. My ministerial status was intact, but I was holding two full-time jobs. It was too much and almost ruined my health.

In 1959 Synod appointed a two-year study committee, which recommended that I could maintain my ministerial status. The Synod of 1961 rejected this decision which Classis Sioux Center then appealed in 1962. For me, as a delegate to that synod, it was an exciting but also tense experience. When the issue of my presidency came to the floor I exempted myself from the discussion and the voting. I'll never forget it. I went to the student union building, just a step from where synod was meeting. Lying on a couch, I waited for the results. The issue ignited a heated debate.

Several forces were at work on the floor of synod in this debate. Some genuinely believed that it was not proper for a minister to be a college president because he wouldn't be fulfilling his real calling. Others, who were not very happy about the rise of Dordt College, felt that if I were not to be president, the future of Dordt College would be in jeopardy.

One person who helped my cause was the late Professor Martin Monsma. Monsma was professor of church polity in the seminary and an authority on church rules and regulations. He stood up and said that not everyone could be a college president. It was, according to him, an office few people could fill. He was convinced that being president of a college and maintaining ministerial status was perfectly in agreement with the demands of the ministry.

The vote was finally taken. I won by just one vote. I vividly recall how my brother Peter came flying out of synod to the student union to tell me the result. But it was not a glorious victory. I maintained my ministerial status, as they say, by the skin of my teeth. As soon as synod gave approval, I accepted the position of full-time president and was installed.

Years later synod dealt with the same issue when Dr. George Van Groningen was appointed president of Trinity Christian College. His request was initially turned down. Trinity appealed the decision, and after another thorough study of the issue, the committee recommended allowing ministerial status for college presidents. That remains the stand of the Christian Reformed Church.

It's rather interesting to note that early presidents of Calvin College, J.J. Hieminga, R.B. Kuiper, and Henry Shultze, were permitted to maintain their ministerial status. Why the church vacillated on this question is hard to say. I think it was not so much a matter of principle with the majority of those who opposed it as it was a matter of politics.

While waiting for synod to decide my ministerial status, business went on as usual at the college. During my early years as president, Dordt College was granted full approval by the state committee on education, who suggested that we seek accreditation from the North Central Association. Although we were encouraged by the approval, we were even more encouraged by the state committee's suggestion that we move toward a four-year college.

Already in 1960 the board had appointed a committee to study the possibility of becoming a four-year college. Interest in a four-year program was growing steadily. Because of this, we did not even try to gain accreditation from the North Central Association as a two-year college.

While we were working to gain state approval, the board decided it was advisable to allow Douglas Ribbens, dean of the college and teacher of education, to pursue a doctor's degree. We were convinced that at least our dean should hold a Ph.D., since he would be the person to head the self-study for the North Central accreditation. While Ribbens was gone we had some difficult forms to fill out for final approval by the state. I was disturbed by this paperwork and wanted Ribbens, who was studying in Colorado, to help me with the study and the report required by the state. He let me know that he was in no position to help. He was too deeply involved in his studies. So it was strictly up to me. I said to our secretary, Miss Miedema, "Well, let's do our best." We worked diligently together to produce a good report. It was a source of great satisfaction to me when, having filled in and sent to the state all these forms—and there were plenty of them—the letter arrived that we had been granted full approval.

Another significant event occurred in the fall of 1960. The college's membership society was organized into seven districts, but we had found it difficult to get enough interest to form a district in Pella. We decided it was time to bring people in Pella into the movement. We called a meeting in the basement of First Christian Reformed Church of Pella. I don't believe there were more than twenty people present, but two significant individuals attended: Gary Vermeer and his brother, Ralph Vermeer. These men owned a rapidly expanding factory, manufacturing farm implements, that later developed into a large operation. Both men supported Dordt College publicly. When asked if they would be willing to become a district, that small group decided to do so. Gary Vermeer expressed a willingness to serve on the executive board of the college. Appointed with him was the Rev. Jack Vander Laan, minister of the Christian Reformed Church of Leighton, Iowa.

You can't imagine what a blessing this was for the college movement. The fact that a person like Gary was ready to be on the board was a welcome boost. It was important enough to Gary that every month, faithfully, in his private plane, he flew with Vander Laan to the board meetings. They always landed on an air strip a few miles south of Sioux Center.

Gary was a person with outstanding abilities. He served on several boards, he possessed remarkable financial insights, and he had experience in building expansions. Furthermore, Gary had common sense and wisdom. I relied heavily upon his good judgment in those early years. I appreciated his counsel and his help in determining which way to go on tough decisions.

I vividly remember when, after he had served on the board for five years, he came to me and said he could no longer serve. "I just can't do it," he said. His own business was flourishing, and he had many other responsibilities. While he served on several boards, he said, there was no board that he enjoyed more than the board of Dordt College. He felt that the men on that board showed a great deal of wisdom and good judgment. They had, according to him, sharp insight when facing problems and, when necessary, dared to make difficult decisions for the welfare of the college. I cannot say enough in the way of appreciation for what Gary Vermeer did and is still doing for Dordt College. Other members of the Vermeer family also did a great deal for the college. Ralph Vermeer played an important role in obtaining denominational quota relief for Dordt. Further support came from Harry Vermeer, another of the brothers.

* * * * *

I mentioned before that holding down two full-time positions became difficult for me physically. The strain soon began to show. On one trip to Michigan for a committee meeting, I developed a serious case of the Asian flu. I was so terribly sick during the meetings that Dr. William Spoelhof said to me, "Bernie, you better take care of yourself."

I was staying at my sister's house. On Friday night I was delirious with a high fever, but I had to get on the plane early on Saturday to be back Sunday to preach. I traveled with Dr. Hulst, flying first to Milwaukee and then to Minneapolis and Sioux Falls. I can't tell you how sick I was. I could barely make it home and once there went right to bed. I said to my wife, "You better get someone to preach for me." We tried to get Rev. C. Ter Maat, but being late on Saturday he did not dare tackle it. My wife said to me, "Why don't you just preach? You've gone through things like this before. You always seem to perk up when you get on the pulpit." So even though I didn't have much time to go over the sermon nor the physical strength to do so, I slowly reflected on my sermon as I stayed in bed.

I felt pretty good on Sunday morning and got ready to preach. I knew I was very weak, but I prayed for strength and thought I could make it through the sermon. Suddenly it was as though a hurricane hit me. In a wave of exhaustion, I broke into an awful sweat. I had just enough sense to fall back into the chair. You can imagine the frightful stir this created in the church. I'll never forget that Peter De Boer, a close friend of mine, was sitting on the front bench. He rushed to the platform, followed by one of the elders. The elder announced a song and dismissed the congregation.

I was taken downstairs, and the doctor was called. When he came he went directly for my heart and said, "No I don't think it's your heart. But you have a bad case of the flu." In fact it was so bad that I was unable to preach for a month, nor could I do any other work. I just stayed in bed.

Later on when I retired and supposedly had my first heart attack, the doctor informed me that I had suffered more than one heart attack previously. Looking back, I think more damage may have been done to my heart when I passed out on the pulpit than what the doctor thought.

I finally returned to work but was terribly weak. Mr. Neal Boersma and I were out raising money for the first major expansion of Dordt College. After being with me for several days, he said to me, "Reverend, are you ever well? Are you always sick?" The work was simply too much. The congregation also began to sense it. We all agreed, even though somewhat reluctantly, that I should move full-time into the college presidency.

It was a year before I really got my strength back again. Even then, I don't know if I could say I was back to normal. But I felt pretty well. The work was demanding and I enjoyed it immensely, but I was always very tired. I now realize that it was just too much. I was traveling all over the country, going to district meetings. In those early years, we would go to various parts of the college constituency to elect officers. We put on a program, and I would give a speech. Several times the weather was very bad. I recall one trip to Prinsburg. It had snowed heavily and the roads were packed with snow and ice. The wind came up on the way home late at night. Huge drifts of snow blocked our path. We were forced to sleep in a hotel in Luverne, Minnesota, only forty miles from home. Those are days and nights I will not easily forget.

* * * * *

During the years when I was moving towards full-time presidency of the college, there was significant growth and development. Enrollments were surprisingly good. Support for the college was getting stronger all the time. Dordt was rapidly finding its place among the people. They were very happy with what the Lord was doing at Dordt College.

Early in my ministry, our family had established a strong friendship with Rev. James Van Weelden and his family. Van Weelden was minister of the Protestant Reformed Church in Sioux Center at the time we first came to Sioux Center. From 1945 to 1955 we worked together to strengthen the

Christian school movement. Toward the end of Van Weelden's ministry in Sioux Center, a big controversy between the Rev. Herman Hoeksema and the Rev. Hubert De Wolf split the Protestant Reformed Churches. As a result several Protestant Reformed ministers left that church and returned to the Christian Reformed Church.

Mrs. Van Weelden was a sister of Rev. De Wolf. They were very unhappy with developments in their church and people in Van Weelden's congregation were becoming tired of the battle. Van Weelden discussed the matter with me, and I agreed to help him apply for entry into the ministry of the Christian Reformed Church.

I was on the classical committee and so had the opportunity to lay the groundwork for Van Weelden's appearance before classis. He was the first of the Protestant Reformed ministers to come into the Christian Reformed Church. The classis meeting was a royal battle. Some ministers were reluctant to open the door for anyone coming from the Protestant Reformed Churches as a minister.

The late Rev. Chris Huissen protested Van Weelden's return. Huissen had been minister of Eastern Avenue Christian Reformed Church, the church Herman Hoeksema served when he was deposed. Huissen was well acquainted with those experiences and harbored hard feelings. The opposition was severe and the atmosphere tense, but after all was said and done Van Weelden was examined. He passed the examination and was permitted to be a minister in the Christian Reformed Church.

After serving several years in Sioux City, Iowa, Van Weelden was called to Red Deer, Alberta, Canada. It was providential that we enjoyed such a strong friendship with the Van Weeldens because it opened a door to students in Canada. Van Weelden asked me to come and speak at a youth Bible conference. The Sunday prior to the camp meetings, I preached in the Lacombe Christian Reformed Church and the Sunday following in the Red Deer Christian Reformed Church. As a result, a large number of Canadian students came to Dordt College. I remember at least nine students who came to Dordt that very fall. Among those were such men as: Case Boot, who is now a professor at Dordt College; the Solomons, one of whom is a minister in the Christian Reformed Church; the Rev. Jacob Kitts; and several others. Later, two of Van Weelden's children also attended the college. What a promising beginning this was. At one time Dordt had over 300 students from Canada, some from every province. There now are Christian colleges in Edmonton (The King's College) and in Ontario (Redeemer College), but Dordt continues to draw students from Canada, though in fewer numbers than before.

The Politics of Growth

The Canadian students were a blessing to the college and added something special. Many of these students' parents came out of the tradition of Abraham Kuyper and were appreciative of the principles for which he struggled. Students from these homes loved to discuss issues. I found it a delight to have them on campus. A few people were not too happy having all these Canadians. I felt this was being extremely short-sighted and quite small. We loved the Canadian students and were very grateful to God for them.

The number of students from the states also grew steadily. Soon we began to enroll children of educators and ministers, most of whom would have gone to Calvin previously. So fantastic and rapid was growth that the call to proceed with a four-year college program was heard on all sides. The work of the committee to study this step began to take on more meaning and urgency.

Not everyone, however, was eager to have a four-year college. If we became a four-year college then we would really be in competition with Calvin College, some said. Although the majority of the people were not at all bothered by this, some were. Among those opposed were a few ministers. Nevertheless, the board was determined to go ahead.

We laid plans carefully. I wrote a document that the board adopted. In testing the waters among the constituents, we found that the various districts of the college were generally in favor of going to a four-year program. But we agreed to call a meeting of the society to allow people to speak their voice officially.

The society meeting was held in the community building in Sioux Center. What a memorable night that was! The document prepared stated precisely the purpose of the meeting and the grounds for our recommendations. We were amazed at the turnout. You will recall that when we organized our society in 1953, 600 men showed up at the Rock Valley First Christian Reformed Church. Now, in 1961, at a meeting to decide on whether to have a four-year college, an unbelievable 900 people were present. It was clearly understood that if the society voted it down there would not be a four-year college. Fifty people came all the way from Pella. We were astounded at the level of interest.

I wanted the people to have an adequate opportunity to speak at that meeting. I knew there was opposition and wanted them to speak freely. We placed microphones throughout the building. I encouraged, even urged, the opposition to speak. We had some heated discussion, but the momentum for the four-year program was overwhelming.

There were humorous moments too. The motion to proceed was made by John Haverhals from Lebanon. Haverhals spoke in broken English but with a markedly positive tone. He could not understand why we had to hold back on this issue. He said, "Why for do we have to get behind K-Nollrest?" The audience roared when he said this, although he didn't realize his mistake. He added, "We must have our own college. We should decide now to go ahead with it." That motion was immediately supported. We gave time for a little more discussion, but I don't recall many comments after Haverhals' motion. We had talked long enough. When the vote was taken, it was a thunderous approval of the four-year program.

Later, I heard an interesting comment about the meeting. I was told that on the way to the meeting, a car full of men from Hull had decided that no matter what B.J. Haan said, they were not going to vote in favor of a four-year college. After the meeting as they were riding home, they said, "We couldn't help it." After listening to all that was said and hearing how the people spoke, they voted in favor of the motion, joining the vast majority who supported the move to a four-year college.

The board immediately took steps to implement the society's recommendation. A great deal of work lay ahead. We had to start proceedings with the North Central Association to gain provisional approval and later, we hoped, full accreditation.

The steady increase in enrollments meant that we needed additional facilities. We also had to hire more professors. A student dormitory was a necessity, and we needed a home for the president of the college. Some difficult decisions had to be made about what should be done first. The process led to some heated debates and hard feelings.

Stanley Boertje was a professor of biology at Dordt College in 1960. Boertje was an outstanding teacher, a strong willed and persistent person. Even though he and I had many good times together, golfing and doing other things, he did not always agree with what the administration was proposing. He differed very sharply with me on more than one account.

It was his strong view that a science building should be a first priority. We thought it was more important to erect an administration building with added music facilities. Boertje felt our decision was a sign we were not really interested in a liberal arts college but were more concerned with public relations and music. Having music in the regular classroom building did not work well. Furthermore, the board was pleased with our choirs under the direction of Mr. Dale Grotenhuis and judged it wise to take care of this particular program first, together with the needs of the administration of the college.

Stanley Boertje, however, made an urgent plea against the proposal. Boertje was a close friend of Gary Vermeer, from Pella, having taught

The Politics of Growth

biology in the Pella Christian High School prior to teaching at Dordt. When Gary came to board meetings he would stay at Boertje's home. We wondered what effect he would have on Gary. However, even though Boertje had presented his case very forcefully and in great detail, Gary Vermeer stood with the board. He had the courage to tell his friend, "You always have this problem when you're expanding. You do the thing you feel is the most urgent for the institution at the moment and then later on, as the movement progresses, you balance it off with expansion in a different direction." In the end, Boertje left the college.

Those were exciting times. You can well imagine how the students, the faculty, and the people felt when they saw the administration/music building, the first dormitory, the first part of the commons, and the president's home going up. Dordt was actually becoming a college campus!

And we hired more professors. By the time we had begun our four-year program, we had made important additions to the faculty. I cannot name all of the changes in the faculty, but I will mention two.

One person who served the college for a long time and fulfilled a very significant role in the life of the college was Dr. Garrett Rozeboom. He taught educational psychology for several years. Later he became Dordt's first dean of students.

While we were adding new facilities and faculty we lost one professor that I considered a serious loss. Peter De Boer, an able scholar and outstanding English professor, received an appointment to teach at Calvin College. Peter and I were close friends. We respected each other professionally and enjoyed each other socially. To this day we hold each other in high esteem. We had gone through a very sad experience together. While a member of my church, Peter and his wife, Joy, lost a baby in a crib death. It was one of the most shocking experiences both of us had to go through, but it brought us close together.

When Peter received the appointment to Calvin College, he really struggled with it. He didn't like leaving Dordt College. I'll never forget the day he told me he was going to accept the appointment. He broke down in tears. Peter was a graduate of Calvin College. He came from out east. He met his wife, who was from Sioux Center, a daughter of E.J. Kosters, at Calvin. Peter had a deep love for his alma mater. Even though he thought a great deal of Dordt College and was strongly behind the movement, he felt that this was a once in a lifetime opportunity and that he should accept it. I told him it was understandable that he would want to accept the appointment. It was a big loss to us, but through it all we found that the college was strong enough to weather these kinds of experiences. It did not critically hurt the college, and we soon found a suitable replacement. With all the other good faculty added to the staff soon after De Boer's departure, we were blessed with a highly respectable faculty and program. The North Central Association confirmed this.

Two federal government programs provided great financial assistance for our building expansion. One, Housing and Urban Development (HUD), gave federal assistance to colleges for dormitories, dining halls and student union buildings. The other, Health, Education, Welfare (HEW), gave federal loans for such things as classroom buildings, libraries, and physical education facilities.

Many colleges depended on such programs in those days. We obviously didn't have the money to pay for all the buildings needed. We didn't have the history or the credit rating to borrow huge sums, nor did we want to take those risks. But borrowing HUD funds at three and a quarter percent interest, with forty-two years to pay back, was easily within our reach. The HEW program charged only three percent interest, but we had to pay the loan back within thirty years. That, too, was a real bargain for us.

Some people were skeptical about receiving aid from the federal government. They thought that any federal assistance would mean federal control and restrictions that would jeopardize our cause. That did not happen. In fact, the federal government was extremely good to us. We were allowed

The Politics of Growth

to teach exactly what we believed. The only thing the government ever required of us was that we were not to hold chapel services, or teach Bible in buildings funded by HEW. To some people that seemed to be a very dangerous requirement. We didn't consider that stipulation to be a threat. We had plenty of facilities paid for by our funds where Bible courses could be taught and where we could hold chapel services.

In our dealings with the federal government, we worked with two people, Mr. Short and Miss Purcell. Some interesting stories can be told about our relationship with these two people.

Mr. Short worked for the Chapman-Cutler Law Firm of Chicago. Chapman-Cutler was appointed by the government to see to it that all the legal aspects of the government's negotiations with the colleges were in proper order. An older man, Mr. Short was experienced and exacting. He insisted that every jot and tittle be in perfect order. Yet Short was surprisingly loving and helpful.

At that time Dordt College was a corporation *de facto*. In a *de facto* corporation, people own and operate the organization. Our college was owned by the members of the Christian Reformed Churches in the local classes. That meant that all of these people were part of the corporation. The government wanted a corporation it could deal with immediately and directly, a corporation *de jure*.

The government required us to set up a new constitution and by-laws in which the sixteen members of the board of trustees would be the legal corporation. They could be elected by the larger voting members board and be under certain restrictions of that board, but the legal corporation would be the sixteen men we called the executive board. To make the change we had to inform our society members of the government's demands and make sure there were no objections to the change. We can thank Mr. R.J. Dykstra for all the work he did for this change. We sent letters to all the churches and the societies in each church. It was an enormous amount of work.

We began to rewrite our constitution and by-laws. Mr. Short suggested that I come to Chicago for a day to work with him and his secretary on the new constitution and by-laws. I must say that this was an interesting experience. We had many good laughs. They questioned me about the college organization and how it operated, and how our church and classes operated. They had a good time listening to my answers and off-the-cuff comments. But we got the job done. Looking back on this experience I think the thing that impressed Mr. Short and his secretary was the fact that my history with the college and the church had given me insight into a subject they found fascinating.

The new constitution and by-laws then had to be approved by the board of trustees. It was in the middle of the summer. Some of the board members were farmers and were extremely busy harvesting their crops. However, the college was hard pressed for time. We needed the money to get our dormitory and commons built. But to get the federal funds, we first had to have our corporation in proper order. We called a meeting, hoping to have a quorum present.

Mr. Short had come all the way from Chicago for the meeting, and we didn't have a quorum. What were we to do? I got on the phone to call a couple of board members who were farmers, busy threshing. I explained to their wives how serious the situation was. They talked to their husbands, and sure enough, at 1:30 we had enough board members to give us a quorum for our meeting. Mr. Short was simply flabbergasted. He could not believe the kind of loyalty, dedication, and commitment these men showed for the cause.

Actions of this kind made a profound impression upon Mr. Short. It was not only the loyalty of these people, but the reason for their loyalty, their religious convictions. Mr. Short, by the grace of God, became very much interested in what we stood for. As we worked with him, he grew more and more interested in and impressed with our beliefs. As a matter of fact, he invited my wife, Deborah, and me to go along with him and his wife on a trip to Europe, particularly to visit Dordrecht in The Netherlands. We could not go. But we did receive a postcard from him sent from Dordrecht, which he specifically visited because of his feelings for Dordt College.

Later on, Mr. Short—and I think the Lord used Dordt College in bringing this about—joined the large church of the Rev. Arthur De Kruyter, an independent Calvinistic Reformed church in Chicago. This church was located in a very wealthy part of Chicago where Mr. Short lived. We were happy to learn about his affiliation with a church dedicated to the principles dear to our college.

* * * * *

Miss Purcell was our contact person for HUD funds. Her office was also in Chicago. She was a fine lady and took a liking to us. Miss Purcell had considerable influence over who would get federal funding. It was a difficult time to get federal aid because so many colleges were seeking funds. We were a bit doubtful that we would qualify. But Miss Purcell was very fair and wanted to be sure that, if at all possible, we got the help we needed. Her interest in Dordt College demonstrates that the Lord was at work in the development of Dordt College.

The Politics of Growth

The fact is, her interest was so strong, that when we were ready to build our third dormitory, (we needed about a half million dollars), we went directly to her in Chicago. She told us that she had both bad news and good news. The bad news was that she was being promoted from Chicago to Washington, and we would no longer be able to deal with her. However, she also said, "The good news is that I told Washington, 'I would like to have a going away present. There's a little college up in Northwest Iowa for which I have a warm spot in my heart. They are very dedicated and committed. The loan is not all that great.'" She told them she would like to see us get our loan before she went to Washington. A few weeks later we received notice that Dordt College would receive that loan. To the government, half a million was not a lot of money, but to us it was an enormous amount. We thanked God for this blessing and for Miss Purcell.

I should tell one more story about Mr. Short. We eagerly desired a student union building, but we didn't have the half million dollars it would cost to build one. So we resigned ourselves to waiting for a more opportune time.

I was in Chicago visiting Mr. Short about a legal matter pertaining to our loans. He had taken me out to the University Club, where we had lunch, a swim, and a back-rub. I was treated royally. Coming out of the University Club building, he said to me, "Rev. Haan, you would like to have a student union building, wouldn't you."

I said to him, "Yes, but we don't have the money for it."

"Well," he said, "I think there is still some money left in the HUD fund. Why don't you go to the office here in Chicago and find out."

It was Tuesday. I immediately went to the office and I asked the person in charge whether it was true that there was some money left in the HUD fund for a student union building. He said, "Yes, there is a little money left in that fund, but it won't do you any good."

"Why not?" I said.

"Well," he said, "the deadline is next Monday." That meant that in order to qualify for the funds, we had to have an architect's drawings of the proposed building, a complete financial statement, a lawyer's opinion, and the approval of the board. It was a momentous job, an impossible one from the government representative's perspective.

I said to him, "But, what if we would get it done and have it in here by Monday?" He looked at me as if I were off my rocker! "How could that possibly take place?"

"Well," I said, "what if we did?" He didn't know how to answer that.

I picked up the forms from the official, left the office building, and went directly to a telephone. I called Mr. Neal Boersma, our business manager, and explained the situation to him. "I'm coming in on a plane tonight and I think we should go for it." Boersma, in his typical Dutch manner said, "All rrright Rrreverrent, we'll take a trrry at it."

By the time I got to Sioux Center, the architects and the college lawyer were there. I got on the phone immediately and called the chairman of the board of trustees and a few others needed for the process. We worked day and night, filling out the forms, and getting everything up-to-date. We flew the forms by private plane to Chicago on Monday. Would you believe it, about six or seven weeks later we received the half a million dollars needed to build our student union building. We had no special committee to decide the decor, the kind of knobs on the doors, the paint on the walls, or any other aspects of the building. We simply relied on what these architects knew about student unions and what we could afford. Despite the fact that we didn't have a single committee, the student union building is one of the most beautiful buildings on campus. I took great delight later in telling the examiners from the North Central Association about that building. How they laughed about it. They could hardly believe it! Well, I went through it, and I couldn't believe it either.

The Lord definitely opened opportunities for us. The door was open, we went in, had the courage to go ahead and, if necessary, take the flak and the criticism that might follow. But we got our money, and we are still grateful for our student union building.

Chapter Seven
Gaining Accreditation and Credibility

Dordt College was now ready to embark on a four-year program. The people were excited, the board was optimistic, and the faculty was enthusiastic. We had added to our facilities. The next step was to increase the number of faculty. Now, too, was the time to begin the process of gaining accreditation from the North Central Association.

One incident in our search for faculty is of special significance to the history of the college. It concerns the hiring of Dr. Russell Maatman.

The coming of Maatman to Dordt College is another illustration of the marvelous leading of the Lord. As we began a four-year program, we were particularly eager to find professors with outstanding academic ability. We already had men of exceptional ability in philosophy, education, classical languages, and music. We particularly wanted to find someone with a Ph.D degree in the physical sciences. Maatman was just the kind of person that we were praying for!

In answer to an ad in the Christian Reformed Church publication, *The Banner*, I received a letter of interest from Maatman. Why would a person with a reputable degree, teaching chemistry in the graduate school of the University of Mississippi, having six students under his supervision working for their master's degrees, and two working for their doctor's degrees, want to come to Dordt College? Here is how it happened.

In 1962, our government was determined to put an end to segregation in our southern universities. Never before had a black student been allowed to enroll at the University of Mississippi. Civil rights backers had chosen the University of Mississippi as a test case, supporting James Merideth's enrollment at the University of Mississippi that year. The story headlined all major newspapers. To insure his safety, body guards accompanied him around the clock. Special agents walked with him around the campus and to his classes.

Maatman and his wife, Jean, decided to befriend James Merideth. This favor shown by the Maatmans to James Merideth brought not only the frowns of the people, but their anger. The Maatmans were socially abandoned and harassed.

At Maatman's retirement 27 years later, Sally Jongsma, writing in the

Dordt College *Voice*, states, "After taking a stand and defending Merideth, Maatman's life was not easy. Distrusted and harassed by neighbors, and even some fellow church members, the Maatmans decided that their five children needed to grow up in a safer environment. They made their decision one Sunday morning on the way home from church. That evening two people were randomly killed by gunfire." Maatman later told us that earlier that year friends had suggested that he apply to Dordt College, but he was not ready to do that. But after this incident he contacted me.

You can imagine my excitement and anticipation when Maatman decided to come for an interview! I was determined to do everything in my power to convince him that Dordt College was a place with marvelous opportunities for someone dedicated to the principles of the Reformed faith.

Maatman stayed at our home. What a stimulating visit it was! We took to one another immediately. We felt like we were of the same spirit, the same chemistry. Obviously, we couldn't show him extensive facilities. Coming to Dordt from the University of Mississippi with all that they had to offer would be quite a change for Maatman. But he listened intently to the story and was, I think, impressed with the board interview and his visits with some of the faculty. That night in my home we pulled up our chairs in the living room, put our feet up on the stools, and had a good lunch and a spirited conversation. It was a beautiful time together. I felt deep down in my bones that Russell Maatman caught our vision and was excited.

There was no doubt that he would get the appointment; the question now was, "What about his wife and children?" I considered it important that Jean come with Russell and spend a weekend with us before he made his decision.

They came a couple of weeks later, at Dordt's expense, and stayed in our home. We felt very much at home with them, and when they decided to accept, Deborah and I went to Oxford, Mississippi, and spent some time with them as they prepared to make the switch to

Gaining Accreditation and Credibility 125

Dordt College. Our friendship with their family began then and continued throughout the years.

Maatman not only brought scientific expertise, but also the ability to get highly-coveted research grants. Furthermore, he read widely—you could hold a conversation with him on almost anything. He was an important presence on committees. He caught the reformational vision and soon became a leader in the faculty. We were extremely grateful for the leading and blessing of the Lord in this experience. I have no doubt that the coming of Dr. Maatman played a large role in attracting other scholars of special ability.

* * * * *

We became a four-year college in 1963. Student enrollments mushroomed. Adding the third and the fourth year programs to our curriculum meant that we needed many new faculty members. The task of acquiring all the needed professors was uppermost in our minds.

In a short time we made a host of additions to the staff. Among those additions were people who are still teaching at Dordt College, persons who were not only highly qualified, but highly committed to our principles and to the cause of Dordt College. Four men holding their doctor's degrees soon joined us: Dr. Willis Alberda, Dr. Aldert Mennega, Dr. Simon Kistemaker, and Dr. Edwin Geels. To demonstrate that Dordt was gaining academic prestige, two of those who joined us were also given opportunities to teach at Calvin College: Dr. Willis Alberda, in the field of mathematics, and Jack Vanden Berg, in the field of English literature. Others who joined us in these early years and are still present with us are Dr. Louis Van Dyke, Mr. Arnold Koekkoek, Mr. Abe Bos, Dr. James Koldenhoven, Mr. Arnold Veldkamp, Dr. Mike Vanden Bosch, Dr. John Van Dyk, Dr. Case Boot, Dr. Dallas Apol, Dr. Syne Altena, Dr. Leonard Rhoda, Mr. Martin Dekkenga, Dr. Charles Veenstra, Dr. Daryl Vander Kooi, Dr. Joan Ringerwole and Mrs. Jo Alberda. Others also served us well, but soon left for other institutions of higher learning.

I deeply loved and appreciated all the persons with whom I was allowed to work during these and later years. In fact, I could well write a separate story about several of these individuals—one of special acknowledgement and special appreciation.

One person who taught for several years at Dordt College, and then left to teach elsewhere, was Dr. Frank Calsbeek. I mention him because of all the work he did to establish a strong physical education program at Dordt College.

Another person who deserves special mention is Mr. Henry De Groot. Henry was willing to leave his position at Sioux Falls College, a liberal arts college in Sioux Falls, South Dakota, to begin a business program at Dordt. De Groot was a highly respected teacher.

Many questioned whether we, as a liberal arts college, should introduce a business department. But the board and I and several others on the staff were convinced that business belonged in a liberal arts college. We believed that the need and the demand was so great that it would be a shame not to go into that field. Mr. De Groot did an outstanding job of setting up the business program. Dordt has had an exceptional number of students in that program and has received recognition through students coming out of that department.

Dordt College was also blessed with competent administrative personnel. I learned early in my presidency the importance of hiring the best qualified persons for administrative positions. My policy was to find such individuals, clearly define their duties, and then allow them enough freedom to creatively carry out their work. I met with them regularly to listen to their ideas and advice. When they were assigned special tasks, I tried not to be constantly looking over their shoulders to check up on them. I wanted them to do their job in a relaxed manner, free from tension. If they made mistakes or failed in certain projects, I wanted to be the first to relieve them of worry over the matter. I didn't believe it wise to reprimand. After all, good administrators are the first to realize their failures and, with friendly encouragement, are quick to learn from their experiences. They made my job much easier. I often said that if I was successful it was due to the fact that I seldom did anything that others on my staff could not do as well or better than I.

One thing was very important to me, however. Although I was careful to learn the wishes of my administrators and of my faculty as well, I reserved the right to make my own decisions and present these to the board of trustees for support when necessary.

Throughout my tenure I was privileged to have on the administrative staff the following: academic dean, Douglas Ribbens; business managers, Neal Boersma and Bernard De Wit; public relations and fund raising, Lyle Gritters and his assistants, Harold and Verlyn De Wit; admissions director, Howard Hall; dean of students, Dr. Garrett Rozeboom and Dr. J.B. Hulst, with his assistant Len Van Noord.

Gaining Accreditation and Credibility 127

All of these people served with ability and were not afraid of work. They gave of their time unstintingly on behalf of the college. They were self-motivated, knew their responsibilities, and carried them out with skill. As president of the college, I received credit and praise for many apparent successes that were being made. However, much of the credit for what was achieved is due to the efforts of these people. Without them it would have been impossible to enjoy the marvelous successes that were ours.

The development of our library was also an important factor in Dordt's growth. When the synod of the Christian Reformed Church appointed a study committee in the late 1940s to study the call for a junior college, one of the reasons it cited to discourage going in that direction was that it would be impossible for such an institution in the "hinterlands" to enjoy an adequate library. When I read this, I shook my head in disbelief. The history of the Dordt library is sufficient proof of the ridiculousness of the study committee's attitude. From the start Dordt paid serious attention to building a reputable library with quality books. We owe much to the dedicated services of Emma Vanden Berg, our first librarian, who later joined our staff and served as assistant to Hester Hollaar, director of the library. During Hollaar's long tenure the library greatly expanded both facilities and volumes. Rather early in our history we reached 100,000 quality books. Already in its first visit to the Dordt campus the North Central Association was pleased with our library budget and the variety of books in our library.

But in addition to good facilities and a competent staff we needed national accreditation. Our credibility and viability as an academic institution rested on such recognition. Although it is possible to place too high a premium on accreditation, it is almost impossible to function without it.

During my tenure as president we went through three self-examination studies to gain and maintain accreditation by the North Central Association. I must confess that at first I approached this matter with a great deal of concern. And with good reason. Those who opposed the establishment of Dordt College were quick to say that it was unlikely Dordt would gain national accreditation.

The fact that I was the president, without an advanced degree, was thought by many to be a severe handicap to gaining accreditation. I put on a rather bold front during this period, but I suffered a good many anxious moments.

Our first encounter with North Central was by no means an easy or a pleasant one. At first, things looked favorable. North Central appointed Dr. Lofthus, from St. Olaf College, to be our counselor and help us complete our self-study. We truly appreciated his guidance and were encouraged by his reaction to our self-study. Dr. Ribbens had the chief responsibility for writing the self-study for North Central. We were fortunate to have him and were cautiously optimistic when the report was sent. As was their custom, North Central appointed a committee to visit the campus to find out whether our self-study was an accurate portrayal of the college.

I think there were four men on the visiting team. They visited classrooms, talked with board members, met with students, checked into our finances, spoke with administrators and, of course, met with me. We sensed that, while the committee was happy about most of what they saw on the campus, they were not pleased that we had only professors who were committed to our point of view. The chairman, in particular, was very upset with this fact. He seemed to feel that if we were to maintain true academic freedom we should have a variety of teachers—maybe even have an atheist on our campus. Neither were they happy with the control the board had over the college. One of the men said that our board should be there simply to raise money.

I was quite concerned about the report the committee sent us and submitted to North Central. Dr. Lofthus was also unhappy with the report of the visiting team. I am quite sure that North Central heard from him. Nevertheless, Dr. Ribbens and I went to Chicago to appear before the representatives of North Central, to defend our self-study over against the visiting team's report. Although Dr. Ribbens gave me moral support, the committee expected me, as president, to defend the report. Dr. Ribbens was not even asked to comment on the work of the self-study.

Gaining Accreditation and Credibility

I came to Chicago with a great deal of apprehension. In fact, I was extremely nervous about the whole affair. We arrived on Saturday, stayed in a motel, went to church on Sunday, and had to meet the committee on Monday morning. It was not a pleasant weekend for me. I was full of anxious thoughts. However, when I entered the room and sat before all of those people, I felt calm and undisturbed. My mind was clear and my voice steady.

As we expected, the questions soon focused on academic freedom. They wanted to know whether or not we believed in a literal interpretation of the Bible. I responded by asking them what they meant by a literal interpretation of the Bible. They had difficulty answering that question. I made it clear that when the Bible was meant to be taken literally, we took it literally, but that often the scriptures did not require a literal interpretation.

They asked my view of creation and the creation days. I told them that there were two views acceptable among us—the view that the world was created in ordinary days of twenty-four hours, but also that these days could be looked upon as periods of time. We did not insist that our professors teach a young earth. Those who believed in an older universe were also given the right to that view.

They questioned me on the freedom professors had to do research that might question some of the views accepted by the college. I told them that we were not afraid of truth and that we were ready to follow wherever truth led us. However, I also made it plain that our convictions were such that we were not about to join an expedition that was out to find the body of Jesus Christ.

I felt that we made a good impression upon the committee. However, they had taken seriously the visiting team's concerns about the lack of academic freedom. As a result, the committee granted us two years of accreditation instead of the normal ten-year period. After two years we would have to submit again to a review by North Central.

A significant thing happened as a result of our visit: North Central appointed a special committee to study the matter of academic freedom. The question was whether or not an institution, in order to be accredited, had to allow teachers on staff who were in opposition to the basic principles and purposes of the institution. In the end North Central decided that an institution did not need to hire teachers who were opposed to the stated purposes of the institution in order to allow academic freedom.

In the meantime, Dr. Ribbens coordinated our next self-study. North Central appointed a committee to come again. What a difference in that committee's attitude toward the college! Their visit was a real delight. When we went to Chicago that time, we didn't have any worries or problems. As a matter of fact, there were very few questions asked. When we finished the meeting, one of the women on the committee said to me that they were very much impressed with our institution. I thanked God and breathed a great sigh of relief.

We received a ten-year accreditation. At the end of that ten-year period we went, once more, through the entire process and found it to be an enjoyable and profitable experience. We had no difficulty meeting the demands of North Central.

* * * * *

One thing that meant a great deal to me was that even the first committee, which was highly critical of Dordt College, was not unhappy with the fact that I was the president, even though I had no graduate degree. They made it very clear that they were not interested in degrees, but were concerned only with the competency of the person who held that office.

Although there were times when I was somewhat embarrassed and made to feel uncomfortable because I did not possess a graduate degree, I don't think I ever allowed these instances to hinder my leadership academically or otherwise. I felt very much ready to meet the challenges of advancement and promotion. And I enjoyed the full backing of the board and most of the people. The majority of the faculty supported me and treated me with loving respect. As time went on I grew more and more secure in my position and the lack of an advanced degree became inconsequential.

Some interesting experiences grew from this situation. When I became the full-time president of Dordt College I did not have a special installation ceremony. I think that was due partly to the fact that I was uncomfortable with my status, but also to the fact that few if any on the faculty or among the board knew the protocol connected with inaugurating a new president. Another incident occurred at graduation one year. Whenever we had graduation exercises or I was called upon to attend meetings where academic garb was required, I wore the robe that was meant for college graduates. I also had a small cape with a cap and a red theological tassel. There was no indication in my academic garb that I was the president of a liberal arts college. At times I found this embarrassing, but I took the lead in my college graduate degree garment for several years.

One year that changed. Our commencement speaker was Dr. Harold Lindsel, the editor of *Christianity Today*. As we were lining up to go into the auditorium, Dr. Lindsel said to me, "Where is your presidential doctoral robe?"

Gaining Accreditation and Credibility 131

"I don't have an advanced degree," I explained.

"That doesn't make one bit of difference," he said. "As president of this liberal arts college you have the right to have a presidential robe." Soon after that incident the college ordered a doctoral presidential robe for me.

* * * * *

Another source of encouragement to me as an academic leader was the way in which the Colleges of Mid-America (CMA) received, respected, and honored me. Dordt College joined this consortium of colleges in 1958, the year it originated. CMA included nine colleges in our area. I met frequently with the presidents, and we participated in a large number of programs that were advantageous to all of our colleges. I can not say enough good about the relationships we developed with these colleges and the people represented at the various academic meetings of the Colleges of Mid-America.

I was particularly pleased to have had the honor of being the president of CMA during my last two years as president. When I retired, Deborah and I received a beautiful painting from the organization. A plaque on the painting states, "To Dr. and Mrs. B.J. Haan, our teachers from 1958 to 1982. The presidents of the Colleges of Mid-America."

During the last year of my presidency I received the Distinguished Alumnus Award from my alma mater, Calvin College. This was a real joy to me, my wife, and my family. We had helped start a college that was looked upon as being in opposition to Calvin College, even though we never meant it that way. To receive that kind of recognition after all those years was certainly a special honor.

Finally, I should say a few words about the honorary doctor's degree that I was offered by the University of Potchefstroom in South Africa. This Calvinistic university learned of Dordt College through the International Organization of Calvinistic Colleges and Universities, which was started early in the 1980s in South Africa at Potchefstroom.

* * * * *

In the early 70s, the Calvinistic colleges held annual conferences. From the beginning, Potchefstroom was sharply criticized for its supposed position on apartheid. The institutions that took the lead against Potchefstroom on this issue were the Free University of Amsterdam, Calvin College, The Institute for Christian Studies in Canada, and some professors at Dordt College.

I became aware of the controversy during the second conference, held at Calvin College in Grand Rapids. My wife and I stayed in a dormitory with several South African delegates and became well acquainted. One evening the discussion was devoted solely to the issue of apartheid. It was a sad meeting. Tensions were high and I recall that, at one point, Elaine Botha, a professor of philosophy at Potchefstroom, broke down while she was addressing the group on the issue. The rector of the university, Tjaard van der Walt, did his best to explain their position, indicating the complexities of the problem and what they were hoping to accomplish in the future. Many at that meeting were not satisfied with what they heard. I felt differently. I was not in favor of apartheid, neither was Van der Walt or Elaine Botha. But I was sympathetic to the people from South Africa. I was asked to close the meeting with the reading of scripture and with prayer.

It had been a stormy session. The battle had raged for at least three hours. Even those who listened were weary, yes, exhausted. I had said little, if anything. I knew many were wondering what I would say now. I arose and proceeded slowly to the podium. For a few seconds I stood quietly and looked rather sorrowfully at the audience. A deadly silence stole over the room. I opened the Bible. Softly, yet clearly, I called attention to the fact that all gathered there were desperately in need of higher help. It was time to listen to the voice of Jesus. I read from John's gospel, chapter 15. The passage begins, "I am the vine, ye are the branches," and gradually and lovingly comes to the solemn and pointed reminder, "without me ye can do nothing." I closed the Bible and pleaded in prayer for the sorely needed guidance and blessing of the Lord in this turbulent situation.

It was as though Jesus arose from sleep at the desperate cry of the disciples battling the raging waters and commanded the sea to be calm. In all my years of offering devotions, I have never experienced a more pronounced awareness of the Lord's presence quieting our emotions and reminding us of our impotence and His power when he asked, "Where is your faith?"

This incident served to strengthen our bond of love with South Africans on both sides of the apartheid issue.

During the four years following the conference at Calvin College, our relationship with South Africa and Potchefstroom became closer and the contacts more frequent. Elaine Botha even taught at Dordt College for a semester, giving us the opportunity to hear her response to the problem of apartheid in South Africa. I once asked her what she thought about the feelings of some of those on the Dordt faculty who strongly opposed Potchefstroom's stand. She said to me, "Rev. Haan, they do not understand the problem." Elaine loved her people and was very opposed to apartheid,

Gaining Accreditation and Credibility 133

but she also saw the enormous complexity of the problem. I could feel her sincerity and sympathized with her.

Sometime after this Tjaard van der Walt, rector of the University of Potchefstroom, also came to visit. He stayed in our home on campus and followed me around for three days. Every once in a while he would say to me, "I like your style, I like your style." I really didn't know what he meant by that. In fact, I was wondering whether he was just amused or whether he sincerely meant it. We kept busy, visiting, playing golf, and attending meetings. At one point he said to me, "B.J. you should write a book on how to be a college president and get away with it." Then I really wondered whether he was just joking or truly meant it.

Not too long after he returned to South Africa, I received a letter from him in the name of the Committee of Honorary Degrees. I was offered an honorary doctor's degree from Potchefstroom University. That meant that my wife and I would go to South Africa for three weeks to enjoy the finest entertainment and hospitality and receive an honorary doctor's degree at the commencement exercises. I was shocked. Obviously I was flattered by the fact that they offered me this honor. The university is no small institution. It has a strong reputation, with approximately 8000 students and over 400 faculty.

However, it was not to be. From the moment I informed the faculty of this offer, several individuals strongly protested. They felt it would damage the image of Dordt College if the president would accept an honorary doctor's degree from an institution that was not strongly opposed to apartheid.

One day six professors visited me in my office, urging me not to accept. I received letters from faculty members at the Institute for Christian Studies in Toronto, Canada. I also heard from a few professors at Calvin College. Dr. Klaas Runia, from The Netherlands, who happened to be visiting in the United States, was even asked to visit with me. Runia was, at that time, president of the International Organization of Calvinistic Universities. I really had the heat put on me, but I persisted in feeling that it was perfectly legitimate for me to accept this honor. I could not understand why so many of my colleagues were so upset about Potchefstroom's supposed lack of willingness to honor the second table of the law that we love our neighbors as ourselves, yet when it came to the Free University of Amsterdam, they were not too disturbed about the fact that this university was liberal in its view of the authority of the word of God and weak on its emphasis of the first table of the law, that we love God above all. In fact while some were arguing that we should not allow Potchefstroom to continue to be a member of the organization of Calvinistic Universities, not one voice was raised against having the Free University belong to this organization. I felt that both institutions should belong, but that we should continue to have dialogue on the issues confronting us.

I was almost ready to accept when one of the professors who stood behind me and recommended that I take it suddenly changed his mind. Nick Van Til came into my office just a couple of days before I made my decision. Nick had read a recently published book called *The Broederbond*, which was very much opposed to apartheid and painted a dark picture of the situation in South Africa. It incriminated such institutions as Potchefstroom University and many of its faculty. He said to me, "I have changed my mind. I am convinced that you should turn it down." When that happened I felt that I did not have sufficient support in the faculty, even though a small majority still favored my accepting it. Considering all the discussion and all the concerns, I felt it was best perhaps that I, even though very reluctantly, decline the offer.

In my letter declining the offer, I tried desperately to explain how I felt about the whole situation. I wanted the people in South Africa to sense my deepest appreciation and my eagerness to accept, but at the same time understand that the situation at Dordt College and other institutions made it impossible for me to do so. It was a heavy blow to my wife and me, for we deeply loved our South African brothers and sisters.

Not long after this I met with the presidents of the Colleges of Mid-America Consortium. I told the presidents about the situation. I was surprised that every last one of them said, "Why didn't you accept? What does apartheid have to do with the acceptance of an honorary doctor's degree from a reputable academic institution?" Their reaction gave me some serious misgivings about my decision. I was convinced that my accepting the degree would not have been frowned upon or sharply criticized and that Dordt's name would not have suffered a severe setback.

The story has an interesting sequel. Not long after this episode Dordt College hosted the International Conference of Calvinistic Universities. Several people from Potchefstroom were present, including the rector, Tjaard van der Walt, and M. Gatshd Buthelezi, chief of the six million Zulus in South Africa. Buthelezi is indeed a sincere, dedicated Christian.

Buthelezi, along with his entourage and several faculty were in our home discussing what to do about Potchefstroom. Some thought we should discontinue any relationship with Potchefstroom and that they should not be allowed to attend these conferences until the matter of apartheid was settled. I asked Buthelezi whether we should really go in that direction. He immediately responded by saying, "Oh, no, after all they are Christians and we must be ready to talk, we must continue to talk." His answer made me feel good because that was my position, too.

I also found it interesting that Buthelezi, in contrast to the members of the Communist Party of South Africa, opposed sanctions. He felt that sanctions would only hinder progress toward the abolition of apartheid and that those who would suffer from sanctions would be primarily black people.

The second incident deals with my honorary degree. When Tjaard van der Walt presented my name in Potchefstroom for a doctoral degree, some questioned my qualifications. When asked, "What has he written to show his scholarly achievements?" he replied, "Dordt College is B.J.'s book." When these men eventually came to Dordt's campus and witnessed what had happened at Dordt College, it was most gratifying to hear Tjaard van der Walt say to me, "My people are fully convinced that you deserve the honorary degree."

Ten years later, after my retirement, a new principal of the university, Carools Reineke, visited the United States. When he came to Sioux Center, he visited with me and some of the other professors in my home. We had a most enjoyable, delightful visit. In fact I offered to take him to the airport the next day. Driving to the airport and having dinner together there, we established a strong bond of friendship. I told him that we would like to come to South Africa to visit. Over the years we had come to know many people from South Africa. Only a few years earlier a professor of law from Witwatersrand University in South Africa, Johann van der Vyver, taught at Dordt College for one semester. We visited with him and his wife, and they urged us to come to South Africa. They told us, "If you come to South Africa we will host you, and we will see to it that you find your way around." We were very interested in going.

When Reineke got back to South Africa, we received a letter from him, telling how he had enjoyed his visit to the United States. To our amazement, we soon received another letter from him informing us that the Honorary Degree Committee at Potchefstroom had again offered me an honorary doctorate. Ten years after I had declined the first offer, they had unanimously decided to honor me again. We were floored! I accepted almost immediately, and we made plans to go to South Africa, all at their expense.

Everything was ready. We had a schedule you wouldn't believe. We were very excited about visiting many friends and places in South Africa, and I looked forward to the graduation ceremony where I would receive my honorary degree.

But it was not to be. A week before we were to leave I suffered a rupture that caused excessive internal bleeding. I had to go to the local emergency room. They worked on me for a long time, finally transferring me to Sioux City for an operation. My doctors told me, "You cannot go on that long trip until this heals." I had to make a call to Professor Reineke. What a difficult thing that was to do. Both my wife and I felt so badly. But Reineke graciously assured me that they would give me the degree in absentia. A few weeks later, Professor Reineke, in the United States with a group seeking better understanding between the United States and South Africa, made arrangements with President Hulst to bestow upon me the honorary degree at Dordt College in the presence of my friends, the faculty, board members, and my family. Hulst graciously agreed and arranged a beautiful dinner. Nearly one hundred and fifty people were present. It was one of the most enjoyable evenings in my life. My children and my wife said that it was even more enjoyable than the big celebration held when I retired eight years earlier.

Since I was no longer president of Dordt College, I did not expect the honor at all. I could only express my sincerest gratitude to the Lord and to those wonderful friends at the University of Potchefstroom. The degree, they said, was granted on the basis of what I had contributed to the cause of Christian education generally and, in particular, to Christian higher education.

* * * * *

A story of special interest with which I want to conclude this chapter concerns E.L. Hebden Taylor, professor of economics and sociology at Dordt for ten years. Taylor was known to students and faculty as Stacey. Taylor was known for his strong commitment to the thinking of both Abraham Kuyper and Herman Dooyeweerd, and wrote a book, *The Christian Philosophy of Law, Politics and the State*.

I was first introduced to the book by Nick Van Til, then professor of philosophy at Dordt. He enthusiastically recommended that I buy the book. A few years later, I heard that Taylor, an Anglican minister living in England, would be available for a position. We sorely needed someone with a solid reformational perspective to head our sociology department. Stacey seemed to be the person we were looking for. I knew that he had lived in Canada and maintained close contact with the leaders of the reformational movement there. These men spoke highly of Stacey. I contacted Taylor and found that he was definitely interested in coming to Dordt. But I had to get recommendations to convince the board of trustees that it was worth the cost to bring him here. Among others, I called Gerald Vande Zande, a popular, intelligent leader of the Christian Labor Association of Canada, who was

Gaining Accreditation and Credibility

a good friend of Taylor. Gerald highly recommended Taylor but told me that Taylor was a real "character" who needed some direction. Vande Zande was confident that under my leadership, Dordt could make good use of Taylor on the faculty.

The board trusted me. Taylor soon arrived, accompanied by his family and his huge dog. Every college needs a couple of "characters" on campus. Taylor was certainly one of these. Although he often gave me fits, he brought valuable insight to Dordt. His method of teaching left much to be desired, but he produced mimeographed notes that were thoroughly reformational. The better students respected his ideas highly. I loved him, but had to keep a tight rein on him. Fortunately, he could take it from me, and we remained good friends.

When I retired, Taylor was not ready to work under a new administration and took a position elsewhere. A few years later he called me and said that he was writing a new book and wanted to dedicate it to me. He asked me to write the foreword. Knowing Taylor, I thanked him, but postponed the promise to write the foreword until he found a publisher. To date I have not heard from him.

It was amusing that later on, when Dordt was in the throes of the so-called AACS struggle, those on the board and in the community who appreciated Taylor, bitterly opposed the Dordt statement of purpose, *Scripturally Oriented Higher Education*. Much of Taylor's thinking colors this document.

Chapter Eight
Expanding Facilities

It was a wonderful experience to watch the rapid expansion of the physical facilities of Dordt College. The city of Sioux Center and, in particular, the late Mayor Maurice Te Paske, played an important role in this expansion. The cooperative spirit that characterizes life in the Sioux Center community and that has been the envy of many other communities was particularly evident in the manner in which the city and Dordt worked together on a number of building projects.

I was respectedly humbled by the remarkable blessing and leading of the Lord. Despite heated battles over Christian education and the American Legion theater, a sense of unity and respect for one another's convictions led to an unusual working relationship in our community. Much of this spirit was due to the leadership of Mayor Te Paske. He was a truly big person. You must remember that he was on the board of Northwestern College in Orange City, which, at that time, was considered to be in strong competition with Dordt College. However, Te Paske sensed that it would be wise to work along with rather than to oppose Dordt. Under Te Paske's leadership Dordt received much help from the city. The city of Sioux Center put in the first streets around the buildings at minimal cost to the college and allowed us a long repayment period at low interest.

The city also provided the boulevard lights that still stand on the original part of the campus. I have often told a story about the installation of those lights. The mayor called me and said, "Rev. Haan, those boulevard lights are here."

"Fine, put them in," I said.

"Yes," he said, "but uh...," then he hesitated. What he really wanted to say was, 'How much light do you want?' 'How close together must they be?' I sensed what he was thinking and said to him, "Well, we want to have them close enough to discourage evil, but not so close as to discourage romance."

He instantly replied, "I know exactly how much light you need." When I told this story later on to different alumni groups, they reminded me that those lights served just such a purpose. Under those lights, more than a few couples began a romance that ended in marriage.

But the cooperation with the city of Sioux Center did not end with those early projects. Greater things were to come. The acquisition of the outdoor athletic complex, the swimming pool, and Te Paske Theatre is another story worth telling.

Early in our history we bought ten acres of land just north of the original campus. Several years later, the city wanted to use the ten acres for athletic programs of the city and the public high school. A deal was made with Dordt College. For a low cost, the city allowed us the use of all of the athletic facilities being built by the city and the public high school. We gained a suitable area for cross country, a beautiful track, a football field that could also be used by Dordt as a soccer field, tennis courts, baseball diamonds with lights for night games, and use of the indoor swimming pool for swimming classes and for open swimming one day of the week. We paid less than $15,000 a year for the use of these athletic facilities. We paid another $15,000 for use of the indoor swimming pool. One day when Dr. William Spoelhof, president of Calvin College, was visiting, he and I took a ride past all of these facilities. I explained how we obtained them and at what cost we were making use of them. He shook his head in amazement and said, "Bernie, you stole this, and it's legal."

The way in which Dordt College, the city, and the public high school obtained the Te Paske Theatre was even more remarkable. The Te Paske Theatre is a beautiful auditorium used for theatrical performances by the high school and the college. The theatre was part of the new public high school and paid for by taxes. Through some strategic political negotiation by the mayor of Sioux Center with the legislature in Des Moines, Dordt College became co-owner of the theatre with the city and the public high school. What was so surprising was that all we had to pay was $40,000 toward light and sound equipment. Dordt has enjoyed the privilege of using this excellent facility for all these years for a relatively small amount of money.

After the theatre was completed we set up a committee to coordinate use of the theatre by the high school and Dordt. We agreed that should a misunderstanding or problem with scheduling ever arise, the city manager, the superintendent of the public school, and the president of Dordt College would get together to resolve it. In all the years we worked together, we never once had to meet to resolve any difficulty.

You can imagine what an enormous saving the use of these facilities has been to Dordt College. Building all of those facilities would have been impossible. In fact, what we were paying and continue to pay for the use of these facilities is less than the interest we would have paid on such facilities, let alone the cost of upkeep. It was a fantastic bargain indeed.

* * * * *

Dordt College was growing and expanding during the presidency of Lyndon Johnson and his Great Society programs. I have already mentioned the two federal agencies, HUD and HEW, that enabled us to borrow funds for dormitories, the commons, and the student union at only three and a quarter percent interest. We also received loans for the library, the original science building, and the gymnasium at only three percent interest and had thirty years to pay them back. I have often said that if it had not been for these government programs it is doubtful that Dordt College would have had the resources to become a reputable institution of higher learning. Our people were simply not able to pay that kind of money at the time. The Lord's providential leading opened the door to these funds for us and helped Dordt College flourish. Along with these increases in facilities and enrollment came an increase in committed supporters, people who were willing to give substantially to Dordt's operational needs. Nevertheless, even if we'd had this support at an earlier stage it would not have been sufficient to pay for all of the facilities the government supplied. Dordt would have continued to exist, but as a much smaller and less influential institution.

Shortly before my retirement I, together with others in the administration and the board, sensed the need for additions to our gymnasium, our science

Expanding Facilities

building, and our library. I was convinced that we should carry out these projects before inflation overwhelmed us. As it turned out, we did a very smart thing. We built a large addition to the gymnasium, the library, and the science building for around $700,000. This was not government financed. We obtained funds for the gymnasium through floating bonds, which were paid back over a period of years at a reasonable interest. The other two projects we simply paid for through income from debt reduction drives.

We sorely needed the addition to the gymnasium. We had small corridors with no large foyer. During half-times and after games, fans had no place to go. We needed an entry, a lobby, and restrooms. The physical education faculty were authorized to work with the architects to draft a plan. They originally wanted to add to the east of the building. But when I was called into the process, I asked the architect, "Didn't we have the west wall of the gymnasium a non-load-bearing wall so that we could cut through it and extend the building to the west?" The architect went back to his office and soon informed us that I was correct. As a result we put a two story addition on the west side of the gymnasium, and we saved a lot of money in the process.

The other two building additions, the library and the science building, were also erected at a low price for the times. My own son, Elson, was the contractor. It was amazing how economically the work was done. But while we were happy about the new buildings, our excitement was clouded by one extremely sad experience. Even after nine years I find it very difficult to write and talk about it. My grandchildren, Elson's two boys, while playing around the construction area, climbed to the top level of the science building where there were some live wires. As they jumped from one place to another, my grandson, Seth, grabbed hold of one of those wires and was killed instantly. It was a horrible shock to all of us. He was very precious to us, as all grandchildren are. He was particularly one of my favorites, always so cheerful and happy. It was a very trying experience, but the Lord was good to us. We all struggled together. Through much weeping we discovered that the Lord is near those who call upon Him and seek His help in times of adversity.

The gymnasium addition provided us with more faculty offices, a classroom, a small basketball or volleyball court, a racquetball court, and much needed washroom facilities. The addition to the science building primarily met the demands of our new agriculture program, with special classrooms, faculty offices, and an enlarged greenhouse with a spacious area for handling plant materials.

* * * * *

Two other building projects seemed to me to be especially significant in the history of the college: the radio station and the chapel. For some time already, a group of people in Northwest Iowa had been interested in radio broadcasting. It began when ten area churches, among them my church, sponsored a radio program in Le Mars, Iowa, twenty miles from Sioux Center. The Reverend Wesley Smedes coordinated what turned out to be a successful program. When Smedes took a call to Michigan, we had to make new plans. The Rev. J.C. Ribbens took over the program for a while, but it began to lose support. However, the idea of a radio station continued to live on.

In those days it wasn't such an outrageously costly business to erect a radio station. Apart from any direct effort on my part, a group formed to build and operate a radio station. The Rev. James Van Weelden, then minister in Sioux City, gave leadership and spirit to the project. For a while things looked promising. I sat on the sideline hoping that the station would materialize. However, as time progressed and differences of opinion arose, I began to wonder if they would be able to maintain the unity needed to carry out such a project. To make a long story short, plans fell apart and the project was for all practical purposes dead.

I was disappointed. But about that time I heard that it was possible for a college to operate an FCC-approved FM educational station. To make certain that I was not interfering with others plans, I called Mr. John Vande Kerk from Rock Valley, who was a prominent member of the committee. He assured me that there was nothing left of the project and that I would be free to go ahead with a college station. He also told me that he would cooperate on anything that we attempted to do.

I immediately contacted Mr. Eldon Kanego from Spencer, Iowa, who was knowledgeable about the building, the equipment, the FCC regulations, and a host of other matters related to establishing a radio station. He was most encouraging and helpful. Then I told the board about my hopes. They did not react one way or the other to the project.

As I often did in promoting a certain project, I gathered representatives from the area to talk things over. Mr. R.J. Dykstra, my assistant at the college, helped organize a large group of influential men who met several times to investigate and discuss the idea. John Vande Kerk was part of this group. I found out that these men, who were successful farmers and business people, were very much in favor of the idea. Their support encouraged me to present a proposal to the board of trustees. After a great deal of discussion and a measure of hesitancy, the board was not ready to

Expanding Facilities 143

move ahead on their own. They insisted that I call a society meeting for approval.

We held the meeting. Attendance was low, but I presented my recommendation. To my surprise and joy, the society voted by a large majority to go ahead.

Before giving final approval, the board set two stipulations. The radio station could not put a financial burden on the college. The station, they said, should be owned by the college but as a separate corporation. As it turned out, the separate corporation was dissolved shortly after the radio station began and KDCR came under the direct control of the board of trustees.

The second stipulation was that we raise the money before beginning to build the station. They did allow us to borrow money on a ten year basis at seven percent interest. The estimated cost was to be $50,000. Mr. Dykstra visited several people and in no time we had approximately twenty individuals who each contributed one or two thousand dollars. The De Stigter brothers, who built the facility at a cost of approximately $10,000, allowed us ten years to pay at seven percent interest.

I was delighted with what was accomplished, due largely to the work of R.J. Dykstra. We decided the station would be called KDCR-Dordt College Radio. A great deal of work went into getting the station approved by the FCC. We had to convince the FCC that the community needed such a station. To do this we contacted several societies and other groups in the area to verify the need for a station. We also had to obtain bids for the equipment. Here again Eldon Kanego from Spencer helped us with the details. Incidently, later Kanego's daughter attended Dordt College. He was impressed with our educational institution and helped us tremendously.

Finally, after receiving bids from two companies, we bought the equipment. But then we had to find someone to operate the station. Here again the leading of the Lord was amazing. Leonard Van Noord, who had attended Dordt College and was teaching at Edgerton Christian High School, was very interested in radio and had some experience. Leonard and his wife, Sue (Vander Baan), were thrilled with the appointment and enthusiastically accepted. Len worked for the college for several years, first as KDCR manager, then as assistant to the dean and college pastor. Len did a remarkable job in a sometimes difficult situation. Constituents, professional people, academicians, and musicians were all ready with advice and criticisms.

We had our problems, indeed we did! The programming committee met long and often about schedules. On the committee were two persons for whom I had a great deal of respect, Dr. Russell Maatman and the Rev. John

Rubingh. Rubingh was minister of the Ireton Christian Reformed Church and chairman of the board of trustees. We planned to be on the air from six in the morning until eleven or twelve o'clock at night. Maatman and Rubingh felt we should begin by just going on the air for half a day. They thought it was going to be difficult for us to get enough programming for that length of time. As chairman of the committee, I vigorously protested. I said, "Why must we be on the air only half a day? If the world can put on a program of that length, why can't we? Are we so lacking in ability and competency? Can we not find enough good material for a whole day of programming?" I insisted that if we were going to go on the air, we would begin from the very first day broadcasting from six in the morning until twelve at night. The board supported this proposal.

When we finally did go on the air, you can imagine how eagerly I listened. I turned on the radio at six o'clock in the morning and kept it on nearly all day and evening. Even though we had many improvements to make and had to learn a lot along the way, I maintain that the very first day we went on the air KDCR had a quality equal to other stations in our area.

From the beginning I wanted the radio station to be more than a broadcast service. I thought it could also provide training for students who were interested in broadcasting and communications. History has shown this to be correct. Dozens of young people have gone through the radio program

Expanding Facilities

and now hold positions at radio and television stations across the country. I also felt that it would be a strong public relations arm, which obviously it has become. I wanted to have that tower, 300 feet high, right in the middle of campus. But I was mostly interested in having a radio station because I believed that the way to promote, preserve, and advance our distinctive, Calvinistic world view, would be to go over the air. From the beginning our motto was "Proclaiming a God-Centered Culture." I hoped that the radio station would be a means to bind people in our area together around the fundamental principles of the faith that we hold dear and that were basic to the academic program of Dordt College.

KDCR continues to attract a variety of listeners not only from our own denomination but from others as well. I know that many people from the Reformed Church of America listen regularly to KDCR. Several Catholics also tune in to 88.5. Both my wife, Deborah, and I have enjoyed the privilege of having our own program. My program was called "Observations"; my wife's, "The Family Room." She gave recipes, devotions, and household hints for approximately twenty minutes every day. In my early morning program I reflected on contemporary issues.

The radio station was a costly venture. At first the board charged the station for all expenses not met by income given directly to the station. This income came from the First Christian Reformed Church and the Bethel Christian Reformed Church for broadcasting their services every Sunday. Beyond that we had to raise money through appeals over the radio and by sending out literature asking for help. The problem was that even though we were convinced money was being donated to the college as a result of the work of the radio station, it was not always sent directly to the station. We could never prove how much support for the college was actually the result of the radio station. After a few years, the amount of money the station owed the college became a bit staggering. Since the college was financially very healthy, the radio station did not become a burden. Finally, after about fifteen years, the board decided to cancel the entire debt.

Others besides Leonard Van Noord have done a great deal for the radio station. Mr. Martin Dekkenga served as a dedicated manager for a few years. Dennis DeWaard, the current manager, has been with the station since 1980. Once again it strikes me that when we went forward to meet a kingdom need, God provided people with talents, gifts, abilities, and the willingness to serve in that particular aspect of His kingdom.

* * * * *

The building of the college chapel is a story in itself. It was not accomplished without strong opposition. Two years before we started building I began to prepare the board and the general public for the project in my annual 'President's Report.' I asked the board for permission to contact an architect and to explore possibilities. I gave him three requirements. The auditorium had to be arranged in such a way that everyone could easily see what was happening on stage; the foyer should be large so that people could stand and talk as they came out of the auditorium; and we needed facilities for the music department, including rooms for choir, band, and orchestra.

I also wanted the building to be white cement with colonnades. I talked this over with my son, Elson. He said, "If you want that kind of building then you have to get a megaphone shaped building." He drew a picture of such an auditorium on a piece of paper. When we presented our ideas to the architect, he was delighted. He said, "Oh, that is wonderful, let's get to work on this." Although many changes had to be made on the original plan, the idea of the building, as originally presented to the architect, remained basically intact.

The time came to present the plan to the board of trustees. Again they rose to the occasion. In contrast, many faculty, at first, strongly opposed building the chapel. They felt we were putting far too much money into a project with funds that could be better spent improving the academic program of the college. I was convinced that we needed this building to round out our program. We not only needed it for our programs, but we also needed

Expanding Facilities

it for chapel services and to bring the wider community together more frequently on the campus for special events. There was no doubt in my mind, or in the mind of the board, that this was necessary.

Another reason for the opposition, I believe, was jealousy of the music department. Some thought that I paid too much attention to the music department. In fact I was accused of favoring Mr. Dale Grotenhuis, "my fair-haired boy." I even said to some who complained about this, that if they did for the college what Mr. Grotenhuis was doing they too would be my fair-haired boys. However, I tried to be careful not to create a spirit of envy, jealousy, and ill will.

I was disappointed in the negative attitude some faculty took toward this project. I found it sad that some of them, at first, refused to contribute to the building. One member of the faculty wanted the chapel to be a showcase for a Reformed view of church worship. He wanted it to be a model church, to illustrate a Reformed, biblical view of liturgy. In his plan, the organ and the choirs would be placed in the back of the auditorium, and we would not have been able to put on major performances in the building. We refused to listen to this idea. The result was that this individual, too, was unwilling to contribute to the project.

It was rather ironic that when the project was finally completed, not one of the men or the women on the faculty was opposed to it. In fact, when relatives and friends came to visit from other parts of the country, the chapel was one of the first things to be shown.

The community greatly appreciated the building, at once making unlimited use of it. I am still amazed at the number of events held there. Furthermore, the Dordt College chapel building is known for its acoustical quality. From the beginning we decided that the building should be suitable for a variety of programming. Although it cost us nearly $20,000, we hired an acoustical architect from Kansas City. It was worth every dollar and more. Included in the acoustical plans was an apparatus composed of many clear panels. It could be lowered over the platform by hydraulic power and tilted to suit the acoustical needs of the performance. The panel originally proposed would have cost us $42,000. We said we couldn't afford that much money, so the architect did some scouting around and finally came up with the panels or "clouds" now in the building. It has served the purpose well for half the cost. By watching the situation closely, we gained a real bargain without sacrificing quality.

When the acoustician came to inspect the building after it was completed, he told us that he seldom had worked with a building where the acoustics were of such a remarkably high quality. We have been greatly blessed by the building. Entertaining groups from all over the country, and even from outside the country, comment on its quality and the joy of performing in it.

We faced two problems in building the chapel auditorium. One was minor and concerned decor. Nevertheless, it caused a great deal of discussion. The other, more substantial, concerned the type of organ we should put in the new building.

We had left decisions about the decor to the architect. However, when the red seats arrived, the purple paint applied to the walls, and the acoustical ceiling clouds installed, we received a rash of complaints. In fact, it was so intense that I decided to call in an interior design expert. When he saw the finished product, he was ecstatic with praise. "For once people have had the courage to choose colors that give warmth and attractiveness to such a facility," he said. That ended all opposition.

The organ disagreement was not as easily settled. Already when the board was planning the facility, the question of an organ came up. A number of members argued for an electronic organ. I'm not opposed to an electronic organ in certain places, but I did not think that we should put an electronic organ in this building. The issue was energetically debated by the voting members board. I asked, "Are we going to put up a large building and put in just an electronic organ? I think that is a big mistake. Our people can't have everything out here. We aren't in a position to have all the kinds of things that other colleges have, but here is an opportunity to do something special. Our people love music. If we put in a big pipe organ, we will get students who want to study organ at Dordt College. And we will serve our people who love music. So let's not be squeamish here. Let's have the courage to put in an organ that will give us some class, some distinction, and still be reasonable."

Fortunately, we won by a large majority. But the pipe organ had to be paid for. We were not sure where to get the money. To my amazement Mrs. Minnie Dahm, a widow, came and offered to pay for half of the organ. The organ we wanted was to cost about $250,000. It was a Casavant, one of the best. Later she came back to us and said, "No, I've changed my mind, I want to pay for all of it." Later still, when we added other pipes and trumpets to the organ, she also paid for these. Her generosity was a tremendous boost. Two hundred fifty thousand dollars was no small thing. A few years later, that organ would have cost us well over half a million. It is a splendid instrument, loved by many musicians. The blessings that organ brought have made it well worth the cost.

To raise the $1.5 to $2 million needed for the building, we initiated our first major campaign, called "Forward Thrust." Two people played major

Expanding Facilities

roles in Forward Thrust: Lyle Gritters, director of development, and Harold De Wit, a farmer who proved to be an outstanding person for this work. These two men, with the help of Harold De Wit's son, Verlyn, raised a handsome sum of money for the project. In fact, by the time the campaign was completed, the building was practically paid for.

They began by calling on a few people from Orange City who responded with large contributions. They went next to Sanborn and to Inwood, Iowa. Supporters in both of these communities provided a truly generous amount of money for the chapel. I recall that about a dozen people in Sanborn contributed $50,000 toward the project. Harold De Wit and I also went to Pella to visit Gary Vermeer. I suggested that it would be nice if someone would donate a certain amount of money for matching purposes, to encourage others to give.

"That's not a bad idea. I'll be willing to go along with that, but I want to stop at $100,000," he told us. We were ecstatic; we had an incentive for encouraging people to give. The matching fund paid huge dividends for Dordt College. Once again we could thank the Vermeers for their generosity, which also continued in later projects.

I should also say that although some faculty were opposed to the project and contributed very little, many others gave liberally to the campaign.

With the funds committed we began construction. While the chapel building was being erected I would frequently visit the site to see how things were going. One day as I came into the lobby, I stood looking around for a bit, sensing that it was too huge an area. The space between the floor of the lobby and the floor of the balcony was enormous, I thought. I said to Gilbert De Stigter, the builder, "Do you mean to say we are going to have all this empty space?"

"That's what the blueprint calls for," he responded.

"I think that it could easily have another floor, couldn't it?" I asked.

He saw no reason why it couldn't be done, so we contacted the architect as soon as possible. The architect also agreed that the idea was a good one. In fact, he said, to put in a mezzanine floor between the balcony and the downstairs lobby would be very inexpensive, comparatively speaking. I went to the board with the idea. They agreed that the addition would give us useful space that could be used for a variety of purposes. Today it is used for Studies Institute offices, the college art gallery, and a place where groups can meet before a performance or event in the chapel. It has served many purposes and did not add too much to the price.

I really wanted to put some stained glass windows in the chapel, so I contacted a Mr. Helder from Michigan who was a master at stained glass work. Although somewhat expensive, the cost was not prohibitive. Three stained glass windows, two in the front of the auditorium on the back corners of the building, are truly beautiful pieces of art. The inscription worked into the window is the passage, 'In Thy Light We See Light.' "In Thy Light" begins on the east panel, "We See Light" continues on the other side. On the front of the building is a large circular stained glass window with the emblem of Dordt College. We often spoke of it as a jewel set right in the center of that building. When the lights are on at night it is a sight of real beauty. The building itself is stately both inside and out. The white structure with its colonnades is visible from a long way off. It stands on the campus as a symbol of the crowning blessings of the Lord. We love the building, and, I believe, are justly proud of it and thankful for it.

After the organ was ordered from Saint Hyacinthe, Canada, a city just a few miles away from Montreal, my wife and I were asked to go and examine it. We had a wonderful time there, staying with Mr. Bruinsma, the organ's designer. It was around Christmas time. We spent a pleasant evening listening to music, singing, and enjoying Christian fellowship. When we asked to see the organ the next day, the workers responded, "Oh, you mean the big one." Our organ in that place, where they were building several large organs, was referred to as 'the big one.' The organ was built in Saint Hyacinthe, taken down for shipping, brought to Sioux Center, and finally

Expanding Facilities 151

reassembled in the new building. What an experience! Only one organ compared to Dordt's in the whole state of Iowa, and that was the one at the University of Iowa. It was the only tracker (mechanical) action organ with a 32-foot pedal division at the time of its installation. Interestingly, the stops on the organ were labeled in Dutch rather than German names. Mr. Bruinsma thought this was appropriate because of our Dutch heritage. It was a real joy to dedicate the chapel/auditorium, knowing that it would be paid for by gifts to Forward Thrust. We were filled with gratitude and enthusiasm. We dedicated the building and the organ in a special, well-attended service. Dr. Joan Ringerwole, who has been professor of music and organ at the college since 1967, gave a recital as part of the service. I made a few remarks, and Mrs. Minnie Dahm gave a beautiful presentation. It was a most enjoyable evening.

I especially remember one person who came to the dedication of the organ, Dr. Stanley Wiersma, then professor of English at Calvin College. Stanley was born in Middleburg, Iowa, not far from Dordt College. As a boy, he would often drive from his farm into Sioux Center, passing the place where the college was eventually built. Stanley used to attend my young people's society on Sunday nights because Middleburg Christian Reformed Church, which no longer exists, was so small that they did not have one. He was a gifted musician and often played the piano for our society meeting. Stanley was very excited about our organ and the new chapel building. He had followed the development of Dordt College very closely, and often remarked that it was such a wonder to him that a place formerly used as a rendering plant was now a college. More than that, it had become a significant cultural center in Northwest Iowa.

Stanley made a point of being at the dedication of the organ. After the program, I happened to bump into him in the foyer. We shook hands and stood there for a few minutes just laughing. We didn't say a word, but we knew exactly what we were thinking—can you imagine this happening here in Northwest Iowa, in Sioux Center? We were filled with joy and delight.

Wiersma wrote the following poem after the occasion:

Villanelle

A life is far too short a time to play
as we were meant to, gamboling along
in what was pasture only yesterday.

A city is abuilding. Work today
as if another day won't roll along.
Then life becomes too short a time to play—

except your play is work, your work is play
because your work-and-play is making song
in what was pasture only yesterday.

When fingers run on ivory inlay,
lead, tin, wood pipes insinuate this song:
"Joan's life is far too short a time to play."

Pachelbel, Sweelink, Eben, and you, too, may
and must provoke the great tradition on
in what, after all, was still pasture yesterday.

Cheer up! Your students' art prolongs your day.
Who knows but organs sound with heaven's throng?—
because life is too short a time to play
in what was pasture only yesterday.

Chapter Nine
The Gathering Storm

It often happens that an institution goes through a titanic struggle over a controversial issue which, at the time, appears to cripple the institution, if not threaten its very existence. Yet when the battle is over the institution becomes stronger. That was the experience of Dordt College when it went through the so-called struggle over the Association for the Advancement of Christian Scholarship in the early 1970s.

I use the words "so-called struggle" quite consciously. Actually the conflict was not so much over the AACS as it was to maintain the fundamental principles upon which Dordt College was founded even before the AACS was in existence.

The turmoil on the Dordt College campus began when a fiercely vocal minority of the faculty, a small representation of students, and a number of irate constituents publicly opposed the AACS. As in all controversies there were two sides. Faculty and students sympathetic to the AACS were quick to add fuel to the fire. They made statements and acted in ways that, although not necessarily wrong, incited strong feelings from those opposed to the AACS. As the controversy raged on I did my the best to steer the boat through the troubled waters. One thing was clear to me: while I did not particularly appreciate some of the statements and practices of the AACS members, I was convinced that they did not threaten the basic principles for which Dordt College stood. In fact, the AACS shared our commitment to the lordship of Christ over every part of life. As leaders in the reformational movement, they were committed to promoting a radically Christian response in all areas of life. This conviction led them to question and often challenge the status quo—in lifestyle, in politics, in academia, in society, and in the church.

On the other hand, those who opposed the AACS gave clear evidence that they did not espouse the biblical Reformed principles clearly articulated in our statement of purpose. Opponents of the AACS, it seemed to me, were more influenced by American fundamentalism with its emphasis on individualism than they were by the Reformed tradition. My concern was to uphold the principles upon which Dordt was established and to stop any attempt to undermine them.

But before I begin to tell the story of this difficult and controversial time on Dordt's campus I should make a few comments. In dealing with conflicts arising from this issue I repeatedly called upon the board of Dordt College to study, review, and make decisions. When individuals or groups would approach me, I would say, "You may come to the board and make your case known, but they will decide." Several groups and individuals immediately tried to influence board members and constituents of the college to take aggressive action against the AACS. I have great admiration for how the board of trustees handled the controversy. They met for hours many times and dealt wisely with the persons and the issues involved.

Ironically, although opponents of the AACS persisted in threatening all kinds of negative repercussions when decisions were being made that they did not like, at the end of the three-year struggle we had our largest increase in enrollment. The prophecies of doom had failed. I was grateful and thankful to God that we gained over 100 students in the fall of 1974.

One other point needs to be made. During this crisis I sensed a strong prejudice among some of our constituents in the United States against the Canadians. It bordered on racism. Some almost exhibited a hatred for Canadians. While it was true that Canadians did come with a somewhat different cultural emphasis, they added very much to the life and activity of Dordt College. I was hurt by the attitude of a goodly number of the people and felt it was truly unchristian.

As I have stated earlier, one of my first goals for Dordt College was to have a clear statement of our educational philosophy. I wanted the college to follow in the tradition of such important Reformed thinkers as Abraham Kuyper, Herman Bavinck, Herman Dooyeweerd, and Cornelius Van Til. Already in 1958 the board had commissioned me to appoint a committee of representatives from the faculty and the board to write such a statement of purpose. That original statement appears in the back of this book. I am convinced that this statement is thoroughly Kuyperian and represents the finest in our Reformed tradition.

Prior to the time of Kuyper and the immigrants that came to America in the early 20s, there was in the Christian Reformed Church a predominantly pietistic strain. This stemmed from those who came from the separatist movement of 1834 in The Netherlands. Later this strain was strengthened by the unhealthy fundamentalistic and individualistic character of American evangelism.

Kuyperian principles strongly influenced the mind and practice of the Christian Reformed Church in the early 20s. But gradually the influence of American fundamentalism with its pietistic, individualistic, non-covenantal emphasis and its lack of kingdom understanding again began to affect the

The Gathering Storm 155

life and thinking of people in the Christian Reformed Church. When I speak of fundamentalism, I refer to those evangelicals who call themselves Fundamentalists. They, like those of Reformed persuasion, believe in the "fundamental" teachings of Christianity as stated in the Apostle's Creed. However, they often fail to proclaim and promote the lordship of Jesus Christ in all areas of life. Their aim, almost exclusively, is to save souls, snatching them out of the world. Theirs is a world flight mentality. In contrast, Reformed Christians believe they are called to be busy in that world not merely by saving souls but by actively reclaiming all areas for Christ, bringing Christ's will to bear upon all of life. One reason for that change may have been an inadequate understanding and application of the teaching of common grace. This led, particularly in educational circles and at Calvin College, to what we called a synthesis philosophy. People began to have a greater appreciation for the thinking of the non-regenerate, non-Christian community. Kuyper always maintained a strong antithesis between regenerate and unregenerate scholarship. Our aim was to counteract both the fundamentalistic and the synthesis thinking that were so markedly present in our circles. We were committed to the truly biblical reformational principles that Kuyper advanced.

Although I was happy that faculty and board members on the statement of purpose committee readily accepted these reformational principles, it was evident that some members did not completely grasp what these principles meant. As time went on, through a great deal of communal scholarship and discussion, these principles become clearer to many of them. But the influence of fundamentalism was still strongly present in the faculty and the supporting community. It was important, therefore, that we looked for faculty members committed to this Reformed perspective.

It is interesting to note that during this time the late Dr. Peter Eldersveld, preeminent speaker for The Back to God Hour broadcast, also saw American fundamentalism as the most serious threat to the Reformed faith in Christian Reformed circles. He was very vocal about the fact that such a view was not Reformed.

Because the college was growing so rapidly, we had to add many persons to the staff. When we interviewed candidates for these positions we frequently found men and women with a good deal of genuine piety, but with little understanding of the comprehensive implications of a Reformed worldview. We hired several of these people, hoping that through communal study and activity they would begin to understand the Reformed principles we held dear and more clearly apply them in their teaching. When the controversy over the AACS developed, it became apparent that this had not happened with a number of faculty members.

Two incidents that occurred during this time further illustrate the mind of the Christian Reformed constituency at the time the AACS controversy arose.

I was asked by the Reformed Fellowship, which was then publishing the *Torch and Trumpet*, today the *Outlook*, to lecture on Calvinism and the contemporary church. They arranged for me to speak in various places throughout the United States and Canada. In my speech I emphasized those Reformed Calvinistic, Kuyperian principles that I believed were no longer being promoted among us. Although this was generally not the case among the Canadians, I found that wherever I lectured in the United States, few really grasped what I was saying. To a goodly number of the leaders and the laymen it seemed as if I was speaking a foreign language. I was not only surprised but disappointed. The incident made me all the more determined to stress these principles on the Dordt College campus.

The other incident was the publication of a book by the late R.B. Kuiper, who was a well-known figure in our circles. He had taught practical theology at Westminster Seminary in Philadelphia for many years; he was a popular minister in our churches; he was one of the early presidents of Calvin College; and at the end of his life he was called in to serve as president of Calvin Seminary. Shortly after his retirement in 1959 he wrote *To Be or Not To Be Reformed*. In that book, Kuiper made a very significant statement:

> Throughout the decades the Christian Reformed Churches welcomed to its membership many thousands of Dutch immigrants. That they have exerted and are exerting much influence on our thinking goes without saying. No less strong has been the impact upon us of Reformed literature produced in The Netherlands. Thus it has come to pass that we, too, in theory at least, set considerable store by the universal mediatorial kingship of Christ. Its recognition has also produced some action. It accounts, in part, for the establishment by our constituency of many Christian grade and high schools, Calvin College, two junior colleges, several institutions of Christian mercy and a Christian labor association. It must, however, be granted that in practice our witness to the headship of Christ over all things is weak in comparison with the witness of Dutch Calvinism, and it certainly is not as vigorous as it ought to be. All in all it is rather feeble. On this score we must confess to a measure of lethargy.

Later on page 163, Kuiper says,

> There is another favorable force operating among us and growing more and more powerful. In recent decades thousands of Dutch Calvinists have immigrated to this continent, particularly to Canada.

The Christian Reformed Church has welcomed them with opened arms. Today they constitute a considerable segment of that church's membership. By and large they stand in the grand tradition of Groen, Kuyper, and Bavinck. That is to say that they strongly stress the mediatorial Kingdom of Christ over the church and over all things besides. In that emphasis they excel, that is particularly true of their ministers. One often hears it said that our Canadian Churches must adjust themselves to Christian Reformed usages and traditions. Of course there is truth in that, but it is just as true that the Christian Reformed Church must learn much from them. By abiding by their presently strong conviction concerning the kingship of Christ and imparting that conviction to the denomination in which they are an integral and increasingly influential part, our Canadian Churches, with the blessing of God, may, I firmly believe, become an inestimable blessing to the Christian Reformed Church, as well as a great boon to the cause of the Lord Christ on this continent and throughout the world.

I was happy to read this passage by Kuiper because it described how I felt also. As a student I had been unhappy to find that at Calvin College very few professors held these views. The one man—and perhaps there were others—who strongly stressed Calvinism by way of Abraham Kuyper, was Dr. H.H. Meeter. I took several courses from him, and I was very pleased with what he taught. In his book *The Basic Principles Of Calvinism*, he clearly articulates the Kuyperian principle of sphere sovereignty, of the kingship of the Lord Jesus Christ, and of the covenant.

Taking into account the decline of Kuyperian Calvinism in our circles, you can imagine how delighted many of us were when Dr. H. Evan Runner came on the scene. Runner was a brilliant student at Westminster Seminary and very much taken with the teachings of the late Cornelius Van Til. He was advised by Van Til to work for his doctorate at the the Free University in Amsterdam and study under Herman Dooyeweerd and Dirk Vollenhoven. At that time Van Til spoke very highly of Dooyeweerd and Vollenhoven.

Later on, tension developed between these men. Van Til believed that in his later writings Dooyeweerd was not holding firmly to the clear teachings of the scripture. He contrasted the earlier Dooyeweerd with the later Dooyeweerd. The earlier Dooyeweerd was to be highly regarded and honored by the students of the Reformed faith. The later Dooyeweerd was to be followed only with great caution. Many of us felt that Van Til's change of mind regarding Dooyeweerd was partly due to the fact that he did not receive as much recognition by Dooyeweerd as he thought he should have received.

When Professor Stoker from Potchefstroom University, a renowned philosopher and dedicated Calvinist, visited Dordt College in the early part of its history, we asked Stoker what he thought of Dooyeweerd and Van Til. His answer was rather amusing. He said, "When I read Cornelius Van Til through and through, I say what a Calvinist, and when I read Herman Dooyeweerd through and through, I say what a Calvinist."

Before Runner came to Calvin, the difference between Van Til and Dooyeweerd was not well known or understood. Strong supporters of Van Til felt perfectly comfortable with Runner, who had thoroughly embraced the Dooyeweerdian, Vollenhovenian approach to philosophy and law. He was a strong advocate of the so called Cosmonomic Law Idea of Herman Dooyeweerd.

In his highly vocal and spirited manner, Runner began immediately to promote his Dooyeweerdian views with great vigor, enthusiasm, and determination. He soon gained a significant following of students. Although many of these students were Dutch immigrants to Canada, there were also a number of them from the United States. They rallied around Runner with a strong spirit of commitment and dedication. Several of these students later became important leaders in establishing the Association for the Advancement of Christian Scholarship. Some, in fact, were members of the first faculty of the Institute for Christian Studies in Toronto.

To give greater credence to the Dooyeweerdian principles and to better promote these ideas, Runner soon organized the Groen Van Prinsterer Club at Calvin. Groen Van Prinsterer had strongly influenced Abraham Kuyper and also Herman Dooyeweerd. Van Prinsterer held a rather high position in the government of The Netherlands. He was an ardent Calvinist and inspired such men as Abraham Kuyper to promote the cause of Calvinism through the idea of sphere sovereignty and the lordship of Jesus Christ over all areas of life.

Runner's emphasis was not welcome in the philosophy department at Calvin College. In fact, when he was up for reappointment a few years later, a committee recommended rejecting him. I was on the board of trustees at the time and, along with several other members, fought a hard battle to keep him on the Calvin College faculty. We were happy that we won.

Although a significant number of ministers and lay people rallied around Runner and his thinking, many were not completely aware of what he stood for. Some, dissatisfied with the liberalism and secularism they believed were getting the upper hand, were looking for any voice that would point to a more Reformed, Calvinistic, orthodox way of thinking. I say this only because some of these early supporters later turned against Runner and his thinking. They had never really felt the deeper pulse beat of the Kuyperian Calvinistic world and life view.

Runner had a large following not only among Canadian students at Calvin College, but also among the lay people and ministers in Canada. Many of these people had lived under Abraham Kuyper as prime minister in The Netherlands and were committed to his vision of reforming society through Christian organizations. They hoped to see those principles promoted here in North America and soon formed the AACS to do so more vigorously and more effectively. As a slightly humorous aside, the organization was originally named the Association for Reformed Scientific Studies (ARSS). However those initials were not acceptable to many and became the object of a great deal of humor and ridicule. The name was later changed to the Association for the Advancement of Christian Scholarship, the AACS.

The AACS was a societal organization of believers whose purpose was to promote a Reformed, Calvinistic, biblical world and life view. They planned to do this through an educational center, the Institute for Christian Studies (ICS) centered in Toronto, Canada. The ICS was intended to be a university where students from various Christian colleges, particularly Calvin College, could do graduate study. Dr. Hendrik Hart, who had studied under Runner at Calvin College and later got his degree from the Free University of Amsterdam, was the first member appointed to the Institute. His field was philosophy.

The Institute for Christian Studies and the AACS soon ran into some serious difficulties which proved to be the harbingers of greater problems to come. The one missing ingredient in the organization was the kind of men who could offer wise and diplomatic leadership. Many of the key players in this movement were brilliant young scholars who possessed a radical bent of mind. They were high-spirited, but sometimes reckless in the manner in which they dealt with God's people. Ardent supporters of the cause soon became some of its most bitter opponents.

Opponents of the AACS often accused faculty members of using shock methods in their approach. An early decision that turned many ardent supporters against the institution was to allow only people with at least a college degree to serve as members of the Board of Curators, which governed the ICS. This was contrary to Kuyper's way of operating. Kuyper insisted that he had to have the support of the "kleineleiden," that is the little people, to be an effective kingdom instrument. Other statements and practices infuriated many older supporters of the movement. I once heard it said that only people below thirty years of age should be eligible for membership in the organization. They believed that anyone older than that was already too much under the influence of another strain of thinking.

Surprisingly, these young radical scholars respected me even though I was already in my forties. They claimed that I was one of the few south of the border who understood and appreciated their mind set. When I said that I was well over thirty they would say to me, "You are an exception." I often said in those early years that while I appreciated very much the basic principles for which they stood, I was not always happy with the way they implemented their program.

It is important to remember that all this happened at the same time as the rise in Europe and North America of the so called Revolt of the Young, the New Left Movement. Many of those in the AACS movement were young people who were also affected by the spirit of their times. All of the colleges in America were confronted with this movement, which at times took on some rather ugly features. The older generation was completely stunned by this movement, characterized by a spirit of anti-establishment, anti-institution, and anti-church. Young people adopted a new form of dress, grew beards and long hair, wore patched pants. Young men and ladies were nearly indistinguishable in outward appearance.

Older people in the church were simply shocked at what was going on. When young people did go to church they came dressed shabbily. Many of them were part of what we called the underground church. They would meet with other young people, supposedly holding hands and engaging in certain forms of dancing. Such reports caused a great deal of alarm among the older generation. This spirit and some of these practices were also endorsed by the young leaders in the AACS movement. A certain iconoclastic spirit prevailed and was evident in what came out of the AACS. It was not so much what they stood for as the spirit in which they operated that aroused people and turned them against what the AACS was promoting. It seemed as if they delighted in arousing the wrath of the older generation.

Faculty members at the ICS often addressed controversial issues and then took a somewhat radical position on these questions. Two books published early in the history of the movement were examples of this strategy: *Out of Concern for the Church* and *All the King's Men*. Many of us found a lot of good material in these books, but others, because of the spirit in which they were written, were terribly disturbed. The editor of *The Banner* at that time, Lester DeKoster, spoke of the lambasting of his mother, the church, on the part of these men. People were infuriated.

But again, we should not forget that this attitude was characteristic of most young people at that time. Many of us were convinced that we had to have

The Gathering Storm 161

patience in this matter. However, those who were opposed to the Canadian AACS movement and who were not delighted with the Kuyperian principles it promoted quickly blamed the AACS for much of what their own children were practicing. They especially accused the AACS teachers at Dordt of fostering bad ideas and practices. To get rid of this so-called rotten influence, many were ready to throw out the good with the bad. I was not about to let this happen. Thank God that there were enough of the right persons in right places of authority to prevent this from happening.

Before going into the actual conflict on the Dordt College campus I want to look at another development around this time, the establishment of Trinity Christian College in Chicago. Trinity began a few years after Dordt College and, early in its history, hired several disciples of Runner, people who had been strongly influenced by Dooyeweerdian thinking. I have in mind such gifted scholars as Calvin Seerveld, Peter Steen, C.T. McIntire, Arnold DeGraaf, Maarten Vrieze, and Robert Vander Vennen.

Trinity Christian College was at that time blessed with a remarkable staff of teachers. At this time Runner and his thinking were still held in high esteem by many of the more conservative members of the Christian Reformed Church. Men like Calvin Seerveld were heralded as the leaders of the future. He was a popular speaker and a strong promoter of Christian education. Christian Schools International often used Seerveld as a speaker, and Trinity flourished. Many students sympathetic to Kuyperian, Dooyeweerdian thinking went to Trinity. Others who became familiar with that point of view at Trinity became ardent disciples of this worldview.

However, when the storm over the AACS broke, and these faculty at Trinity continued to promote that thinking, a real battle developed on the Trinity campus. At that point things were still very quiet on the Dordt College campus. We were aware of what was going on, however. The presidents of the three CRC-related colleges at that time, William Spoelhof of Calvin College, Gordon Werkema of Trinity College, and myself, met twice a year. It was only natural that we should talk about the problem facing Trinity. I recall very well how in that debate I urged Werkema to move cautiously, to have patience, not to get rid of these men but to ride out the storm if at all possible. But Dr. Spoelhof appeared to be of a different mind. He felt that these men threatened the well-being of the institution, and that perhaps it would be better if they left the college. Werkema took Spoelhof's advice, and the result was that practically all of these men left Trinity. The only one of the Dooyeweerdian stripe who stayed was Vrieze. McIntire, DeGraaf, Seerveld, and Vander Vennen joined the staff at the Institute for Christian Studies in Toronto. As a result the enrollment at Trinity for a long period of time dropped appreciably. Few students came to Trinity from Canada after these men left. One wonders whether it was wise of Trinity to have dismissed these men.

What struck me as a strange anomaly in this controversy that raged at both Trinity and Dordt was how Calvin College continued to be practically untouched and unharmed by it. Yet the mainspring of the AACS movement, Dr. Evan Runner, was teaching at Calvin, and a significant number of sympathizers of the movement were on the Calvin faculty. Perhaps the general public was certain that the prevailing emphasis and philosphical-religious perspective at Calvin was safe from a thoroughly Kuyperian, reformational influence.

Trinity Christian College eventually chose to distance itself from a vigorously reformational stance, being satisfied with a more modified, "safe" commitment to Christian principles. Dordt, however, vowed to be true to those reformational principles that it was convinced were the best in the Reformed tradition and held the best answers to the fundamentalistic thinking that had invaded our circles and still threatens our educational institutions today.

As the AACS storm moved out of Toronto, Canada, and on to the Trinity College campus, the heavy reverberations of the storm rudely awakened spirits throughout the Christian Reformed denomination. The Dordt community, as already pointed out, was poised for the storm. I saw the eye of the gathering storm with its ominous dark clouds moving toward us. When the first angry flashes of lightning signaled the arrival of the heavy downpour with its fierce winds, I knew it was time for the board to close the shutters and await the outcome.

* * * * *

Against this background of the rise and development of the AACS movement I feel it is necessary to insert my early appraisal of the situation, presented to the board of trustees in the spring of 1972.

Special Report of the College President on the AACS Issue
Just at the time when our nation, our churches, and our educational institutions were to be severely shaken by perhaps the greatest revolution in world history, the Association for the Advancement of Christian Scholarship, centered in the Institute for Christian Studies in Toronto, Canada, appeared on the scene. Headed by a group of young, brilliant intellectuals from the Christian Reformed Church,

The Gathering Storm

this new movement, stimulated by the philosophy and vision of Abraham Kuyper, Herman Dooyeweerd, and D.H.Th. Vollenhoven, set out to "reform" our churches and academic institutions, to free our people from the dominating influences of secularism and scholasticism, and to promote a new life-style that would be more in agreement with the demands of the Scriptures. With youthful vigor they began to promote their philosophy and advance their program of "radical" Christian action.

One hardly knows which force has been more jarring to our Christian Reformed constituency—that of the general revolutionary movement in our land or that of the AACS. It is generally agreed among responsible Reformed scholars that there is a good deal to be said in favor of the AACS philosophy and position. However, some very serious questions and objections have been raised concerning certain emphases, attitudes and actions of the AACS proponents. Needless to say, this situation creates a formidable problem. Do the questions and objections expose problems of such a serious nature that they overshadow what is good in the AACS? Or is the good in the AACS of such value that we should have patience in dealing with the problems? We ought certainly to proceed cautiously. For one thing, it may well be that the AACS movement, coming at such a crucial time in the history of the church, has provided a necessary antidote to the fracturing effects of the great revolution by arousing all of us to re-examine our beliefs, institutions, and practices—upsetting as this may be. We ought not dismiss this possibility too readily. Especially when there are trusted leaders who recognize in the AACS, with all its faults, a religious spirit and motivation which are of the genius of our Calvinistic heritage.

Dordt College is determined to remain true to our Reformed faith. But, since there is so much in our day which threatens to undermine and destroy this precious heritage, we need to utilize whatever we can to maintain, refine, and advance our distinctively Calvinistic, Biblical faith. Is the ACS representation on the Dordt staff an asset or a liability in achieving our goals? There are those who are firmly convinced that the AACS is a liability. Others, not necessarily in agreement with all that the AACS advocates, believe that the AACS constitutes a positive and healthy asset. Still others do not have strong feelings in either direction. It is obvious, however, that the issue is very much alive.

One factor which makes it difficult to engage in a responsible appraisal is the widespread unrest and heated debate which is taking place concerning the AACS. In educational institutions and journals, in church assemblies and publications, in our homes and on the street corners, the AACS has become a subject of heated debate and discussion. Furthermore, new flames of resentment continue to burst forth because of the added fuel which advocates of the AACS bring to the fire by fresh acts of indiscretion, wrath-provoking articles, and statements which are denunciatory in character. Students do not always make matters any less difficult. They have a way of taking recourse to extreme measures, which is characteristic of their immaturity and their youthful eagerness to see something accomplished at once. They are often guilty, not only of misrepresenting their tutors, but also of going recklessly far beyond them, even though their basic motive is commendable. The Dordt campus and constituency know something of the explosiveness of the situation.

In this complex situation we as board members are called upon to make a wise and responsible assessment of the matter. In doing so we must not be swayed by emotions nor be guilty of rash decisions. Our college and constituency need and deserve calm, firm, and judicious leadership.

In general, we cannot ignore the fact that the synod of our church has continued to recommend the AACS to our churches for financial support through offerings. The church has not officially questioned the Reformed, biblical character of the AACS. Rather it has officially endorsed this cause as a legitimate kingdom movement. We should also take note of the fact that Classes Sioux Center and Orange City have granted licensure for preaching to one of the most "suspect" proponents of the AACS position. (Classis Sioux Center granted the licensure this past September after a thorough examination of the brother concerned.)

We know, too, that, more and more, as time goes on, misunderstandings are being removed and the cardinal issues involved in the discussion are coming into sharper focus. Both "sides" are attempting to understand each other and resolve the issues within the context of an increasingly unified spirit and atmosphere. Admissions of mistakes and apologies for irresponsible statements and actions are now readily being voiced. There is evidence that former opponents are beginning to find each other in seeking and promoting the best in our Reformed tradition.

The few ardent advocates of the AACS on the Dordt staff (six perhaps out of the fifty professors), some to a greater degree than others, have aroused considerable disturbance. (Although one wonders who is more at fault, the AACS men or those few who have irresponsibly aroused some of the students and of the constituency against the AACS men.) It is not necessary to review what has happened. The board of trustees is well aware of the problem.

Whatever one may say concerning the words and actions of indiscretion on the part of the AACS proponents, or concerning their philosophy and program, no one has been able to establish that they are teaching contrary to the Reformed confessions. This is, of course, a crucial matter.

Although there are faculty members who are diametrically opposed to certain emphases of their AACS colleagues, a large number look upon the AACS approach with favor. They also have high regard for the scholarly ability and Christian commitment of their AACS colleagues. (It is well known that the AACS men are wholeheartedly committed to Dordt's statement of purpose and to Christian education on all levels.) The majority of the faculty members appreciate their AACS colleagues from another point of view. They believe that one of the essential characteristics of higher education is a variety of emphases and approaches within the boundaries of our Reformed confessions. Life is diversified. This diversity should come to expression in the thought patterns of a Christian college so that the entire Christian community may be enlightened by it. It is also worthy to note that for the first time in Dordt's history, one of our students (a philosophy major) received the highly coveted recommendation of the Woodrow Wilson Scholarship Foundation. This indicates something as to the quality of scholarship of our three philosophy professors, two of whom are strong AACS proponents.

We can add that, despite the few on campus who seem to be "terribly disturbed" by the presence of the AACS men and have raised a storm of protest over it, the AACS emphasis has stimulated Christian scholarship and a more serious reflection upon our faith and life. This is desirable, for sin has eaten its way almost imperceptibly into the fabric of our thought and life patterns. Often what is unquestioned in our thinking and traditions and thus has become identified with Christian piety constitutes a hindrance, a roadblock, to the promotion of a truly God-glorifying life. It is the calling of all, and especially our Christian colleges, to engage in an in-depth examination and evaluation of the sources and development of our traditions and the possible non-biblical and/or irrelevant elements which have crept into them. Nothing is more detrimental to the Christian calling than to be dominated by a stereotyped mentality which feels frightened and threatened by every challenge, and, under the cloak of "godly concern," perpetuates the "status quo." If Luther and Calvin had been governed by such a mentality, we would perhaps still be in the Roman Catholic Church today. The AACS advocates have perhaps, in that respect, contributed something praiseworthy to Dordt College. It would be extremely difficult to justify the removal of this emphasis from our academic community. But neither must it be the only emphasis. It would be unwise to allow this emphasis to dominate, and sufficient steps have been and are being taken to prevent this.

In this connection there is one issue which would become a serious matter and bears watching. We refer to the "radical" Christian action not only in all other spheres but also in the realm of the academic. According to AACS thinking practically all the products of scholarship, past and present, reflect the predominant influence of scholasticism and humanism. This is supposedly true also in theologians in the Reformed tradition. In fact even the past and present curricular structures evince the ever dominant influence of scholasticism and humanism. We cannot deny that the penetrating analysis on the part of the AACS advocates indicates their scholarly ability. And one cannot help but recognize the truth in much of what they say. However, their insistence that, unless we accept and apply their "radical" principle of evaluation and restructing, we are doomed to fail in our Christian academic calling, poses a threat to academic freedom and could force us into an unhealthy academic straitjacket.

This kind of "radicalism" also reflects itself in extreme attitudes and statements concerning the instituted church, our Christian schools, our homes, and our life-style. These "institutions" also, supposedly, are saturated with the leaven of secularism, scholasticism, and humanism. There could be more truth than fiction to this claim. But this does not justify the way in which the proponents of the AACS speak or their "shock-treatment" approach. It is this failure to honor the good in our churches, schools, and homes, and the readiness to condemn on all sides which has touched off an almost uncontrollable volley of wrath and resentment. Obviously we cannot permit such a situation to continue.

* * * * *

What I have written in this chapter is necessary to walk understandingly through the next chapter. Some material already related will have to be brought back into the story, albeit in a different context, shedding light on the rise, the development, and the final playing out of the struggle with the AACS on the Dordt campus.

Chapter Ten
The Storm Erupts and Subsides

When the AACS movement first started, many of us, as I stated earlier, were happy that the Kuyperian principles were once again being talked about and promoted. Dordt College, from its inception, honored the Calvinistic world and life view, which holds that all of creation is under the dominance and kingship of our sovereign Lord and Savior, Jesus Christ, and that every area of life should reflect obedience to the laws that God established for his creation. For a couple of years we made significant strides in developing a greater interest in these principles. During the early days of the AACS, the Reverend Louis Tamminga, a minister in Edmonton, Alberta, began the Christian Action Foundation (CAF), an organization to promote the very principles that Dordt held dear. I wrote several articles in the CAF publication and gave a clear statement of the principles on which Dordt College was operating.

Tamminga was impressed with what he saw developing at Dordt College and was enthusiastic about the possibilities available here for advancing the work of the CAF. In 1965 he accepted a call from Bethel Christian Reformed Church in Sioux Center and was minister there for about five years. When Tamminga arrived we immediately began to organize a group of people to promote the CAF. We had amazing success. We not only built up a large membership in Northwest Iowa, Southeast South Dakota, and Southwest Minnesota, but also had contact with some people in South Holland, Illinois. Tamminga and I traveled to that area more than once and held some profitable meetings with people interested in CAF. We also sponsored a number of conferences at Dordt College, and CAF grew to a membership of almost 800 people.

Interestingly enough, we even had the support of a few of the more conservative ministers, notably the Reverend Harry Van Dyken and the Reverend John Byker. At the time, Van Dyken was minister in Winnipeg, Manitoba, and his children attended Dordt College. Byker was minister in the First Christian Reformed Church of Rock Valley, Iowa. At the time these preachers were very kindly disposed toward the AACS.

Although I was fairly well acquainted with the men associated with the AACS and I liked the basic direction of the movement, I had some misgivings. I had a great deal of respect and admiration for most of those men, but I made it clear to them at a meeting in Chicago that I had doubts about some of their attitudes and actions. In fact, at one meeting when they put pressure on me to go their way I finally smiled and said, "Listen, you men go your way for ten years, and we at Dordt will go our way for ten years. Then we will compare notes and see where we are. If you are doing better, then we will take another look."

However, men like the Rev. Harry Van Dyken were more strongly in favor of the direction of the AACS. I visited with Van Dyken twice, once at Dordt, the other time at his home in Winnipeg. During one of those meetings he told me that his daughter who had been attending Dordt was not going to come back but would enroll at Trinity Christian College in Chicago because of the reformational professors there. His daughter had studied during the summer in Seattle, Washington, under Dr. Maarten Vrieze, a Trinity professor and an ardent proponent of Dooyeweerd's philosophy. Van Dyken told me that Dordt would never really amount to much if we didn't get men of that calibre on our staff.

I said to Van Dyken, "You are more conservative than I, and yet I am a bit hesitant to put these men on our faculty at this stage." We had interviewed Maarten Vrieze and decided that Dordt was not quite ready for such a person. Although it was perhaps not the wisest thing to have done, we had heard rumblings of what was going on at Trinity and were a bit hesitant to bring such a struggle on our campus. Van Dyken and Byker, however, became so enamored with the group that they both accepted calls in the Toronto area to be closer to the AACS. Within a few months these two ministers formed an entirely different opinion of the movement and became vehement opponents of it.

Incidentally not only did Van Dyken and Byker become extremely antagonistic to the AACS movement, they also became strong critics of the Christian Reformed Church, especially when it adopted the famous Report 44 on the nature and authority of Scripture. They were convinced that Report 44 seriously undermined our belief in the comprehensive view of the authority of Scripture. Van Dyken and Byker eventually left the Christian Reformed Church and started a new denomination called the Orthodox Christian Reformed Church. That church is very much opposed to the AACS and to what it considers to be false teaching in the Christian Reformed Church. Nevertheless, it was the initial fervor of men like Van Dyken and Byker that led me and others at Dordt College to consider AACS supporters for teaching positions.

Something else happened on the Dordt College campus that encouraged us to work together with AACS people. Dr. Simon Kistemaker, now a professor at the Reformed Theological Seminary in Jackson, Mississippi, joined the Dordt College faculty and was soon promoting the AACS. In fact, he started the first AACS chapter on the Dordt College campus. He, too, later withdrew his support and had no part in the further development as far as I know. But, at the time, the fact that a man so highly respected, fully trusted, and completely dedicated to the Reformed faith was promoting the AACS had an effect. Many of us joined the organization and became members of the local chapter. I also spoke at AACS sponsored activities on various occasions, and no one complained about it or saw anything wrong in it. They were, in fact, pleased with the idea.

One thing more needs to be said before we continue with the story of the conflict. The Dordt College statement of purpose, *Scripturally Oriented Higher Education*, came under intense attack during those years. This statement, written for the North Central Accreditation Association, covered not only the basic philosophy of education of the institution, but also applied that philosophy to every aspect of the college: curriculum, extra curricular activities, administration, and campus life. I had appointed a committee from the faculty to help expand our original statement. The committee was composed of Douglas Ribbens, the academic dean; Nick Van Til, professor of philosophy; Merle Meeter, assistant professor of English; Norman De Jong, assistant professor of education; and John Van Dyk, instructor in classical languages and philosophy. As in the earlier statement, I would write sections of the document and then present them to the committee. Members of the committee went through them with a fine-toothed comb. We changed many words and phrases and clarified many ideas. But not once in all of these meetings did anyone on the committee raise objections to the substance of the document. Principles such as the covenant, the kingdom of God, the lordship of Jesus Christ over the entire creation, and the teaching of sphere sovereignty were clearly enunciated with no objections from any member of the committee. When the document was completed and presented to the faculty for adoption in 1969, it was unanimously accepted. One faculty member, who later became a leading opponent of the document, came up to me and said, "Boy, Bernie, this is really good stuff." Within two years after its adoption, however, the document came under intense attack. Ironically, those most critical of the statement of purpose included two members of the revision committee. It was obvious that these men never fully understood or appreciated the Reformed tradition of Calvinism via Van Prinsterer and Kuyper.

As I pointed out in the previous chapter, those were volatile times.

The Storm Erupts and Subsides   171

Throughout the United States and Canada, students were rebelling. College students seemed to be anti- everything. A few of the Dordt faculty appeared to agree with that mentality. Concern about that spirit forced us to be very careful. The board of trustees had taken a solid stand against long hair and beards on campus. I remember that I objected to this rule and expressed my concern by saying, "I hope that because of this stand some of you men will not find it difficult to get your own children to come to this college." I had the feeling that the extreme reactionary spirit of the time would pass, and that we should patiently ride out that storm. However, I sympathized with the board. I, too, felt that some students looked grubby and were no credit to the campus as far as their dress was concerned. But, at the same time, I realized they were young people who were seeking their identity. I wanted to move more slowly. The very next fall, a national merit honor student, a high school graduate from the Pella area, whose father was one of the members who had argued strongly in favor of the no-beard policy, absolutely refused to come to Dordt College because of that rule. Although this student didn't have a beard, he said he would not go to a college that took such a position. His father came to me soon after and said, "Now I know what you meant when you urged us to be careful and go cautiously." The board soon rescinded its decision on this matter.

In 1966, John Van Dyk had come to replace Dr. John Zinkand, who was teaching for a few years at Westminster Theological Seminary. Van Dyk was qualified to teach Greek, Latin, English, Dutch, and German. He was a valuable addition to our faculty. I vividly recall meeting Van Dyk's plane in Sioux Falls and quickly becoming good friends. I had the highest regard, and still do, for John Van Dyk. He has done great things for Dordt College.

Initially, Van Dyk seemed to have little interest in the AACS movement. He did come with a firm world and life view, however. With his teaching ability he soon captured the imagination and the support of many students, particularly the more qualified students.

One person who influenced Van Dyk a great deal and sparked his interest in the philosophy of Dooyeweerd was John Vander Stelt. Vander Stelt came to Dordt two years after John Van Dyk. Encouraged by some of the more conservative ministers, I felt that it was time to gradually add more so-called AACS 'types' to the staff. We advertised for a position in philosophy and theology and an application came from John Vander Stelt, who was at that time working for the AACS in Toronto. We interviewed him and found no reason not to give him an appointment. He accepted. These two men soon had a profound influence upon the thinking and the living of a good number of the finest students at Dordt College. I sensed at the time that this was going to create some problems, since the shift toward these men by many of the better students was obvious. In fact, some professors who had previously enjoyed the respect and admiration of students were soon criticized for their supposed lack of a thoroughly Reformed world view perspective. This did not surprise me, but such criticism did not sit well. Others on the faculty and the board, however, received Van Dyk and Vander Stelt's thinking with appreciation. They considered it a good stimulus on the campus.

One summer in the late '60s, my wife, Deborah, my daughter Katie Lynn, and I went to one of the conferences held by the AACS in Bolton, Ontario. We heard some very fine speeches, but we did not totally appreciate the style of the young people at that conference. We left the conference a day early because we were tired of some of the activities associated with the conference. I had an uneasy feeling at that time that we were headed for some difficulty. Trinity was already in the throes of its struggle and had suffered a great deal from the conflict. Other signals gave me the feeling that everything was not as it should be. I awaited the trouble.

When it came, four men played predominant roles in opposing the AACS on campus: Norman De Jong, Gerald O' Donnell, James Veltkamp, and Merle Meeter. Others sided with them but did not take an active role in the battle.

As is often the case in conflicts, the battle over the AACS served as an occasion for some to vent their grievances against individuals in the administration and on the faculty. Much personal bitterness surfaced in the conflict that ensued. It should be said, however, that when the fight was on, the men on the side of the AACS showed a spirit of cooperation and willingness to discuss matters in a friendly way. Not once during the entire struggle, in all of the investigations that took place, were Vander Stelt or Van Dyk charged with teaching contrary to the Scriptures, our creeds, or the Dordt College statement of purpose. They were, indeed, accused of teaching contrary to scripture, the creeds, and our statement of purpose, but not by those officially assigned to deal with the question. Although we did not always place the same emphasis on certain issues, when we talked it over, we could usually come to an agreement.

Three significant developments in the conflict occurred between 1970 and 1972 while Norm De Jong was on leave of absence to work on his doctor's degree. As news about the controversial activities of the AACS and the opposition they were receiving filtered back to Sioux Center, the CAF began to lose members. That made some of us very sad. Secondly, the AACS began to sponsor their Discovery Lecture Series. Speakers from the Institute for Christian Studies in Toronto came to several communities to speak on a variety of topics. The lectures were, in many ways, very stimulating, but they also created questions and doubts among community people and faculty members. A third development was the beginning of the AACS student conferences held at Lake Okoboji. Several professors attended these conferences to learn more about the movement. Some were not altogether happy with what they heard and saw. The tension grew when a Dordt College graduate was asked to teach temporarily at Western Christian High School and said things in the classroom that caused an uproar and, eventually, his dismissal. Professor John Vander Stelt was unjustly accused of being the cause of this young man's thinking. People often forgot that there were many influences at work among the young people, especially college students. These sometimes led to unwelcome and unacceptable views.

Sometime during this period the Rev. Louis Tamminga and John Vander Stelt came to visit me. They felt that the people of our community were too traditional, too dualistic, and too legalistic in their thinking. Convinced that we were desperately in need of radical reformation, they suggested that I, in my position of leadership, should forge the way. I was to confront people forcefully with our distinct calling and responsibility as God's people in our age. Since it was dinner time, I suggested we go to lunch and that I give my reply later. After reflecting on the conversation for a day or two, I met Tamminga, and told him that my answer was no. I said, "All of our people have these shortcomings to a certain extent. Yet, when I see all that God has accomplished through these people, when I think about their commitment to the church and Christian education and, generally speaking, the lives they live, even though we must work for renewal and reform, I am convinced that if the whole United States and Canada were like these people it would not be such a bad world." Although I frankly disagreed with Tamminga and Vander Stelt's proposal, it did not minimize my sincere affection for them nor did it diminish the high respect I had for them.

In the meantime the struggle was already proceeding on its own. The first sign of unrest came through a protest from the First Christian Reformed Church of Rock Valley, Iowa. Their consistory urged us to take a close look at what was going on among the representatives of the AACS on the Dordt campus. Shortly thereafter a group of nineteen men, spearheaded by the Rev. Cornelius Van Schouwen and businessman Elmer Duistermars, formulated a protest against those faculty who were members of the AACS and, in particular, the Canadian teachers on the Dordt staff. Although most of the Canadians were loved and appreciated, you must remember what I said earlier about some of the community's dislike for Canadians. It seemed to me that some of the opposition to AACS members was not over issues and principles, but stemmed from deep prejudices and personal grievances that readily fired emotions into a flame of resentment.

One of the leading businessmen in our community told one professor who supported the AACS that he would not be satisfied until he ran him out of town. His comment was not made primarily because of the professor's teaching, but because of personal dealings they had with each other. Others involved in the struggle seemed hungry for recognition and power; they quickly used the tension to seek their own ends. Many pious phrases and accusations flew around that I believed were not born of a spirit of love or a desire for truth. Thankfully the board of trustees dealt wisely with the matter, and I was supported by an overwhelming majority of the people.

Even one of my closest friends was among the ardent opponents of the AACS supporters on campus. He tried desperately to convince me to get rid of these men. He came into my office one day, presenting himself as a person very much concerned about me and my welfare. He told me that I could leave the college in a blaze of glory if I would only listen to those opposed to the AACS and get rid of the Canadians. I replied that I would like to go out in a blaze of glory all right, but that I was not intending to do so in that way. I was convinced that I had to deal with this matter carefully and let the board handle the issues. A few weeks later, he came and tried again to change my mind. This time he said, "Men out there are saying that since we can't get Rev. Haan to go along with us we're going to have to get rid of him. He has too much influence and power in there." Rumor had it that they were even grooming two people from the staff, who were opposed to the AACS, for president and dean of the college. I found this somewhat amusing, but it goes to show how far these men were planning to go. They worked overtime to enlist the support of people but without much success.

In response to the letter from the Rock Valley consistory and a protest from the nineteen men from Sioux Center, the board of trustees appointed a special study committee to look into the situation. The committee interviewed the five Canadians considered to be the chief representatives of the AACS movement: John Van Dyk, John Vander Stelt, Case Boot, Hugh Cook, and John Struyk. I never believed that all five were involved to the same degree, but since they were all Canadians and under the critical eye of several people, they were thoroughly investigated by the committee and given only one year appointments. Perhaps the fact that Boot, Cook, and Struyk were grouped with Van Dyk and Vander Stelt was due to the fact that students recognized the same basic priniciples in their teaching and were attracted to it.

The Storm Erupts and Subsides

All five were eventually declared innocent of any heresy or of teaching contrary to our Reformed principles and the statement of purpose of Dordt College. But the board urged them to be careful, to watch their conduct, and to avoid giving any occasion for the opposition to further pursue their aims and intentions.

Things seemed to be settling down somewhat until Norman De Jong returned from his studies at the University of Iowa. By the fall of 1973 we had discontinued the Discovery Series Lectures on the campus and no longer cooperated with the AACS on the conference at Lake Okoboji. But I sensed that the tension was still close to the surface. A few faculty members harbored deep suspicions toward those professors who supported the AACS. De Jong reopened the battle. During the summer before he returned to Dordt, he taught a course in Canada with Arnold DeGraaf, a member of the AACS faculty. DeJong came back poised for battle.

Trouble erupted when the staff of the Dordt faculty publication, *Pro Rege*, refused to print an article by De Jong refuting an article written by Dr. J.B. Hulst on the Kuyperian principle of sphere sovereignty. Angered, De Jong tried to have the article printed in the student paper, the *Diamond*. Janet Vlieg, the student editor, also refused to publish it. So De Jong went to the board, convinced that I, as president of the college, had ordered Vlieg not to print the article. When De Jong presented his case to the board, Janet Vlieg was brought in. She stated emphatically that when asked about printing the article of Dr. De Jong in the *Diamond* I had said, "Go ahead, print it." It was her decision not to print it.

Because De Jong was causing such a furor over the issue, the board took a forceful stand at that time, declaring the principle of sphere sovereignty to be a vital part of the Dordt statement of purpose. I was very happy that the board stood strongly behind me on this issue, since I had insisted all along that the real struggle was not over the AACS but whether we were to maintain the principles upon which Dordt College was founded. I was convinced that if we lost those principles the basic purpose of Dordt College would be lost. Now I had to demonstrate to the entire faculty that these principles were not foreign to our Reformed tradition but were an integral part of our history. I had to prove that those opposing the AACS were really opposing the best in our Reformed tradition. I reiterated that the original statement of purpose placed a strong emphasis on sphere sovereignty and that the college from its inception had operated on that basis. Sphere sovereignty was not something new or something that only these Canadians from Toronto were promoting among our people.

I called a meeting of the entire faculty to discuss the issue. I wanted it to be absolutely clear that I was fighting for the statement of purpose and that those opposing the AACS were opposing the statement of purpose. I began by quoting an excerpt from the late Dr. Henry H. Meeter, professor of Calvinism at Calvin College. I quoted from the chapter on the "Sovereignty of the Social Spheres," from page 157 of the book, *The Basic Ideas of Calvinism*: "An expression which has become a favorite watch word among Calvinists is 'the sovereignty of the organic groups in society each in its own sphere.' By this is meant that the family, scientific organizations, commercial, industrial, agricultural, philanthropical organizations and whatever other groups naturally develop out of the organic life of human society, as well as churches, do not owe their origin, existence or principle of life to the state. They have an inner principle and cultural task all their own entrusted to them by God. They are authorized directly by God for the pursuance of their tasks. Upon this sovereignty given by the Creator the state may not infringe."

After reading this quote, I gave my reasons for supporting these views. To my utter amazement the key persons who were against the AACS violently disagreed with what H.H. Meeter taught. I was simply dumbfounded. A few of them even called it heresy. I then let it be known that it was absolutely clear to me that all this talk about the AACS was nonsense. The real issue was our Calvinistic Reformed tradition. Those who opposed it were coming from a non-covenantal, non-kingdom, non-organic approach to Christian higher education. I sensed a strong spirit of modern day individualism at work that was contrary to the genius of the Reformed faith.

That meeting gained me the support of the large majority of the faculty. Although most of them had always supported me, this meeting seemed to answer many questions. The board of trustees also supported me fully. I thank God that the Rev. Edward Blankespoor was the chairman when we were facing the brunt of the storm. His knowledgeable understanding and calm yet firm demeanor were a blessing.

But De Jong, O'Donnell, and Veltkamp kept the struggle alive. Working closely with some members of the community, they met together, planned together, strategized together, plotted together, and continued to encourage one another to keep the battle going. In addition to the encouragement they received from some in the local community, they were spurred on by opponents of the AACS throughout the denomination. One of the most vocal of these was the former editor of *The Banner*, Lester DeKoster. DeKoster, a known opponent of Kuyperianism, once said to a group of us that Calvin would refuse to walk on the same side of the street with Abraham Kuyper.

As I watched the opposition continue to grow, I knew we were in for a

The Storm Erupts and Subsides

titanic struggle. Nevertheless, I was confident that we would win in the end. At the height of the conflict someone said to me, "Why don't you do something, why don't you get out and speak about it?"

I replied, "When you're in a blinding snowstorm the best thing to do is to stop the car and wait alongside the road until the weather clears and the roads open again." In a battle so filled with emotions it is often useless to try to speak out. We can be grateful that those responsible for steering the course were men of wisdom, patience, and determination. They were not swayed by the clamorings of a few vocal people.

I did my best to answer those faculty members who raised objections and carried on the fight. I worked hard to keep some unity among the faculty so that we could continue our work of educating young people. Even though I did not agree with the thinking of those opposed to the AACS, I was not about to ask for their resignation. These men, too, were brought up in the Christian Reformed Church and had learned many of their ideas through Christian Reformed education. I felt that it would be foolish to try to eliminate them from the faculty. They were, after all, Christian Reformed, they were committed Christians, and they believed they were right before God. Yet no matter what I tried, it didn't seem to be enough to satisfy the more radical members of the faculty in the midst of this struggle. At the same time I sympathized with those men who were being accused. They were very uneasy. Their families also became the targets of intense emotions in the community and were deeply troubled. I know that they held group prayer meetings frequently. I attended one of those meetings and was deeply impressed with the spirit and attitude of these families.

Several incidents illustrate how the controversy unfolded and the spirit that accompanied them. The precise order in which these incidents occurred is not important here; my main point is to give a sense of the inner workings of this controversy.

After De Jong was refused the right to publish his article in the Dordt faculty journal *Pro Rege* and the Dordt *Diamond*, he came to my office and announced that he was going to lead the fight. I was utterly amazed at his confidence and composure. He told me that I was not nearly as influential with the board, the constituents, and the faculty as I thought I was. He felt that some faculty were looking for a leader in this struggle, and that he was capable of giving that leadership.

De Jong saw himself as a skilled debater who knew his philosophy. He had written a book, *Education in Truth*, that spelled out his perspective. He was ready to accept the challenge of the battle. I asked him if his family knew about this. Yes, he said, he had talked it over with his wife and with his children, and they were determined together to go ahead. I said, "Well, I would be very careful, you could be at the other end of the stick when it is all over." That comment did not move him one bit.

I told De Jong that the board would be dealing with this problem and that he would have the opportunity to present his arguments to them. I also told him that he could present his case to the Purposes Committee of the faculty. It was the responsibility of the Purposes Committee to advise the president and the board on the basic direction of the college.

De Jong took advantage of both opportunities. He appeared before a committee of approximately ten men, among whom was Dr. Gerard Van Groningen. Although Van Groningen had misgivings about the AACS, he felt more concerned about the direction of those opposed to the AACS. I was happy he was on the committee. I introduced De Jong and told him he was free to present his ideas to the committee. He was extremely confident as he began. After about ten minutes into his long discourse, Van Groningen interrupted and said, "Mr. Chairman, do we have to sit here and listen to this? This isn't Reformed."

I replied, "I have given Dr. De Jong the freedom to address this group, so let him say what is on his heart." So he proceeded. A little later Hugh Cook, one of those considered to be an AACS supporter on the faculty, interrupted and said, "Mr. Chairman, do we really have to listen to this? Is that what we are here for?"

Again I said, "I gave Dr. De Jong the privilege of the floor, and we are going to hear him out."

What really surprised me was that De Jong remained as cool and collected and confident as you could imagine. The Purpose Committee did not agree with De Jong. The board likewise did not agree with his position and told him that he was to discontinue all efforts to stir up unrest and division among the constituents and the faculty. That very night De Jong called a meeting of about twenty faculty members at Oak Grove State Park to discuss the AACS issue. Some of these faculty members felt that such a meeting might bring some harmony again. Others joined because they were strongly opposed to the AACS. Most were not aware that the board had forbade De Jong to carry on such meetings. Several of these faculty members, who later heard that De Jong had gone against the board's decision, came to apologize and explain why they were at that meeting. They had intended no harm.

But De Jong was not the only vocal opponent of the AACS. Gerald O'Donnell also strongly opposed the AACS and persisted in his pronouncements against it. He began distributing materials against the organization, and in fact, used the college Media Center to duplicate materials and send them out. I happened to run into him in the Media Center when he was busy with this one day and noticed that he was ill. He had a bad case of the flu. I told him that he should go home, stay in bed for a couple of days, and get over this sickness. He looked a bit uneasy when I came in the Media Center. I think he felt a bit guilty. He was also surprised at my concern for his health.

Within a few days he came to my office. I'll never forget how he sat across from my desk and said that he was surprised at my kindness to him considering what he was doing, especially since he was using Dordt equipment to further his purposes. But then he said to me, "I feel sorry for you. I would like to help you by giving you some advice." He continued, "What you should do is what I did. Just put all other books aside, take your Bible, and sit with it. Read and pray until the Holy Spirit gives you light. I know there are men out there who are misguiding you, but I believe that if you follow this method you will find help. I did and it surely helped me."

I was astonished, nearly dumbfounded by how he thought I should deal with the problems. But I thanked him, and he left my office. This same teacher would go into the classroom after John Vander Stelt finished teaching and before beginning his class would pray that the Lord would remove the demons from that room. I decided something radical had to be done. We could not tolerate that kind of attitude and action.

A third faculty member, James Veltkamp, came to my office at least two times during this struggle to register his concerns. He was so troubled. He would come into my office and pour out his heart. I said to him, "Well, Jim, you have the same privilege as others. You can go to the board and you can present your thinking on the matter to see how they respond to it."

"Well," he said to me, "I'm not really a philosopher or a theologian." He was hesitant to write up his views and present them to the board. I told him that he had better keep still if that was the case. He didn't listen. A short time later, maybe three or four months, he came to my office again, terribly upset, wringing his hands in anguish about what was happening, fearful for the future of Dordt College and for our faith. I told him again that he should go to the board. He refused to do so, and I said again, "Well, then you better not complain about it."

"But you ought to know, Bernie, how much I pray about this," he said to me. He had said the same thing the time before.

"Jim, I'm sorry, but I'm not impressed by that," I said. "After all, the men whom you are opposing are praying too. I know how much they pray."

Another individual, a member of our supporting community, who played a major role in the conflict was Bernie Postma. An immigrant from The

Netherlands, he was a competent, gifted individual. He had hoped for a position in the business department at Dordt College, but we did not have a place for him. When this struggle came up, he joined those opposed to the AACS. He was not an easy person to deal with. He aggressively dug up all kinds of material to support his position. I allowed him to come before the board, which he did, and in an amazing way calmly and confidently presented his point of view to the board. He even went to The Netherlands to visit his relatives and took the time to meet with the late Dr. Herman Dooyeweerd. In our Dordt College statement of purpose, we had referred to the Cosmonomic Law idea of Dooyeweerd. We also adopted his view of science for our scientific task as Christians. In his visit with Dooyeweerd, Postma obtained a letter in which Dooyeweerd among other things, related his view of the Scriptures. In this letter Dooyeweerd said that the Bible is not the Word of God but contains the Word of God. We at Dordt did not accept that view and neither did we have that as part of our statement of purpose. We took from Dooyeweerd that which we believed was consistent with our Reformed view of the Scriptures.

You can imagine how Norm De Jong and the others opposing the AACS reacted to that letter of Dooyeweerd. It was widely circulated. It's too bad that Dr. Dooyeweerd did not live long enough to explain what he meant by that statement in his letter. It would have been interesting to hear his response.

Petitions were written and public slander abounded. Accusations from both sides were bandied back and forth on the streets of Sioux Center and on Dordt's campus. I received my share of criticism, too. I had served as pastor of the First Christian Reformed Church of Sioux Center for eighteen years and had lived in a loving relationship with its members for all those years. But now some opponents of the AACS who were members of my church and had been good friends of mine, visited others, telling them how I had changed—that I was not the same person anymore. When some of the older people, particularly the ladies of the church, would say, "Yes, but he preaches soundly," they would reply, "Yes, when he's on the pulpit he's sound, but as soon as he leaves the pulpit, it is a different story." It's no wonder that many board members throughout the area began to ask where I really stood.

One day while these insults against my character were floating around, I stopped in at Mayor Te Paske's law offic. He knew what was going on. In a genuinely sympathetic tone he asked how serious the situation was. I told him things could be a lot worse. He let me know then that the mayor of Orange City, Chester Van Peursum, a Dordt constituent, had just told him that Rev. Haan had the situation pretty well under control. With a slight smile and a sigh I agreed, but then referred to one person whom we both knew very well was making it tough for me. Te Paske told me to remember what his father, also an attorney, once told him in a similar situation: "When you are in a pissing contest with a skunk, you're outclassed." This earthy comment seemed most appropriate at the time. In the midst of a mud-slinging match all of the participants seem to betray something of a skunk-like odor.

Before long the consistories became involved. On March 22, 1973, the board sent a report to the constituents:

Esteemed Brethren,

Recently, members of the executive committee of the Dordt Board of Trustees met with ministers and elders from the churches of Sioux Center to discuss the petition presented to the executive committee of the board concerning recent activities of the AACS. The petition is attached. After a lengthy discussion the following was decided.

1) That the constituents of Dordt College be publicly informed as to the time when the executive committee of the board of trustees meets for special matters so that anyone wishing to convey concerns regarding college matters can avail himself of an audience with the executive committee and if necessary with the board. This is the Biblical and only acceptable method of dealing with these concerns and is the only procedure which is in the best interests of those involved in institutions of our Lord's Kingdom.

2) That the circularization of petitions as a means to register grievances against kingdom institutions, particularly against the actions of persons associated with these institutions, is contrary to the Word of God and cannot be tolerated regardless of the nature or even the justifiability of the grievance.

3) Only when the Biblical method is honored can justice be preserved and the peace and welfare of the church and kingdom be enhanced. Only then can brothers and sisters in the Lord and kingdom institutions be protected from rumors, falsehoods, half truths, misrepresentations, and the arbitrary will of individuals which can seriously damage the reputation of individuals and jeopardize the kingdom institutions concerned.

4) Finally it is the hope and prayer of this committee of the board, the college administrators, and the consistory representatives, that all of our constituents continue to labor together in

the wholesome spirit of Christian love and understanding to promote a truly biblical, Reformed, world and life view at Dordt College. The Lord has richly blessed Dordt and we are convinced that the graduates by and large reflect genuine loyalty to our Reformed faith.

I should note here that Dr. P.Y. DeJong, then minister of the First Christian Reformed Church of Sioux Center, served the board on a special committee dealing with this matter. He wrote much of the report and did an exceptional service to Dordt College. However, as before, nothing that was said or done by the official bodies seemed to be able to stop the activity and work of those opposed to the AACS.

All the while I continued to do my best to bring about peace and harmony. I still did not want to see any of the men dismissed from the faculty. We held committee meetings and faculty meetings, openly discussing the issues. But nothing seemed to help. As I left one meeting where we thought we had reached an agreement on some crucial issues, O'Donnell met me and simply said that he didn't trust these people, that he was not convinced. In other words he was going to continue the fight. Because of his attitude and actions I early made up my mind that I was not going to recommend him for reappointment.

Whenever I was invited, I took the opportunity to go out among the people to explain what was happening and where the board of the college and I stood in the matter of concern. Dr. James Koldenhoven and Dr. Russell Maatman accompanied me on one of the more significant and productive trips to the Pella area. I knew at lot was at stake here since we had for a long time enjoyed solid support from this area. Knowing the people and their thinking, I was fully aware of what I was about to meet. I carefully prepared for these meetings.

The first meeting was held in Prairie City with the Christian Reformed ministers of the area. The second was held in the Second Christian Reformed Church of Pella before a sizeable number of people. When I finished my speech the ministers were given time to make comments and ask questions. Although much was at stake, I thoroughly enjoyed deliberating with the ministers and others on the burning issues facing us. I recall especially the comments of the late Rev. John Geels, then minister in Sully, Iowa. He and I were genuinely respectful of each other. He arose and said that he agreed with practically everything that I had said but still harbored misgivings about the AACS. I was convinced, however, that the boil had been broken and the core was out. The possibility of healing seemed promising. That people were still leery was understandable considering the on-going battle

The Storm Erupts and Subsides

between leaders in our denomination in the United States and the men in Toronto. People's reaction and the support of Koldenhoven and Maatman were a huge boost to my morale.

One of the worst speaking experiences I ever had was during this period on a visit to the Midland Park Christian Reformed Church in New Jersey. Some rabble rousers from the Orthodox Presbyterian Church, under the influence of Dr. John Frame, an outspoken opponent of the AACS and the Cosmonomic Idea of the Law, were primed for a fight. They rudely interrupted me in the middle of my speech. I was quoting from some of our forefathers, Abraham Kuyper and Louis Berkhof, when they shouted, "Forget about those men; we want to know what the Bible says." Emotions were so high and the intensity of the atmosphere was so great that I simply sat down and discontinued speaking. Dr. J.B. Hulst, who was present with me, stood up and tried to bring some kind of order to the meeting. But to no avail. I was convinced at that time, and still feel, that many of those from Westminster Theological Seminary were not well enough versed in the Dutch history of theology or the development of Reformed thinking as it came by way of Dutch theologians to present a respectable critique of the writings of men such as Kuyper, Dooyeweerd, and Vollenhoven. After this incident I called one of the chief representatives of the faculty at Westminster to tell him that although I had a high regard for Westminster, I was not pleased with the conduct some of the men displayed in dealing with the AACS problem. Their thinking, in my opinion, was not governed by what many of us considered to be the best in our Reformed tradition.

In a determined effort to bring about peace and unity in the faculty I called for another special meeting right after the vacation period in January, 1974. We met in the first week of that month, and representatives from both sides spoke. It appeared as though we were reaching a point of understanding and agreement. Immediately after that meeting I left with the Rev. John Hellinga on a trip to Eastern Canada to recruit students for the college. Hellinga was a board member and well acquainted with the churches and schools in that area. We were having an enjoyable time and a good deal of success when I received a call from my wife. She told me I had better come home as quickly as possible. Dr. Ribbens had called to say that the storm was brewing again. De Jong had visited him and tried to convince him that I was a changed man, that my thinking was no longer really Reformed and that I should not continue to receive his support. I later found out that Dr. Ribbens told Norm De Jong he was dead wrong. He let De Jong know that he had known me since he came to Sioux Center in 1955 when the college began. He had heard me speak to the board, he had stayed at my home, and he had visited with me at length about the college, its goals, its purposes, its principles. Nothing had changed. I was a strong Kuyperian at that time and through all the years he had worked with me I had never changed my commitment to those principles.

Hellinga and I left for home the morning after my wife called. We discussed the situation at length. While we were eating supper I made up my mind to ask for the dismissal of those men who were causing all the trouble. Hellinga wondered at the time whether I could actually accomplish what I proposed, but I was positive that it had to be done and that in the end we would have the support of both the board and the constituency.

When I returned home I immediately conferred with Dr. Ribbens to get a firsthand report of his visit with Dr. De Jong. During the next few days I also talked with several other faculty members to find out what was being talked about and what the anti-AACS men on the staff were doing. Then I knew for certain what action had to be taken. My decision was confirmed by one significant event. Nine highly respected professors, who were not branded as AACS supporters, appeared before the board to register their dissatisfaction with what was happening on campus. They felt it was time for the board to do something positive and put an end to the struggle that had come to dominate everything on campus. On January 14, 1974, I came to the board with a proposal:

Esteemed Brethren,

> That which is always a major concern to Dordt College is how to be and remain a truly effective Reformed Calvinistic institution of higher learning. This is also and always has been the chief objective of your college president. As board of trustees, administrators, and faculty we have worked hard together in seeking to define and realize our purposes. Throughout our history we have demonstrated determination to remain true to our basic religious commitments. But pressures of various types have been exerted to force us to take action which would be detrimental to Reformed scholarship. Recently these pressures are of such a character that the board of trustees and the faculty have had to spend an immense amount of time on them. What is more disconcerting is the fact that these pressures center around a few faculty members whose points of view and manner of conduct continue to create and promote a spirit and climate which make responsible Calvinistic academic work exceedingly difficult if not impossible. Furthermore, these few faculty members have contributed not only a little to the unfounded distrust that is present

among a number of our constituents and the improper unchristian methods being used to force the board of trustees to dismiss professors who are associated with the AACS. At least two of these faculty members, who are so violently opposed to men with an AACS appreciation, have also engaged in action against these brethren, administration, and board action which either violates academic freedom, and/or promotes schism, and/or is a breech of professional ethics, and/or is insubordinate. Their conduct unquestionably places them in a position where the rules for dismissal apply, namely that 'dismissal of teachers holding tenure shall be for cause. These causes are: (1) moral turpitude, failure to conduct themselves in all matters in a Christian manner, or a failure to reflect the Reformed interpretation of the Scriptures in their teaching, (2) unsatisfactory performance of duties.'

There have been serious attempts to resolve the problems which have confronted us as an academic community. A few years back some of us were concerned about certain actions and teachings of the AACS-oriented teachers. The board has made a thorough study and investigation of the matter, and its decision should have settled the issue. Opportunity has also been given to those few anti-AACS faculty members to present their concerns and objections to the entire faculty. Each time these few have not only failed to substantiate their fears but have provided ample evidence of their own questionable scholarship and more seriously their own sharp departures from Dordt's statement of purpose.

The fact is that a clear majority of the faculty has run out of patience with these colleagues and refuse to carry on further discussion with them on basic issues because of the irresponsible methods being employed. If it is true that the AACS philosophy needs further investigation, which is very well possible, the faculty and the board of trustees will not be able to do this in an honorable manner with these contentious men present. Just two weeks ago the faculty met for two days. The discussion centered around the very issues that have been the cause of agitation. The debate was open and to the point. At the end of the two days the AACS men were not only exonerated by the overwhelming majority of their colleagues, but also the faculty expressed a strong desire to put an end to false accusations and work together in a healthy Christian spirit of unity. We left that meeting thankful to God. However, two or three members of the faculty who had given a shoddy display of scholarship and had alienated colleagues who had previously been somewhat sympathetic to them, began shortly following the meeting to sow dissension and promote strife.

We have reached the point where we can no longer tolerate such a situation. Our patience and long suffering have reached the limit regardless of the immediate disagreeable consequences of the radical action we ought to take. These are minor compared with the present conditions under which all of us are forced to work. But far more important to us is the fact that Dordt College can never be a powerful influence for our Reformed faith, a light shining in the darkness, a clear voice for our Calvinistic world and life view unless we clean our own house. A house divided against itself cannot stand. Our people deserve a united college standing on the solid foundation of Scripture and our Reformed faith. Only then can we truly honor the name of our God.

Therefore in the light of and on the basis of the above analysis of our situation I recommend that Dr. Norman DeJong, not be reappointed on the ground of insubordination.

Since the board had earlier decided not to reappoint O'Donnell, I recommended that both Norm De Jong and James Veltkamp be dismissed on the ground of insubordination. The board hesitated to dismiss Veltkamp because it did not think there was sufficient evidence of 'cause' to dismiss one who was tenured. However, both Meeter and Veltkamp sensed the board's feeling and very soon accepted positions elsewhere.

After I finished my report and made my recommendations, members of the board of trustees breathed a great sigh of relief. They said to me, "We were waiting for you to come with this months ago." They were quite amazed that I had the patience to work as long as I had to try to bring about healing and to avoid dismissing anyone. My recommendation was adopted by all but one member of the board. Those dissatisfied with the board's decision now had to wait until March when the final decision was to be made by the voting members board. Those opposed to the AACS worked hard to gain the support of as many voting board members as possible. On matters of such grave importance the voting members board of over fifty men had to approve a board of trustees decision.

Dr. James Veltkamp went out speaking on the issue just prior to the voting members meeting. He gave a speech in Rock Valley, Iowa, and seemed to receive a good response from several of the people. You may recall that the First Christian Reformed Church of Rock Valley had sent the initial complaint about the AACS-influenced teaching on the Dordt College campus.

The Storm Erupts and Subsides 187

I also went out to speak, because people wanted to know what was going on. One of the worst experiences I had was in Edgerton, Minnesota—an experience not unlike the Midland Park, New Jersey, meeting I mentioned earlier. Many people attended, and I could feel that the majority of them were ready to listen objectively and with the right spirit. But a smaller group of people had already made up their minds. Norman De Jong had taught in the Edgerton Christian School for several years, and he still had many friends there. He had, according to reports, also worked to solidify support for himself in the Edgerton area.

I delivered my address, explaining our purposes and what was happening on campus. As soon as I finished, a few people voiced strong opposition to what I had said and to what I supposedly was doing at the college. One person in particular, Cornelius Verbrugge, stood up and said that I had lied to him, and that he was going to reveal that lie to the board when they met in March. Verbrugge was a member of the voting members board.

I said to him, "If I lied to you, tell me what that lie was." But he would not do so. "Well," I said, "all these people now believe that I told you a lie. I don't know what it is. I have no chance to reply. I think it is your Christian duty to tell me what that lie was." But he would not respond. His actions did not win him a great deal of support. Many were very angry about the way he conducted himself. About two weeks later he made his accusation against me at the board meeting. He said I had told him that Rev. Hellinga and I were only going to Canada to recruit students and not to recruit more AACS professors. That had not been true, he said. Actually we had not contacted any prospective faculty during our visit to Canada and produced evidence to prove it.

Verbrugge's accusation was false, yet he had told all these people that I had lied. However, I must give credit to Cornelius Verbrugge. He apologized to me more than once after that incident. He even came to see me one day and suggested that if his church in Leota, Minnesota, was vacant at the time of his death he would like me to preach the funeral sermon. Strange as this seemed to me, it did make me grateful. Cornelius and I subsequently worked together on a very cordial basis.

The meetings in Rock Valley and Edgerton created quite a stir in the broader community. Veltkamp took advantage of this unsettledness and went to Edgerton to give a speech. However, I think he was somewhat shocked to find that several of the Dordt faculty had driven up to Edgerton to confront him and let people know the truth of the situation. When he finished speaking, Mike Vanden Bosch, who had earlier been sympathetic towards Norman De Jong, stood up and, in a very gentle, loving voice, clearly explained what was actually going on. Veltkamp evidently was taken aback. I was not at the meeting. Faculty members had gone willingly to take up the battle on behalf of the college and me.

Another series of events kept the conflict alive and influenced several of the voting board members. Lester DeKoster, the editor of *The Banner* at that time, had talked and corresponded regularly with Norman De Jong, James Veltkamp, and the others. He was bitterly opposed to several men in the AACS. I remember setting up a conference at Dordt College in which twenty-five leading figures in the denomination participated. Lester De Koster and the late Dr. Bernard Zylstra, president of the Institute for Christian Studies in Toronto, carried on a lengthy but interesting exchange of thought. I and many others felt that Bernard Zylstra clearly had the stronger presentation and position. DeKoster was not happy about the situation. DeKoster was so incensed that he walked out of the meeting and only returned when one of his close friends prevailed upon him to return. Later, DeKoster attempted to throw a roadblock in our path, one that was successful in arousing a threatening response from our more conservative friends. He told my son-in-law, who was at that time studying in Grand Rapids, that it was Dordt's refusal to rehire these men who opposed the AACS that inspired him to write articles in *The Banner* opposing the Cosmonomic Law Idea of Herman Dooyeweerd and supporting those who were fighting against the AACS. These articles did real damage to Dordt College. Many of my conservative friends thought a great deal of Lester DeKoster, and so they began to raise all kinds of questions about me. Knowing me so well, having lived with me through all those years, and having heard me speak and preach on many occasions, they simply couldn't understand what was going on. So you can see that I was a bit apprehensive about the upcoming meeting of the voting members.

We decided to set aside an evening session to deal strictly with the AACS problem. Regular business of the voting members board would be held for the next day. I came to that meeting with a calm spirit. As I said before, often when I had to go through these experiences, the Lord gave me a quiet and calm spirit. Although I had been warmly greeted by all of the members, there was obviously an air of tension as the meeting opened. After devotions we immediately began to deal with the issue. One of the first questions was raised by the Rev. Harold Hollander. He was the voting member from the Northcentral Iowa classis and a minister in Wellsburg. Having previously served a congregation in Neerlandia, Alberta, Canada, he had worked with a group of men there who were strong advocates of the AACS movement. His stay there had not been easy, and he was not too sympathetic

The Storm Erupts and Subsides

to the AACS thinking and movement. I have a lot of respect for the Rev. Hollander. He was always a good friend and always a strong supporter of the college. I can understand why he felt the way he did. Sometimes the people who were the supporters of the AACS could be very difficult to handle and very demanding, very critical. He stood up and had in his hand our statement of purpose, *Scripturally Oriented Higher Education*. I knew the document well and could almost see from where I sat the place where he was reading. He said he had one question first and then would follow it up with others. I thought to myself, when I get through I don't think he will have any more questions. I stood up to answer. They tell me that I spoke for forty minutes and sat down.

Hollander quickly arose and replied, "I agree with every word that you have said, but I don't read it in this document."

I said, "Then you don't understand the document, because I wrote the document and that is exactly what it says." He had no more questions.

I don't recall how long other questions were entertained. But it wasn't much later that they declared recess. During the break, the voting board members flocked to me. I was overwhelmed. Many said, "We should have heard this a year ago, we could have avoided all the trouble." I wasn't too sure about that, but I knew the board members were satisfied. They voted almost unanimously to affirm the decision of the board of trustees. I had to leave the meeting for a few minutes, and during that time the voting members board made a motion to give me a vote of full confidence. You can imagine my pleasure and my gratitude when I returned and was told of the vote.

Even though I was grateful for this, I was sad about the situation. Norm De Jong, whom I still highly respect in spite of all that happened, wanted us to reconsider our decision and pleaded to be reappointed. His plea surprised me in a way because at the beginning of the fight he had talked to me and declared emphatically that he was going to battle all the way, come what may. He definitely had been left on the wrong end of the stick. But he changed his mind, and he wanted to stay. I felt very sorry for him and especially for his wife and children. In fact, several of the men on the faculty knew my feelings, and they warned me strongly not to change my mind or ask the board to reconsider the decision.

We had come through the eye of the storm and had survived, so to speak. The situation was still a bit shaky, and the aftereffects of the battle were still to be faced. We lost about six faculty members. Although they claimed that they did not leave because of the situation, I felt the struggle had a lot to do with their departure for some other position. Now we could look more calmly and objectively at the AACS group. To do this I asked the board to appoint a committee with no faculty members on it, only local ministers, educators, and some laymen. It was a large but interesting committee. We met about three or four times and, already after the first meeting, I could sense that the bitter feeling against the AACS was gone. In fact, many felt that although we should continue to watch certain things, we did not have to oppose the AACS movement or the men who were supporters of it. In fact, within the committee we found that some of the men most opposed to the AACS presented ideas that the group at large could not accept. Many saw that ideas that had been considered dangerous to the Reformed faith and espoused by the AACS, were fundamental principles in our Reformed history. The committee served its purpose. It quieted the waters, and we could go on again with the business of Christian, Calvinistic, Reformed biblical higher education.

This is a good place to say something about a very important factor in my life and labors—my wife Deborah. I am not known to be one who engages in much talk or complaint about the amount of work I had to do. It is obvious that I was kept very busy. Much of my time was spent debating issues of weighty significance. I moved in an academic community highlighted by a good deal of philosophical and theological argumentation, often controversial in nature. Because at crucial times I was too busy caring for the general welfare and direction of a Christian higher educational institution, I frequently had little time to do the research and study necessary for giving leadership. My wife was an enormous help to me. We lived so closely together in the work of the college and the church that we increasingly thought alike and anticipated issues and problems that would arise. Deborah knew my mind, my goals, and my sources of information. She knew my library. When I was in the heat of a conflict, needing to be armed with appropriate materials for discussion and debate, I only needed to hint at what I was looking for and she would come up again and again with references and quotations that were exactly what I needed. She was interested and excited about this research work. In fact, she couldn't wait to let me know when she found something good. Frequently my colleagues would comment that I had the right references on key issues at the right time. God did, indeed, provide me with a true helpmeet.

Students, of course, were quite interested in what was happening during this whole struggle. The campus was alive with discussion and argumentation. In a sense it was good. It stimulated a lot of thinking. A few students opposed the AACS and sided with Norman De Jong and those with him, but the vast majority were on the other side. They were very kind and sympathetic to me during this struggle. One time during the heat of the battle I walked into the room where they were holding chapel and to my surprise all the students stood up and I received a round of applause. No one ever told me why it was done, but it was a very encouraging experience for me. I'll never forget it.

Chapter Eleven
Beyond Liberal Arts or Vocational

During the later years of my presidency, five programs were initiated that I think have been of real merit to Dordt College. These five were the computer program, the theatre arts program, the engineering program, the agriculture program, and the Lectureship Institute now known as the Studies Institute.

We sensed already a few years before my retirement that computer science would become a major program on the campus. We started slowly with mathematics professor Dr. Willis Alberda teaching the first courses in computer science. At the same time we researched what the program should include. After I retired the program mushroomed. An addition was built to house equipment and classrooms. The program has been quite successful and continues to grow; we thank God for that.

I was more deeply involved with the development of the dramatics, engineering, agriculture, and the Lectureship Institute programs. These programs, with the exception of the Institute, grew and developed greatly after my retirement.

* * * * *

Of all the Christian liberal arts colleges in our country, there are few that can point to a theatre arts program that is as comprehensive as the one at Dordt College. The program was initiated under the leadership of Dr. James Koldenhoven. He, Verne Meyer, and John Hofland presently make up the theatre arts department faculty. The staff shows an enormous amount of creativity and, over the years, has produced outstanding performances of a variety of different types of plays. Shirley Matheis has also been an important part of the department. She has designed and made the costumes for many years. I am amazed at the talent they have been able to cultivate over the years.

It took several years before Dordt College was ready to begin a full-scale theatre program. But to this day I am very happy that we did, even though it created some difficulties for me.

A theatre arts program on a Christian college campus is not the easiest thing for a college president to deal with. No other program has more potential danger for public relations. In fact, dealing with reactions to performances can easily give college presidents gray hair.

To indicate the kinds of problems drama departments can create for a college president let me tell you about two experiences I had with other presidents. While we were building the college chapel, we went to Kenosha, Wisconsin, to look at an organ. I decided to stop at a nearby Lutheran college to visit with the president. During our discussion, I asked him if they had a dramatics program. He responded immediately and emphatically, "Oh, yes, we surely do. It's the one program that gives me more problems than anything else on campus. I wish that I could have one man in that department over whom I had complete control and who would put on just one play a year." He continued to tell me that every time they put on a play, he was scared to death. He had more problems with his constituents over plays than over anything else.

Not long after that, at a meeting of area college presidents, we found ourselves talking about plays and dramatics on our campuses. The president of Yankton College told us that there were times when he had been ready to crawl off his seat and hide underneath the bench, he was so embarrassed. We all had a good laugh. We knew what he was talking about.

It was because of such reactions that we studied the situation carefully before going ahead. We had many meetings, set up many study groups, and always ended up deciding to wait a little longer.

However, even though we didn't have a theatre major, we did put on plays and offered some excellent productions. I would hesitate to say that none of them gave us problems; we always faced the possibility of a strong reaction among the constituents. However, as time went on people became more conciliatory. Many even came to appreciate the difficulty of selecting and producing plays in such a way that you do justice to the play itself and at the same time don't offend people.

As the process dragged on, Dr. Koldenhoven became frustrated by our hesitation to move ahead and establish a theatre major. He came into my office one day, and he was furious. He had just come from a visit with the dean of the college, Dr. Ribbens. Dr. Ribbens was an extremely qualified man and one whom I trusted very much, but he could be a bit caustic in dealing with faculty about matters that were open to question and debate. The administration was coming closer and closer to approving a dramatics program, but more work still had to be done. Evidently when Dr. Koldenhoven began to push to get the program moving, Dr. Ribbens put up some resistance. Koldenhoven walked out and came directly to my office. I could see on his face that something was wrong.

He said to me, "Rev. Haan, I will never, and I mean never, go into Dr. Ribbens' office again to talk about dramatics." I told Koldenhoven to sit down and listen. I assured him that while Dr. Ribbens may have discouraged him, the fact of the matter was that we were beginning to make plans to move in that direction. I assured him that we would soon start serious action with respect to a dramatics program.

We immediately set up a committee. As part of the program, I wanted the faculty to spell out the guidelines they were willing to follow in choosing plays to perform. As much as possible, I wanted to meet the standards of our constituents.

We did draw up some excellent guidelines. The faculty was pleased with them, the board was very happy with them, and we made the decision to go ahead. I must say, however, that even though we had those guidelines, and we were assured that they would be honored, I did not think they were always adhered to. I certainly do not want to accuse the members of the staff for being dishonest; I am sure that they meant well, but there were occasions when the productions raised quite a stir among the people and among some of our clergy. I had to spend a good deal of time bringing together community leaders, ministers, and the theatre arts staff to settle differences that arose because of objections to a production.

I must tell you of one experience that illustrates some of the public relations problems that arose. We had decided to put on a play called

Purpleleanie, based on the book by the late Dr. Stanley Wiersma. It was a story about life in our church communities here in the Midwest, especially in the Orange City and Sioux Center area. Some people who read the book thought Wiersma was making fun of the church. Others felt differently. They appreciated the humorous insight into practices and traditions in our community and churches. One of the theatre faculty, Verne Meyer, decided to make a play out of *Purpleleanie*. When the play was performed in our area, the chairman of the board of trustees, the Rev. Thomas Vanden Heuvel, was very upset. He became even more disturbed when he learned that we intended to take *Purpleleanie* to Grand Rapids and put it on at Calvin College. He was convinced that we were making a big mistake and would do untold damage to the college. To gain support for his view, he talked to several other preachers in the area.

After a phone conversation with him, I suggested that we get together for lunch and talk it out. Those present were: John Piersma, then my pastor, Dr. P.Y. DeJong, Thomas Vanden Heuvel, John Sittema, Henry Vander Kam, Edward Knott, and Henry Vanden Heuvel. Incidentally, all of these good friends of mine were leading spirits in the establishment of Mid-America Reformed Seminary. The meeting was a most interesting one. I knew that at least two of the ministers often went with their wives to see Shakespearean plays in Stratford, Ontario, Canada. So I raised the question, "Well, what about plays?" One of the ministers who was highly respected by these men said that he thought that all plays were wrong. So I asked the other men what they thought about it, and whether they still attended the productions up in Canada. They said yes they did. I had the house divided against itself, and I could sense that it would not be long before I would overcome the criticisms that had been raised.

However, I did want to take their concern seriously, so I suggested that they meet with the theatre arts staff and discuss their concerns. I was told that it was a worthwhile meeting.

We went to Grand Rapids with the play. It was a smashing success. My sister, who was widely read and knowledgeable about such things, told me that it was one of the most interesting plays she had ever attended. We came out of the whole episode smelling like a rose, as people say.

Dordt has continued to make a good name for itself in the field of theatre. The community of Sioux Center is proud of what the college is presenting, and our productions are well attended.

* * * * *

For some time the college had considered introducing an engineering program. Already early in the history of Dordt College, Dr. Marvin De Young had taught some pre-engineering courses: Engineering Graphics and Descriptive Geometry. But beginning a full engineering program always appeared to be too big for us to undertake. We had heard from educators in sister colleges that an engineering program demanded an unusually gifted faculty, that the students had to be exceptionally well qualified, that the demands of the engineering accrediting agencies were rigid, and that the cost would be almost prohibitive. However, I never closed my eyes or my mind to the possibility of introducing engineering. I had the feeling that we had students out there who would like to be at Dordt College and would be ready to come if we had such a program. It bothered me that these qualified students were going to other institutions. I also felt that having an engineering program would give a certain kind of sophistication to our science program and benefit the academic stature of the college.

The decision to go ahead with an engineering program came unexpectedly. It is amazing how the Lord works and how he opens doors. Dordt College was a member of the Association of Reformed Colleges, which was made up of eight colleges of Reformed background. We met once a year and had interesting and profitable discussions. In these meetings each president reported on items of special importance happening on his campus. One year, the president of Geneva College referred to their newly established engineering program. I knew that Geneva was smaller than Dordt, enrolling less than 1000 students, so I was eager to hear what he had to say. He described a full-fledged, successful engineering program. Dr. Ribbens, our academic dean, was also attending the meeting, and we immediately began to ask questions. We continued discussing the matter on the way home.

Upon our recommendation, the board decided to bring in the head of the program at Geneva College as a consultant. We wanted more information about their experience and wanted help evaluating the feasibility of beginning an engineering program at Dordt. The consultant spent two days with us, reviewing our entire program. He looked at our science faculty in mathematics, physics, chemistry, and biology and was very impressed. He also look at the quality of our students, the number of the students we enrolled, and our organizational structure. Based on our academic program and the type of students we appealed to, he concluded that we were almost in a better position to go ahead than they were.

That report was enough to set the wheels in motion. We appointed a special study committee to investigate the kind of program we should offer. In the spring of 1979 we decided to advertise for a faculty member in engineering. Mr. Charles Adams applied and was eventually given the appointment. He was just the right person for the job, bringing not only excellent qualifica-

Beyond Liberal Arts or Vocational 197

tions, but also a truly biblical, reformational perspective. Even today I know of no one more dedicated to that perspective than Mr. Adams.

During Adams' first year, 1979-80, he taught physical science courses for Mr. Richard Hodgson, who was on leave of absence. During that year Adams also led a curriculum study for the engineering program.

Some members of the faculty harbored doubts about the wisdom of beginning the program. Others of us were more optimistic, and we persisted. Today I am thankful that we did not give in to those who were pessimistic, because it is being abundantly blessed. At present, there are nearly seventy students majoring in engineering. It is the third largest program on campus.

While writing this chapter I received a copy of the self-study conducted for the Accreditation Board for Engineering and Technology. I was simply astounded by this volume. It shows that we have truly done our homework. We have an outstanding faculty in the department.

In order to qualify for accreditation, a college has to demonstrate that it fulfills a variety of criteria set up by the accrediting board. Dordt College qualifies in all areas. By August of 1991 the official notification of accreditation was announced. Needless to say, when I witness what is happening in the area of engineering on the Dordt College campus, my heart is glad. I thank God for all that is being done in this significant field of study.

* * * * *

How the agriculture program came to be is another story. It is probably most fascinating to me because of the role that I was privileged to play in the history of that program. The idea of an agriculture program on the Dordt College campus was something I envisioned already years before it became a reality. Early in our history, I would look at the farmland adjacent to us and dream of owning that land for an agriculture program. But I was ahead of my time. When I talked about it, I got very little support from the administrators of the college or from members of the board. So I forgot about it for the time being. In the meantime, practically all of the land east of us was purchased by real estate people. Housing developments sprang up all around the college.

During 1977-78, we began to take a closer look at the possibility of introducing such a program. I talked with the development officers of the college; I discussed it with a few of the board members; and I began to sense that there was a new interest in the idea. Enrollments continued to grow, the college was financially strong, and the time seemed to be right to consider the possibility.

I was eager to start an agriculture program for several reasons. I knew that a goodly number of possible students were interested in agriculture. In fact, many would not come to Dordt College or any other college that didn't offer agriculture. I felt that we should do something about those

I was eager to start an agriculture program for several reasons. I knew that a goodly number of possible students were interested in agriculture. In fact, many would not come to Dordt College or any other college that didn't offer agriculture. I felt that we should do something about those students. I was also convinced that many farmers, although they supported Dordt College, were not taking much interest in the college. I knew that we could garner the financial support of dairy men and cattle men, as well as other farm-related people from across the country. I was also convinced that Christians needed to deal with issues and problems related to agriculture, such as the question of pesticides and the question of third world agriculture. And there were many agriculture jobs available for students in co-ops and agri-businesses.

Beginning an agriculture program was not outside the domain of academics. Iowa State University had a full-fledged agriculture program and even offered advanced degrees. I was convinced that agriculture need not be outside of the boundaries of a liberal arts college. As a faculty we had discussed such programs and had become convinced that using the terms theoretical and vocational led to a false dichotomy. Such a notion was more compatible with Greek thought than with a Christian view of God's creation.

To get an agriculture program started required an immense amount of work and demanded a great deal of financial support. We not only had to convince people of the validity of the program, but we also had to have their commitment to contribute large sums of money. To use an apt metaphor, we needed to prepare the soil properly before getting started. The first step was to get the approval of the board of trustees and the voting members. This was not difficult to accomplish. The next step was to build a strong tie with representatives among the constituency. As with the chapel, I worked hand in hand with Mr. Lyle Gritters, who was vice-president for development, and Mr. Harold DeWit, our development representative. We decided to invite a fairly large number of successful and respected local farmers and their wives to a special dinner. After a meal punctuated by good fellowship and humor, I talked about the proposed agriculture program. I began by saying, "This is a free dinner, but it will probably cost you more than any dinner you have ever had before." The remark drew a good deal of laughter. I then went on to present our plans and, after the presentation, gave a good deal of time for discussion.

In these situations I always hoped for a visionary leader who would inspire confidence in others. Mr. Evert De Vries, from Edgerton, was such a person that afternoon. He had served many years in the consistory in Edgerton; he was on the school board of the Christian school;

and he was always actively involved in any kingdom activity being promoted.

De Vries asked for the floor at a strategic moment in the discussion and made a little speech. He said something to this effect: "We have been able to put up a large chapel with a large organ for people who love music, why can't those of us who love agriculture and farming get together and put this farm program into being?" I could tell immediately that he struck a chord in the hearts of those present and knew that this group would be a big help in getting the program started. A few board members who were present at this meeting later gave the board their appraisal of what had happened. The board was filled with new enthusiasm for the project, as were Lyle Gritters, Harold DeWit, and myself. We were ready to go to work.

The first thing we had to do was purchase a piece of land. We were able to buy property a few miles northeast of Sioux Center. Although we knew this property was not the permanent location we wanted for the program, we worked the land for a couple of years to get the program underway. Meanwhile we had our sights set on another property along Highway 75. After a couple of years we negotiated a trade with the city of Sioux Center and obtained the property now known as the Dordt College Agriculture Stewardship Center. Later, we added more land by purchasing the farm of John Broek, which lay along Highway 75, a little north of the main farm.

It took some work to convince the board and those closely associated with the farm program to buy the land from the city. The land was costly. You must remember that at that time the farm economy was booming, land prices were high, and everyone was optimistic. However, there were signs that the situation would not stay so promising. Only a couple of years after we purchased the land, we ran into a very serious farm recession. Land values dropped considerably and many farmers found themselves in deep trouble. In fact many farmers went bankrupt and lost everything. I have heard that 25-30 percent of the farmers in the area went broke during that time. Fortunately we had raised enough money to get the program on its feet and make it through the crisis. Even though we suffered from the recession, it was not enough to cripple the program.

As soon as we purchased the first piece of ground, Gritters and DeWit went out among the farmers of the constituency to raise money. When we finalized the purchase of the present property on Highway 75, we moved quickly to put up the buildings needed for a dairy farm. It was a most successful and extremely exciting experience. I had no idea that so many of our constituents, especially dairy farmers, would give so lavishly to the program. I am told that the development office raised between $1.5 and

$1.7 million. Close to seven hundred people contributed two thousand dollars and a few contributed up to five thousand dollars. It was simply unbelievable. In addition, we received donations of over three hundred cows. Some of these were calves 600 pounds and over, others were mature cows, fifty of which were registered holsteins. These animals came from dairy farmers in California, Oregon, Washington, Montana, Wisconsin, Iowa, Minnesota, Canada, and South Dakota. Bringing these animals to Sioux Center was quite an undertaking, and we still marvel at the manner in which the donors put the animals onto trucks and trains and shipped them into Sioux Center. One large shipment of cows even made the evening television news in Sioux City. It was something that stirred the hearts and minds of many people.

We held a special ground-breaking ceremony on the Stewardship Center property. It was a truly thrilling experience. We set up bleachers for people who attended. The Iowa state secretary of agriculture was present and spoke appreciatively of the project. But for me, the highlight of the evening was the fact that the president of the agriculture club at the college, Ida Kaastra, a student from Ontario, held the plow in the ground-breaking ceremony. After graduation Ida Kaastra traveled to Africa as a missionary and applied much of her training to agriculture in the third world.

What an experience! I think it is still true that Dordt College is the only Christian college in our country that has an agriculture program such as we have. Graduates of the program have not only gone into farming, but also into a variety of agriculture-related careers.

Not all of the plans I envisioned for the farm were realized. I had hoped that we would have a restaurant specializing in Dutch food on the farm. We got as far as the drawing board for a building to be located on the northwest corner of the property, right off Highway 75. Included in the design was not only the restaurant with its dining facilities and coffee shop, but also a miniature convention center, including motel rooms. We even dreamed about including a special area where we could make cheese and special kinds of sausage to be served in the restaurant and sold from the coffee shop. We had even selected the name for the coffee shop, 'Eet smakelijk,' Dutch for hearty eating. Special foods were to include pig-in-the-blankets and "Ole Kuchen," or "Vet Bollen." But the recession brought an end to all of those plans.

One of our main concerns was to be able to find competent, qualified people to teach agriculture courses on the college level. Some were afraid this would be very difficult. Here again we were surprised. Soon after we advertised, we received a reply from Duane Bajema. Duane had been involved in agriculture work in the third world, working in Mexico for five years with the Christian Reformed World Relief Committee. He was the kind of person we wanted, and although at first he hesitated, he finally accepted and came to Dordt College. Soon after, we received an application from Henry DeVries, who had done graduate work in agriculture at Cornell University. Henry worked with us for a couple of years and then went back to school to complete a doctoral program. Throughout our history we have been reminded that when we had a real need, God provided the proper persons to carry out that program.

I had high hopes for the agriculture program and was convinced that with the proper management we could be very successful. One of the problems a college faces, when going into a program like agriculture, is that academicians may not exercise the necessary precautions to avoid undue expenditures. Individuals who don't have an overview of the college tend to spend more easily than those responsible for the welfare of the entire institution. We spent a good deal of time setting up the program. The budget for the farm was also clearly established and the limits were set. Those in the program had to live within those boundaries.

When I retired in 1982, the agriculture program was well on its way. Of all of the things I hated to give up when I retired, this program was the most difficult.

* * * * *

I helped initiate one other program just prior to my retirement and that was the Lectureship Institute. The board gave approval to proceed with the establishment of the Institute as early as March 1, 1979, three years before my retirement. As president I considered it my chief responsibility to promote the principles and goals for which Dordt College was established. To achieve that goal, I was determined to promote high quality academic activity on campus so that we could give leadership in Christian higher learning. One way to do this, I felt, was to have individuals who would stimulate such scholarship on campus. I knew that some on the staff did not fully grasp or implement in their teaching the basic principles of our statement of purpose. Most of these individuals had the potential to do so, but needed something to quicken them. We needed some way to continue to hold before them these purposes of the college. Even those committed to the statement of purpose needed prodding to consciously apply it in their teaching so that students would understand those principles.

One other matter influenced my thinking about the lectureship idea. Enrollment projections noted that there would be a sharp decline in college enrollment within a few years, lasting for nearly ten years. I was determined to find a way to keep Dordt College a strong, reputable institution that would be influential in propagating those Reformed biblical perspectives that were so dear to us as an institution.

I recommended to the board of trustees that we set up a program to bring scholars who were wholly committed to our Reformed biblical world view on campus each year. These individuals would teach courses and also present general lectures on campus. They would be given time to write articles or books that would develop those basic principles in specific areas. Depending upon the circumstances, these individuals would be on campus for a semester, year, or possibly for a longer period of time.

The board decided to inaugurate three such lectureship chairs: the Abraham Kuyper chair and two others in political science and history. It was our intention to have those chairs funded by individuals with money and commitment. The advancement representatives of the college believed this goal was realistic. This program brought to the campus Dr. McKendrie Langley in the Abraham Kuyper chair, Dr. James Skillen in political science, and Dr. Rockne McCarthy also in political science. Dr. J.B. Hulst was chosen to be the director of the Institute.

However, the program never really got off to a good start. We had qualified men, but the faculty, generally speaking, were not receptive to the idea. Some of them felt that they were being neglected and others were getting the attention. It was difficult to integrate the Lectureship Institute into the total academic program of the college. We ran into many snags and spent a good deal of time trying to resolve the problems and make the Lectureship Institute effective.

After my retirement the concept was modified, and it became the Studies Institute. Today the Institute not only allows the college to bring other scholars onto the campus, but also gives the faculty released time to spend on special projects and study. I still feel that the original idea was a good one. It could have been a powerful force in the promotion of our distinctively Reformed principles of higher education. But I am grateful to the Lord, nonetheless, for the good that did come of it.

Chapter Twelve
Observations

When I retired after twenty-five years as president of Dordt College, the presidents of the Colleges of Mid-America consortium invited my wife and me to a special farewell dinner. After the meal they asked me to relate some of the highlights of my presidency at Dordt College. It was a most gratifying evening, since they could often relate appreciatively to my experiences. Much of what I said to the presidents and their wives makes up this last chapter.

I have called this chapter "Observations," and I intend to talk about my connection with Christian Schools Internationals, the relationship I had with the Dordt board, my life with Dordt faculty and constituents, and, of course, my experiences with the students.

Let me say at the outset that life on a college campus can be a most fascinating one. It certainly was for me and my family. We not only enjoyed living on campus, but thoroughly relished the contacts we had with hundreds of constituents throughout the United States and Canada. The joys we experienced far outweighed the pain.

Part of what I enjoyed about the presidency was the variety of activities in which we participated. I was interested in sports, I enjoyed music, I appreciated dramatics, I liked study, and I relished getting together with people to discuss issues. As president I moved freely about campus, eager to be part of everything that was going on. It was also a pleasure to be involved in the broader world of academia, including pre-college Christian education.

* * * * *

While I was president, I was especially committed to the organization called Christian Schools International (CSI), formerly the National Union of Christian Schools (NUCS). During those years I did everything I could to promote this cause. I often worked closely with the leaders of CSI. Early in Dordt's history I had regular contacts with John Vander Ark, who was the director of NUCS when I became president. I also worked very closely with Vander Ark's successor, Dr. Michael Ruiter. We formed a good working relationship, and when I retired from Dordt College in 1982, I was privileged to represent CSI among schools in the south for about two years. I promoted CSI among people in the Presbyterian Church of America who were also interested in Christian education.

One of my last public addresses was delivered at the CSI convention held

Observations

on the campus of Covenant College on Lookout Mountain, Tennessee. In that speech I recommended setting up a task force to be sponsored by the CSI. It was to deal with crucial issues facing the Christian school community. The task force was composed of members from all of the Christian Reformed higher education institutions, Covenant College, and other prominent Christian education leaders. It was an influential group. This task force met for ten years and did some outstanding work in spelling out the nature and purpose of Christian education. It also helped to resolve some pressing problems confronting the Christian school movement.

One such issue, causing serious disagreement, was whether the confessions of the church, the "Three Forms of Unity," were an adequate basis for Christian education or whether Christian schools should have their own educational creeds. Such a creed obviously would not go contrary to the creeds of the church, but would recognize the purpose and special responsibility of education within the kingdom of God. We came to the conclusion that schools should have a special statement of purpose but, at the same time, should maintain strong support for the creeds of the church. I presented our position to the national convention of the CSI in Ottawa, Canada. The proposal was well received. Many school boards subsequently wrote educational creeds for their schools. These statements described the nature of biblical, reformed, covenantal education and how it should be implemented.

After Dr. Michael Ruiter retired, CSI decided to disband the task force because they felt it lacked a specific focus. I was disappointed in this decision. I felt that the group could continue to exert a positive influence on the growth and development of Christian education. It could have been a strong ally of CSI.

Just prior to my retirement CSI had its national convention on the Dordt College campus. During one of the afternoon sessions Ruiter and William Gritter, the secretary of the Grand Rapids Christian Schools, presented me with a carved rooster (Haan means rooster in Dutch) with an inscribed plaque in the center. I was deeply honored. Of all the awards I have received, this one had special significance to me because Christian education and the Christian school movement have been two of the focal points of my life.

* * * * *

My life was filled primarily with presidential duties and responsibilities at Dordt College. Much of my time was spent working with the college board. I was firmly convinced that the board of the college, chosen by the constituents, should have final authority on all matters involving the personnel, principles, policies, and direction of the college. I considered the position of president to be a liaison between the board and the faculty. I worked closely with the board, making sure that nothing of significance happened without their approval. They were kept fully informed of the issues we were facing and the problems involved.

Although the faculty made recommendations on academic matters, the board had the power to approve or turn down those recommendations. The board could also institute educational polices of its own. Although it didn't happen very often, there were occasions when the board took a position that was not to the liking of some of the faculty members. Usually it was something I felt strongly about, and the board supported me. The Reserve Officer Training Corp and the Lectureship Institute are examples of two programs the board favored but the faculty did not.

I always had the utmost confidence in board members. A board elected by the people is, almost without exception, composed of individuals who are respected, experienced, and wise. I always felt that when board members came together there was enough insight, wisdom, and understanding to carry out their responsibility. Dordt College was blessed with many dedicated and competent board members and chairmen. One who deserves special mention for many years of service as chairman of the board is Dr. Arnold Boeve. He has provided wise and outstanding leadership.

* * * * *

My relationships with members of the faculty, generally speaking, were enjoyable. At times members of the faculty strongly disagreed with what I was doing, but usually these differences were resolved amicably. Committee meetings were relaxed. We debated issues openly and frankly, without bitterness. It is still a pleasure to attend social gatherings of the faculty. Even after my retirement we have been enriched by our contacts with them.

During my presidency, my wife and I spent a great deal of time socially with the faculty. In the early years, Deborah would have all faculty members and their wives to our home for dinner. These were enjoyable occasions. We were also privileged to host guests from foreign countries. During our years in the president's house we entertained people from Korea, South Africa, The Netherlands, and Germany. Our children, too, enjoyed these visits and loved to listen to the stories and conversation these experiences provided.

As the college grew we had to hire many new faculty members. Over the years I participated in literally dozens of interviews. I learned early, as president, to avoid the temptation to focus only on the one individual that seemed to be most qualified. It is relatively easy to sell others on a

Observations

prospective appointee by stressing the negative aspects of the other candidates. However, if the favorite declines the appointment, it is then difficult to revive interest in the other candidates under consideration. Yet many times those initially passed over turn out to be very effective teachers.

In those early years when Dordt was small in size, we were almost like members of one family. Frequently faculty members would want to visit with me. I always tried to keep my door open to them. Sometimes they were concerned about an issue or an administrative decision. Sometimes their concerns were more personal. I made it a policy to listen attentively, to make a few comments, and then suggest that we both think about the matter for a few days. I usually left the matter with the understanding that, if the professor considered it necessary, he or she could come back to me. I never promised to contact the professor about it later. If I did that, then failure to do so would be considered indifference or neglect on my part. It often happened that our initial discussion would be the end of the matter.

Over the years we hired several professors who had been former students at Dordt College, most of whom graduated from the college. Almost without exception these individuals proved to be competent teachers. They were not all exemplary students at Dordt. But I liked some of these students. They were basically good fellows with promise. I well remembered my mother's distinction between clean dirt and dirty dirt. Clean dirt, she used to say, is easily gotten rid of, but dirty dirt is something different. She applied this analogy to students. Some students are like dirty dirt. They need to be watched and occasionally dismissed. But others, though not always on their best behavior, were students of promise. I didn't forget this last group of students. I would keep an eye on them after they graduated, believing they could be of real service to the college someday.

One such student was James Schaap. Today Schaap is known as an outstanding writer and is highly respected in our circles. He has been an elder in his church and has proven to be a very effective teacher. However, when he was a student at Dordt College he liked to have a good time. One day, in his third year at Dordt, I received a telephone call from his father and mother. They were each on a phone. Sounding somewhat desperate, they told me that Jim had decided to quit school and join the army. They were convinced the decision was a mistake and wondered if there was anything I could do to help change his mind—but I was not to tell him that they had called. I was obviously in a rather difficult situation, but I assured them that I would do my best. I called Jim into my office and, although I don't recall exactly what I said to him, I do remember that I spoke to him very openly. I chided him and told him that it was foolish for a man of his talents and abilities to do such a thing. Although he didn't show it right away, our discussion must have had an impact. You can imagine my relief and happiness the next day when my secretary opened the door and said, "Jim is going to stay." He not only stayed, he graduated and went on to teach and get his doctor's degree. Within a couple of years, he was named the outstanding teacher of the year in the Phoenix, Arizona, high school system.

Some time later we needed a replacement in the English department. I proposed that we contact Jim for an interview. Some in the administration and on the faculty were skeptical, wondering if I had forgotten his student days. But I felt that he was the person we needed. As it turned out, he had an excellent interview.

I enjoy telling this story because it indicates how careful we should be in judging students. Good qualities will often manifest themselves later in life and give us an entirely different opinion of a person.

Some other interesting situations also arose in my dealings with the faculty. I remember one young man who was quite subdued and mild during his first couple of years on the faculty. Gradually, however, he began to gain confidence in himself. One day he came to my office with a document in which he proposed some significant changes in his department.

I said, "I'll read it. Come back in a couple of days and we'll talk about it."

He was back within two days. I told him that the document was well-written and a credit to him, but we simply were not in a position to add faculty and increase the budget as his proposal would have required. A day later I found a letter of resignation on my desk. I read the letter, went to the academic dean, and said, "Put this in your file, but just leave it alone." March and contract time came. When the young man's name came up, I recommended that he be reappointed. He was reappointed, and he accepted. It was about a year later, as I was walking beside him on campus that I said to him, "You know, you and I had some rather interesting experiences together haven't we?" He stopped short, gave me a quick look, and said, "Yes, we really have." He remained at Dordt during the rest of my presidency.

I should make one more comment about how I tried to relate to the faculty and other college personnel. I made a point of visiting faculty members and administrators in their own offices. I also walked around campus, eager to stay in touch with those who worked on campus. I also used the telephone frequently. I did not like to use memos. That was not my style. If I had something to say to someone I would call them on the phone and get it settled. This allowed me to maintain personal contact with people, which

I felt was essential at that point in Dordt's history. I also stayed abreast of the financial situation of the college, which meant that I spent a considerable amount of time with the business manager. We talked over building plans, discussed various funds, and debated where to invest money. I wanted to stay informed on all financial matters so that as we planned for the future I knew exactly what the situation was and what the possibilities were financially.

One policy that I followed religiously was never to speak negatively about faculty members to others. If I felt it was necessary, I would call a professor into my office and speak openly and honestly about their conduct or, upon occasion, what they were teaching. But I tried never to speak derogatorily about the faculty to others.

* * * * *

I was privileged to have very qualified secretaries while I was president of Dordt College. I have already mentioned Henrietta Miedema, now Mrs. Douglas Ribbens, who came at a crucial time in our history. When she became Dr. Ribbens' secretary, Gertrude Visser worked with me for a short time. She was pleasant, kind, and eager to help, always loyal to me. During the last ten years, Nancy Vanden Bosch was my secretary. Her husband, Mike, taught English at the college. I greatly appreciated Nancy. I tended to "let off steam" occasionally when I became exasperated by a person or a problem. I knew I could trust her never to repeat any of my railings to others. She was also an extremely intelligent and competent secretary, one with whom I could discuss issues and even problems. She had a calmness about her that eased tensions. She helped me get through some of the tougher years with a certain amount of grace and relaxation. I owe a great debt of gratitude to her.

* * * * *

Of all my work at the college nothing pleased me more than to be around students. There is something refreshing and challenging about student life on a college campus. I attended as many events as possible. I went to many ball games, and I listened to many recitals. I tried to be a part of their lives. My mother had given me some helpful advice for this part of my job, too. She told me that when dealing with young people it is best not to see everything, but sometimes to look through your fingers. She added, "Don't worry so much about the little mistakes, but don't allow them to make the big mistakes in their lives." She also warned me not to forget to have a sense of humor.

For nineteen years our home was next to one of the dormitories, right in the middle of the action. We would often lie in our bed on warm spring evenings, listening to the talking and laughter on campus. Nothing is more refreshing and heartening than the joyful laughter of young people.

I remember one night, lying in bed with the windows open, when the girls' dormitory had a fire drill. All of the boys came flying out, too. Since the boys' dormitory was right next to our bedroom we could hear the conversation. A couple of students were standing just outside the dorm watching everything that was going on. We heard one say to the other, "Ah, let's go back in, they've got more on now than they have during the day."

Our children also loved the activity on campus. As soon as the weather was warm, water fights would begin. The children, already in their pajamas, would sit by the windows and direct the students to the hose and the water buckets. They were fascinated with the water fights. It was wonderful bedtime entertainment.

Once in a while, however, things would get out of hand. I remember lying in bed, perhaps around midnight. The clamor on campus reminded me of Moses when he came down the mountain with Joshua and Israel was busy serving the golden calf. Joshua thought the sound was that of battle but Moses thought differently. At times I, too, thought that the noise on campus held an ominous ring. I would first go downstairs and switch on the back porch light. Often that signal was enough to let them know I was aware of what was going on, and things would settle down. If that didn't work, I would put the dog on the leash and take him for a walk across campus. I would come upon groups of students, and all I would do is say, "Hi fellows, nice evening isn't it? Having a good time? Well, be careful." And then I would walk on. Almost without exception it was enough to make them quiet down and soon go back to their rooms.

You learn to expect pranks on a college campus. But even though I expected them periodically, they could still be a bit disconcerting. I made it a policy to have one of the maintenance people look over the campus and see what had taken place during the night. That way if anything was amiss it could be taken care of before the students were up and around. But the students soon caught on to this and outsmarted us. One morning I came to the college and found that a group of students had hoisted a piano to the ceiling in the old gymnasium. There was no way the janitors could get it down before the students came to class. Everyone laughed in amazement and wondered how they got the piano to hang up in the rafters.

Sometime later, as I walked onto campus early in the morning I noticed several people looking up at the radio tower. On the top of the tower was a bicycle. That tower is 300 feet high. I was amazed. The students thought the prank was wonderful. I joined the laughter, too, because it was really quite an accomplishment. But I knew we would have to hire someone to get that bicycle down. I let it be known to the students that it was going to cost a couple hundred dollars. The next morning when I got up and looked at the radio tower, the bicycle was gone. The students had had their fun; they had created some excitement; and they were satisfied. They did not want the college to have to pay the cost of getting it down, so they went up themselves and brought the bicycle back down.

A college president should always stay in close touch with the student newspaper. Publication of the *Diamond* began early in Dordt's history. Students took the opportunity to express their opinions, and the paper soon became a source of interest and sometimes controversy. I decided early that we should not be too restrictive about what was printed in the college paper. We had to let students experiment and sometimes create a bit of a stir, to learn to think and express themselves. In one of the early examinations by the accrediting agency, we had been pictured as a bland, colorless college. That bothered me. I wanted the campus to be an exciting, challenging place. My philosophy was that if there was no noise in the chicken coop, you didn't get any eggs. So, I was very willing to allow students to create a stir.

I even tried to encourage discussion occasionally. I remember laying the seeds for discussion on a few critical issues. Unaware that I was doing this, the students would take these issues on in the *Diamond*, often making critical accusations against the administration's position, and feeling happy for having spouted off. I knew that when they talked about the administration, they often meant the college president. My wife and I would read these articles and chuckle, happy that they were raising some issues.

But I set limits. A faculty sponsor kept an eye on articles to be published, and if he thought it could cause a serious problem, he would let me know. I only remember this happening two or three times. When I did decide the piece would not be published, I would meet with the *Diamond* staff and give my reasons. I told them more than once, "Fine, I'll give you lots of liberty, but when you're going to smash vases and I have to pick up the pieces, I'm going to decide which vases are to be smashed." I knew that people wouldn't go to the students, they would come to me. I wanted to have some say in such situations.

Sometimes, students would come to me upset about something going on. I allowed that. I recall one time a student came into my office, complaining bitterly. I listened for some time. Finally, I got out of my "presidential" chair and said to the student, "You sit in that chair." The student looked at me strangely. I said, "You sit in that chair. I think you could be the president of this college. With your insights and your wisdom you could do a good job." The student got the message. Later, we both smiled about the incident, but the point had been made.

Generally speaking, the students treated me and my family with respect and love. We lived on campus for nineteen years, and the students never mistreated us. I found that admirable. In fact, there were times when they showed real thoughtfulness. On my sixty-fifth birthday, I came to my office, opened my door, and found the room filled with balloons. One of the students drew a huge caricature of me and had it signed by hundreds of students. I was flabbergasted! Since not everyone had seen the card, I took it with me the next time I spoke in chapel. As I was expressing my appreciation for their thoughtfulness, I slowly lifted that great big picture before the student body. A roar of laughter filled the building.

As the caricature of me illustrated, students are quick to pick up peculiar mannerisms. On several occasions they played up my way of speaking and some of my idiosyncrasies. I never felt offended by these actions, and, in fact, came to appreciate them as a sign of camaraderie and respect. But the students weren't the only ones who imitated me. Some of the faculty were good at it too. Mike Stair, who taught in the theatre arts department near the end of my presidency, became an expert at imitating me at faculty celebrations. It was done in a loving spirit and was incredibly funny. It's good to be able to laugh at ourselves.

The students all knew that one of my favorite expressions was the term "Wonderful." I was asked to give the commencement address during the last year of my presidency. At the end of the service, all of a sudden, a huge banner unfurled from the chapel ceiling high above us. On that banner was written the word "Wonderful" with a big exclamation mark. It was a fittingly playful conclusion to a good relationship between myself and the students.

In the early years of the college, I handled all student discipline problems. When you're dealing with young people, most of them between the ages of seventeen and twenty-three, you can plan to have some problems. College campuses reflect the behavior of society in general. As I dealt with these students, I always tried to remember that most of them came from godly homes where parents were very much concerned about their children. Most parents wanted us to have a strong disciplinary policy, but not so tough that it might endanger their children's academic status. I found that parents can be very stern and demanding about discipline when their children are not involved. However, when their own sons or daughters become objects of discipline, they plead for mercy and become very defensive of their children's actions. They will sometimes try to put the blame on the rules of the college, the campus environment, or a lack of counseling.

Over the years a number of parents and constituents have told me that Dordt College was not strict enough. They wanted more stringent rules. I remember visits with parents who had serious complaints about something that was going on at the college. We would be accused of being too lenient. I would listen carefully and instead of being defensive I would say, "Well, I'm sure glad you don't know all the bad stuff going on on this campus that I know, because then you'd be really angry." Frequently they would say, "It isn't really that bad, is it, Reverend?" I'd reply, "Well, they are your children and my children, and that isn't all good." And before I knew it, they were defending me and speaking more kindly about what was going on on the campus.

A few times students were guilty of misdemeanors that involved the law. It is difficult to explain how sons and daughters of good parents can become so quickly involved in bad conduct, yet it happens. But, even though we had our problems, I know of very few Christian colleges where discipline is taken more seriously, and where more effort is spent counseling students and dealing with them in a Christian manner when they go astray.

Such discipline and encouragement is not limited to the faculty and administration. I can't say enough good about how the student body dealt with fellow students who were becoming delinquent. I recall one occasion when a girl in trouble left the college. Another student said to me, "We feel badly about this, because now she will not have a whole dormitory of girls praying for her and trying to help her." It happened more than once that some of the men students would talk to me about a fellow student who was causing trouble and not behaving as he ought. I remember them saying to me, "Reverend, don't worry about it, we're working with him, and we're going to see that he gets straightened out." And I tell you, in several instances that's exactly what happened.

Even though I took discipline cases seriously, some humorous situations arose. I recall a time a student was heard using God's name in vain. It was reported to me, so I called him into my office. He must have been at least 6'8'' tall. I could tell immediately that he was not very happy with himself for what he had done, but nevertheless I pointed out to him the seriousness of the situation. I said, "You know, I think I should call your dad." I knew his parents fairly well. He immediately said to me, "Oh please, don't call my dad. He'll kill me." I said, "Your dad will kill you? You great big, tall, strong fella?" "You don't know my dad!" he said. I couldn't help but smile inwardly. I was confident that this would not soon happen again. After talking to him for a bit, I said, "All right, I'll let it go, but if it happens again, you're going to be in real trouble." He said to me, "Don't worry, it won't happen again." I was always happy that students didn't want me to call their parents. I thought it showed that they had respect for their homes and for their parents.

When people would speak negatively about the college, I often responded by saying, "We are not perfect because we do not have perfect young people. But I hope that you consider Dordt's graduates before you draw any conclusions." The majority of Dordt students proved to be good examples. When the college began, many ministers and educators hesitated to send their children to the college. But as students returned from Dordt and became capable Christian school teachers, committed church members, and strong Christian school supporters, ministers and teachers began to change their way of thinking. One person said to me, "If these are typical of the students Dordt College produces, we will take another look." It didn't take long before a large number of ministers' and educators' children began attending Dordt. Generally speaking, my life with the constituents was most rewarding. I loved to work among the people, to associate with them, to talk with them, to listen to their problems and concerns, to be with them in times of disappointment, and to share their times of success and prosperity.

I didn't mind when they came to me with complaints. I always stressed the fact that this was their college, and my door was open to them at any time. I recall a rather interesting experience with a woman who was bringing her daughter to college for the first time. The dormitory to which her daughter was assigned was not completed when school started that fall. I had to make the difficult decision whether to let the girls go into the dormitory even though it was not ready, or to place them in homes all around the area, and then maybe, two or three weeks later, transport them back to the dormitory. I decided to let them stay in the dorm, even though it was not finished. Beds were in the hallways; there was no good place to store their belongings; and construction workers were around all day. It was not the best situation.

The mother came into my office in a huff, expressing her displeasure and anger. She said, "Here I bring my child to college, and what do I find? This situation is awful." She spouted off for a few minutes. I looked at her and said, "Well, you came to the right person, because I made the decision that they should go into the dormitory," and I explained why I had made the decision. She left the office, not exactly satisfied. About two hours later she came back to my office and apologized. She had gone from my office to the dormitory, where many mothers and daughters were busy moving in, making the best that they could of the situation, and becoming good friends. She said to me, "It couldn't have been nicer. We learned so much about each other, I want to apologize." Sometimes these experiences do more good than you can anticipate.

Since these girls had no place to hang their clothes for two or three weeks, my wife suggested that they hang them in our garage. We had a double garage, so we parked our cars outside. For the next few weeks the girls would come into our garage to get their clothes. That turned out to be a real blessing. The girls got to know us and quickly felt at home.

When parents brought their children to Dordt, it could often be a touching event. After saying good-bye to their daughter, one couple from Canada came to me and the mother with tears in her eyes said pleadingly to me, "Rev. Haan take care of her. She is our most precious possession." I was moved by this and felt again what a responsibility we all had as Dordt faculty and administration. What a rewarding experience it was when this young lady walked across the platform four years later to get her degree with her parents present.

I could write about a host of other incidents, events, and individual people with whom I had personal dealings during my twenty-five years as Dordt president. I am tempted to write about many of these people, but that is not the purpose of my memoirs. I have tried to make references to individual persons only when I felt that in so doing something of the nature of my work in the history of the college was illustrated. I am confident that the many persons with whom I labored so intimately and with such personal satisfaction will understand.

* * * * *

I lived a full life at the college. As I watched it grow I also saw the love of the people grow for Dordt College. I had to provide leadership in times of success but also during reverses. I was president in times of rejoicing and in times of sadness. Through these memoirs my wish is to share as much of my varied experiences as possible with all the people whom I loved.

It would not surprise me, however, if there are those who lived and worked very close to me, who, when reading what I have written, would have a different version of what transpired. Nevertheless, I have done my best to give you what I saw and what I experienced. These are my observations.

How effective was my presidency? How do I evaluate myself? I realize, of course, that in the final analysis the judgment of my effectiveness has to be made by others. I am fully aware of many weaknesses I had as Dordt's president. I could perhaps justify some of these weaknesses by claiming that I was busy with too many things with a rapidly growing college. And it would be partly true. My schedule was so loaded that I was forced to let certain things go. To be perfectly frank, I never considered myself an outstanding president. And my weaknesses were regularly pointed out by others. Colleagues and others would reprimand me for things that I failed to do or that I should have done better. I tried to receive these comments graciously, although at times I felt hurt by criticisms I thought to be cruel and unjust. My main interest was always the future of the college. I was willing to accept some of the more painful aspects of my office to ensure that the college remained rooted in the principles upon which it was founded. I also received much credit for things that others accomplished.

One of my strengths was having a grasp of the total picture and not being too much absorbed with details. I think my goals reflected this. The Lord taught me early in life not to be too concerned with doing big things but rather to take hold of the challenges immediately before me and do everything possible to meet those challenges. From Abraham Kuyper I learned that the kingdom of God was an organic unity. The unfolding of kingdom life was seen in the context of that organic wholeness. Taking hold of one aspect of that kingdom and working hard at it would open up many other possibilities and challenges within the kingdom. That which took place in my early life and in my tenure at Dordt are abundant proof of this.

Humor played a significant role in my ministry and presidency. To me, humor is a remarkable gift. To be able to laugh at yourself and to laugh with others is a great blessing. When difficulties arose, I often sensed that the problems were more emotional than rational. In such situations, tensions build up quickly. Being able to inject appropriate humor at the right time often averted what could have resulted in a painful and damaging situation.

Another possible strength of mine, I believe, was a keen sense of the importance of timing. I firmly believed that we had to be ready to strike when the iron was hot. There is no place in the movement of the kingdom for hesitancy once the Lord has opened the doors. Some people, when failure strikes, give up, and hardly dare to try anything new again. Thankfully that was seldom my problem. I could relate many failures in my life history, even though I would rather not speak of them. However, they did not stand in the way of vigorously attempting new ventures. And even in the most trying circumstances, I was, as many who worked with me observed, full of optimism.

The day of my retirement finally arrived. Under the able supervision of Lyle Gritters, who was vice president for advancement at that time, a number of celebrations were held in honor of my retirement. One was a dinner with all the board members and their wives and the faculty and their spouses. Three other retiring faculty members were also honored: Nick Van Til, Hester Hollaar, and Henry De Groot. A second, more public celebration, was held in the chapel. A program outlining my years at Dordt was presented. These were truly delightful occasions that we will long remember. We were especially happy that several of my brothers and sisters could share the evening with us. We happened at the same time to be celebrating our fortieth wedding anniversary and forty years in the ministry. It was indeed a most memorable and enjoyable experience.

The board was truly generous to us. Upon retirement, we were presented with a small motor home so that we could travel and enjoy our retirement. But even more pleasing to me was the fact that they set aside $20,000 for a ten-year B.J. Haan Lectureship Series on Christian education. Special lecturers were to be brought in to speak on the topic of Christian education. At the end of the ten years, a book would be published which contained a summary of all that had taken place in the ten-year lecture series program. The board also encouraged me to use the time God would give me in my retirement to write my memoirs.

And now I am at the end of my story. The Lord has blessed me and my family with abundant spiritual and material gifts. We have enjoyed much appreciation and encouragement from God's people. It is, to be sure, heartening to receive praise, and we certainly had our share of it. But I have often remarked that it takes an enormous amount of grace to handle praise with humility. One of my greatest fears, one with which I struggled all my life, was that I might be guilty of robbing the Lord of the praise due His Name. There is always the danger when people commend us that God is pushed into the background. Nothing is more repugnant and unjust. I know, and all who labored with me know, that God is the one who made all these happenings possible. Occasionally certain individuals accused me of seeking my own glory. It was like the thrust of a dagger to my heart. I knew full well that this sin always lurked in my labors. After such remarks, I wrestled much in prayer to find peace with the Lord and maintain the strength to carry on my duties effectively. My earnest prayer and desire has been that, in spite of all our sinful claims to honor and glory, when we come to the end the Lord Himself will say, "Well done, thou good and faithful servant."

Educational Task of Dordt College

Fundamental to the understanding of the educational task of Dordt College is the commitment of its constituency to the Word of God. That Word of God is divinely inspired, the infallible and only rule for faith and practise. In the face of varying interpretations of God's Word, membership in the Christian Reformed Church, including all faculty personnel at Dordt College, is bound by the interpretation of God's Word as stated in the Three Formulas of Unity--the *Belgic Confession*, the *Heidelberg Catechism*, and the *Cannons of Dort*.

These Formulae of Unity are in agreement with the flow out of the Calvinistic interpretation of the Scriptures. Calvinism, which finds its source materials primarily in John Calvin's *Institutes of the Christian Religion*, is a broad system of theology, often called a world-and-life view, which rigorously applies the principles of God's Word to all areas of life. The Sovereignty of God is the basic principle in this system. Members of the Christian Reformed Church are strict adherents to this position. The basic propositions which are fundamental to the educational system of Dordt College, if not precise formulations of the Calvinistic pattern, are either direct implications, commonly accepted, from the Calvinistic position, or modifications which are oriented to the Calvinistic system.

Propositions

The following propositions or principles shed light upon and undergird the entire educational program of Dordt College.

1. The origination and interpretation of all things is found ultimately in a personal, absolute, sovereign God. All things having been created by God, He alone gives meaning to all things.

2. Man, created in God's image, possesses the faculties necessary for the explication of meaning which is implicit in the universe, and for the under standing of the relationship between the various spheres of life and their ultimate relationships to the sovereign creator.

3. Man, created in God's image, is God's vice-agent representative king, in the universe and is given the mandate, often called the cultural mandate, to subdue the earth bringing all things to serve God's glory. This calls man to the task of searching out all things and relationships, leading to this proper development of God's creation to its appointed goal.

4. Man, in his responsible position, must be properly developed so that the cultural mandate will not only be carried out, but that man himself may realize his potential as king of creation and as God's masterpiece.

5. Sin has dealt a ruinous blow to God's image in man, not only crippling him in his task as God's representative king to fulfill the cultural mandate, but also setting him at variance with God's law and purpose. Fallen man lives and dies unto himself, exalting himself as the master of his own fate. By reason of man's representative capacity, the entire cosmos was affected by man's sin. The curse of sin has, therefore, impeded the perfect development of the natural order.

6. To counteract the influence of sin and to carry out His original program, God has engaged in the plan of redemption and recreation, centrally effected in His only begotten Son, Jesus Christ. In Christ fallen man is effectually called back into a living relationship with God, is restored through the representative king, and is committed ti the task of reclaiming all of life for God's service and glory in accordance with His law.

7. The redemptive work of Christ has cosmic significance. He not only restores fallen man to his kingly position and activity; Christ also, as the new representative head and king of creation, by His atonement provides the basis for the restoration of the cosmos. By the restoration of man through the regenerative work of His Spirit, He enables man to understand and interpret His special revelation, the Holy Scriptures. Through the medium of the Scriptures man can interpert himself and all of nature (cosmos) in the context of sin and Christ's redemptive work. Man can cooperate with Christ's Spirit in the transformation of nature, leading all of creation to its consumation, ultimately achieved in the renewal of all things when Christ returns.

Unregenerate man cannot discern the pattern of larger spiritual and transcendent meaning. But he too, under the blessing of Christ's recreation, can find moments of truth in the various realms of human endeavor. He may, for example, accomplish great things in the sciences or in the arts. But it is the Christian alone who finds for these truths their ultimate meaning and reference. This is his broadest educational task.

8. In the recreative work of God, His special revelation is the only rule for faith and life. That revelation is basically the key to

the understanding of all meaning. It contains principles which govern all of life's relationships. And through it alone Christ's redemptivebenefits can be enjoyed personally and in their cosmic reaches.

9. In the training and development of the redeemed in Christ the Holy Scriptures are basic, since they are indispensable to the proper realization of the individual's capacities and the proper fulfilling of his responsibilities. All education must be Scripturally oriented.

10. The redeemed look upon the whole universe as the object of their responsibility. No area or sphere is excluded. The cosmos is Christ's kingdom. In each sphere the principles of His Word must be applied. To guarantee this application of God's Word to all areas of life, as well as to bring about the reclamation of fallen man, Christ has instituted His Church. It is the solemn responsibility of the Church to propagate and maintain the truth as revealed in Scriptures; to see to it that her membership is instructed in the knowledge of Scripture; to demand an education for her children and youth which is Scripturally oriented; and to inform her members of the principles of God's Word as they apply to their various labors and activities in God's kingdom.

11. While the instituted Church informs her membership concerning their responsibilities in God's kingdom, it is not her task to engage in specifically kingdom activities. The instituted church normally does not control and operate institutions of mercy, educational institutions, etc. Her membership as citizens of the kingdom organize into societies, where necessary, to implement the kingdom programs.

12. God's kingdom is divided into specific spheres. There are spheres of education, state, church, home, mercy, labor, etc. Each sphere has its distinct task. What belongs to one sphere should not, normally, be transferred to another sphere. Each sphere wherever necessary should have its own society for the implementation of its task. The church, though in a sense part of the kingdom, holds a unique position in the kingdom in that it speaks to all spheres, delineating the principles of God's Word as they apply to them.

13. Although God's kingdom is divided into several spheres, one must guard against viewing the spheres as static, in a compartmentalistic sense. The various spheres are organically related. They are governed by the same laws of interpretation and mean-

ing. And they flow into one another in a dynamic and vital context. While each sphere has its distinct task, there is bound to be a measure of overlapping and shifting of peripheral responsibilities from sphere to sphere, resulting from changes in our dynamic, rapid moving social order. That which is self-evidently the distinct task of each sphere would be zealously honored and respected as the solemn right of the sphere.

14. Education as a distinct sphere in God's kingdom has a specific task to perform. Its task is that of contributing to the development of Christian culture through the nurture of the rational-moral character of man. This is achieved by the refinement of his mind, his manners, his morals and his tastes, through the use of the various disciplines and skills of learning, and the transmission of the scholarly knowledge of past generations to the present, together with the necessary evaluation and application, enabling the individual to realize himself as God's image bearer and to fulfill his purpose in human society commensurate with his capabilities and opportunities.

15. The subject material for education is the entire universe, nature and man. This is often called God's general revelation in distinction from His special revelation, the Bible, made necessary by sin. The latter is basic to the understanding of meaning in the former. The ad must be developed and equipped through the various skills so that he may be led into the many areas of general revelation, often referred to as the fields of learning. Employing the tools of scholarship he gains an understanding and appreciation for all spheres as they reflect God's glory. He is inspired to make effective use of this education as qualifications, opportunities, and resources permit.

16. Since all children born of the members of the church are brought into a living covenantal relationship to Christ by birth, which is signified in their baptism, and are both members of the church and citizens in God's kingdom, their entire education, from the kindergarten through higher education should aim toward their development and training for proper kingdom service through teaching that is thoroughly Scripturally oriented.

17. Education is specifically a kingdom sphere properly sponsored by a society of the covenant community. Yet it stands more closely to the instituted church in its relationship to the other spheres of the kingdom in that it too is fundamental to all spheres. It is

preparatory to virtually all kingdom activity. Even the instituted church depends upon the sphere of education of the execution of her task. This explains the instituted church's serious concern relative to the education of her youth. Without education her task cannot be performed. Without a Scripturally oriented education for her youth, the effective realization of her responsibilities is critically endangered. Consequently the alliance between the instituted church and education must be very close. Where necessary the instituted church stands ready to give official support through her resources and even to assume official control of education.

Adopted by the Faculty and Board of Trustees in 1961.